PATHWAY TO ECSTASY

Also by Patricia Garfield
CREATIVE DREAMING

PATHWAY TO ECSTASY
THE WAY OF THE DREAM MANDALA

Patricia Garfield, Ph.D.

with Illustrations by the Author

PRENTICE
HALL
PRESS

New York   London   Toronto   Sydney   Tokyo

Illustrations on p. 149 and p. 163, The Psychic
Centers of the Human Body and the Psychic
Energy System, respectively, are both from Philip
Rawson, *Tantra: The Indian Cult of Ecstasy*,
New York: Avon, 1973.

Illustrations on p. 162, p. 175 and p. 176, The
Gall-Bladder Meridian, The Black Midline
Channel, Tu Mo, and The Front Midline Channel,
Jen Mo, respectively, are from Academy of
Traditional Chinese Medicine, *An Outline of
Chinese Acupuncture*, Peking: Foreign Languages
Press, 1975; available in the U.S. through China
Books and Periodicals of San Francisco.

 Prentice Hall Press
15 Columbus Circle
New York, New York 10023

Introduction copyright © 1989 by Patricia Garfield

Originally published in 1979 by Holt, Rinehart
and Winston

PRENTICE HALL PRESS and colophon are
registered trademarks of Simon & Schuster, Inc.

Library of Congress Cataloging-in-Publication Data

Garfield, Patricia L.
    Pathway to ecstasy: the way of the dream mandala/
Patricia L. Garfield.
      p. cm.
    Includes bibliographical references.
    ISBN 0-13-653155-5: 12.95
    1. Dreams.   2. Mandala.   I. Title
BF1091.G3 1989
135'.3—dc20   89-39650
                                       CIP

Designed by Joy Chu

Manufactured in the United States of America

10 9 8 7 6 5 4 3 2 1

First Prentice Hall Press Edition

To Zal,

In the garden
of the Alhambra
grow two tall trees

Roots separate,
their trunks blend
branches embrace,
juices mingle.

Centuries pass--
they still are one.

So will it be,
for our ever,
lovingly entwined.

acknowledgments

Bringing forth this book has been a long and difficult labor. My journey to uncover the secrets within dreams led to unlikely activities, and the people who assisted in this wide-ranging quest have come from varied disciplines. To all of them I owe deep gratitude.

Detlef Ingo Lauf, professor of comparative religion at the C. G. Jung Institute in Zurich, enriched my knowledge of Tibetan sacred art during his visits to the United States.

Professor Stephan Beyer, of the Department of Indian Studies at the University of Wisconsin, recounted some of his experiences of life in a Tibetan monastery.

Professor Joseph Campbell, in a workshop at the Westerbeke Ranch, extended my comprehension of mythology.

Tarthang Tulku Rinpoche, founder of the Nyingma Institute in Berkeley, gave me some practical experience in the Tibetan Buddhist techniques that I had until then only read or heard about.

Magaña Baptiste and her staff introduced me to the pleasures of belly dancing; Khadija Rabanne helped me to expand and refine my dance movements; Mary Ellen Donald taught me Middle Eastern drumming rhythms.

My acupuncturist, Dr. Tsun-Nin Lee of San Francisco, did more than insert needles and improve my general well-being: his techniques literally sent currents of energy coursing through my body; his effectiveness stirred me to explore the fabulous wealth of Oriental philosophy and methods.

Professional colleagues have been both challenging and stimulating. A chance remark by one of them first called my attention to the archetype of the Horned Goddess in my dreams and set me off on a new avenue of research. Paul Verdone, of California State College, Sacramento, took physiological measurements of my dream state in his sleep laboratory. Fellow members of the Association for the Psychophysiological Study of Sleep kept me in touch with the fact that dreams are also biochemical events—a useful grounding as I sailed through myths and mysticism.

When my experimentation with Eastern meditation led to alarming symptoms, as I will describe, I was fortunate enough to meet K———, a Chinese master of Taoism, now living in San Francisco. He swiftly alleviated the problems and was extraordinarily kind and supportive.

I learned a great deal from the "dream seance group"—Gayle Delaney, Stephen Walsh, Alan and Diane Vaughan (and their baby, Lauren, after a few months), my husband, Zal, and myself. We shared in depth, and Gayle's method of "dream interviewing" helped us all to interpret the symbolism of dream content more rapidly than ever.

Our children, Linda, Steven, Wendy, and Cheryl, played vital roles in the daytime and dreamtime search. And it was my mother, Evelyn, who inspired my original interest in dreams.

Charlene Ho's excellent typing was invaluable. Karen Mickleson and Jeanne Perilman Pinault helped bring about order in my various papers so that I could attend to writing. Artist Sheldon Schoneberg offered suggestions about the illustrations. Fred Cline and his staff at The Society for Asian Art in San Francisco were endlessly resourceful. Hsiu-Ming Lee, devoted housekeeper and friend, constantly freed me from demanding household duties—and occasionally advised me on the meaning of some mysterious Chinese character.

William Abrahams, my editor, coaxed from me with infinite patience and skill exactly what it was I was trying to express but had not yet clearly formulated.

My beloved husband, Zal, listened to dreams at breakfast; he talked ideas at dinner; he comforted me when I was discouraged; he rejoiced with me when I was inspired; and he fretted over me when I was in trouble. Despite the clutter of books in our bedroom and paintbrushes in our study, he could still manage another good-natured art critique or chapter reading. "Father" of the book, he provided the circumstances—a nourishing environment—that made it possible for me to create it.

—Patricia Garfield

San Francisco
Christmas Day, 1977

CONTENTS

Introduction to the Second Edition of
Pathway to Ecstasy: The Way of the Dream Mandala

Since *Pathway to Ecstasy*[1] was first printed in 1979, it has evoked passionate—and contradictory—responses. Over the past ten years I have been privileged to speak with hundreds of the many people who read and understood this book. Invariably they comment: "This book changed my life." Some people tell me they kept *Pathway* on their bedside table and read from it each night because the events of my personal history evoked responses within their own lives. Others say they went into psychology or became dreamworkers because of the impact of this book. Still others say it was supportive during a traumatic divorce by demonstrating the possibility of a truly loving relationship.

However, some people were repelled by *Pathway*. They found the degree of orgiastic passion it contains abhorrent.

One group specializing in dreams banned it from their members. Others objected to the spiritual element the book expresses. I even received hate mail.

My first book, *Creative Dreaming*,[2] had totally altered my husband's and my life by putting me into the intense public spotlight. Then came the highly mixed, and equally strong, reactions to *Pathway*. Perhaps such intensity is bound to have repercussions. For me, it eventually led to a need to withdraw into a more contemplative way of life, one in which my work with dreams and approaches to the spiritual path continue to produce a number of profound and surprising transformations.

The Way of the Mandala

I mention these reactions because reading this book will also produce profound changes within you. Most especially, your dreams will shift. This is because we'll be working with the mandala, an ancient and powerful system of self-transformation. As we do so, I will present aspects of my life as a teaching device. Reading about my crisis points will very likely create deep repercussions within your own life. However, if you will open yourself to it, this resonance can lead to positive experiences of growth.

Mandala is an ancient Sanskrit word meaning "circle" or "center." It is symmetrical in design, usually circular, surrounding a clear center. Contained within it are subtle or precise references to cardinal points, the number of which may vary. Mandalas may be artworks or forms found in nature. The Aztec calendar stone is a mandala, as is the Earth when viewed from space. The compass rose is a mandala, and so is a snowflake, a sand dollar, the human eye, and a pattern of iron filings gathered around a magnet.

For centuries, Tibetan Buddhist monks have created mandalas in artwork, weavings, and designs made with colored sand, much as Navajo shamans have done in the New World. The Tibetans use these designs as meditational devices for centering the mind so that it may pass, one step at a time, through the many dimensions of space, time, and consciousness to the freedom of pure "being" that lies at the center of all things. This is always, no matter how often you have taken it, a journey of profound inner change, marked by new insights into one's self and the nature of life.

It was Carl Jung who first introduced the idea of the mandala to Western dreamers. In his autobiography, *Memories, Dreams, Reflections*,[3] Jung tells how he painted his first mandala in 1916, and that two years later he was painting a mandala in his notebook on a daily basis. He found that each new design evoked his inner life at that moment, and he used them to chart his "psychic transformation." Eventually Jung concluded that the path of the mandala is the path to our center, to becoming a unique individual.

Mandala work develops a rhythm of its own, and this book is designed to keep pace with it. Our journey to the center begins slowly as we enter the sacred precinct and make our acquaintance with the ever-deepening levels of the unknown universe that lies within us. Our voyage may occasionally hit snags and blocks as we face our own resistance to change. We may momentarily revert to old ways of seeing and being that are now threatened by new perspectives. But then the understanding of our lives begins to pick up speed. The closer we come to the center of the mandala, the more powerful its gravitational pull. Then, with a powerful release of pent-up energy, we experience light, freedom, joy, peace, and unity.

Keeping a Dream Journal

I strongly urge you, if you do not already do so, to begin keeping a dream diary. Equip yourself with a pad and pen at your bedside, and a more formal notebook to hold finished dream records. It's a good idea to make an entry in the formal journal at bedtime. Put down the day and date, with a few brief remarks about what you did and how you felt during the day.

During the night, jot down notes on your small notepad about any dreams you may have. This is done easily in the dark with your eyes closed if you hold the pad horizontally and extend the little finger of your writing hand to prevent lines from overlapping. With your nonwriting hand gripping the short side of the pad, your pen-holding hand can feel its way back to the beginning of the next line, like a typewriter carriage returning. At the very least, try to write down the key events of the dream, and any unusual words or phrases.

If you have time when you awake in the morning, take notes while still lying down with your eyes closed—your recall will be more complete. If you must move, do it gently so your mind can cling to any dream remnants. Try recording your dream from the last thing you recall, no matter how trivial, and from there describe what happened before it. Memories of a dream often return in reverse, with the most recent portion being the clearest.

That morning, or sometime during the day, or even in bed that night before you fall asleep, copy your notes clearly into your permanent dream journal. This dream description will follow after your entry on the events of the day preceding the dream. Some people use the dream note-taking method, then later type up their more complete dream descriptions on a typewriter or computer, and insert them into a three-ring binder. The computer method allows you to search for and compare similar dreams more easily. Other people like to put their dreams into a bound blank book.

Although this process may seem too troublesome for those of you who've never kept a dream diary before, you will find it is well worth the effort. You'll be creating a document that no one else in the world can write—a book about your inner life. This dream record can teach you much about yourself, providing a rich resource for creative work. As if watching a grand drama, you will see your fears, your desires, your ambitions—and perhaps even encounters with your spirit— acted out upon your dream stage.

Your journal can become your personal manual of self-transformation, where you will be able to discover the lesson, purpose, and meaning of your life. Even if you do not have the time to keep a continuing dream journal, you may wish to set aside a month, a vacation period, or at least a few week-ends, to investigate the treasure house waiting within your dreams.

Developments in Dreaming Since the Original Publication of *Pathway*

The Dreamwork Movement

When I first began to write books about dreams, there was no such thing as a professional dreamworker. There were, of course, psychiatrists, psychologists, and social workers who worked with dreams. But few, if any, did so exclusively. Today, there are thousands of professional dreamworkers offering workshops, leading ongoing peer, self-help, and dream-appreciation groups, or providing dream-focused counseling.

Hundreds of dreamworkers have banded together in their own local, regional, and national organizations, such as the Association for the Study of Dreams, which I cofounded.[4] It is now possible to undertake specialized training in dreamwork, for instance, at the Lucidity Institute at Stanford University.[5]

The Bodywork Movement

Another bright strand in the tapestry of time woven since this book first appeared is the growing appreciation of the physical body. Alongside the intense interest people in the United States have developed regarding personal health and fitness, there has evolved a new valuing of the body as the interface between the physical and spiritual worlds—a central topic in *Pathway*. A glance at the current titles on bookstore shelves reveals how widespread the interest in luminous body energy has become.

We have discovered that our bodies are delicate instruments, capable of registering subtle energy flows as well as simply reacting to the foods we ingest. To glory in the vitality of our bodies is part of living fully. As centers of radiant energy, our bodies will speak if we listen. They can become sources of wisdom and instruction. You may find that the same energy vibrations that are tapped in acupuncture, stirred in meditation, or activated by crystals, may also be accessed in dreams—especially in lucid dreaming.

The Growth of the Women's Movement

Parallel with the growing dreamwork and bodywork movement, there has been a renaissance of the women's movement. Women in today's society are particularly in need of role models, figures of strength, power, inspiration, and guidance. I felt certain that the goddesses who began to appear in my powerful dreams were supplying a much-needed balance to the patriarchal protestant religion in which I was raised, in addition to the Eastern ones I began to explore.

Long before Sylvia Brinton Perera wrote *Descent to the Goddess*,[6] and Jean Shinoda Bolen wrote her fascinating *Goddesses in Everywoman*,[7] these amazing creatures were striding through my dreams. I believe they lie sleeping in all women's dreams, until summoned by the dreamer's growing sense of self. Women in the United States are now becoming more aware of how to awaken the goddess within. Men are also discovering that they need positive female figures in their dreams.

This does not necessarily imply that one must embrace paganism—although large numbers of men and women have done so. More important is the realization that inner strength grows out of inner work. This inner strength can fit into many spiritual systems, or fashion its own.

Candid Self-Examination

"The life which is unexamined is not worth living," advised Socrates, the ancient Greek sage.[8] But to confront one's internal demons takes courage. At the time I wrote *Pathway*, there were few contemporary books available where the authors reflected on their intimate life in a forthright manner.

Shirley MacLaine turned the tide in 1983 with her trendsetting book, *Out on a Limb*.[9] By exploring her personal life and risking public derision by including the psychic dimensions, MacLaine touched off an avalanche of self-confessional spiritual biographies. In different ways and with different problems, other prominent figures, such as ballerina Gelsey Kirkland in her *Dancing on My Grave* (written with Greg Lawrence in 1986),[10] began bravely exploring in print the dark corners of the mind.

Candid autobiography is now in fashion, yet the implications of self-examination are classic. By facing our problems and crises, we begin the process of transformation. To look at the life being lived is like becoming aware that we are dreaming within the dream. Once we "awaken" to our emotions and to the consequences of our behavior, we can consciously begin to choose our direction. Awake and asleep, our minds clarify.

Current Open Attitude

Many of the concepts and traditions that were unfamiliar or seemingly foreign to my readers when I first described them in *Pathway* are commonly discussed today. In the city of San Francisco, crossroads of the East and West, practitioners of acupuncture can be found on almost any commercial street. Books on such subjects as Chinese medicine, Taoism, acupressure, Tibetan Buddhism, kundalini energy, yoga, and Tai Chi proliferate. Numerous people in the United States are following some Eastern spiritual path, guru, or martial art. While some of the leaders of these sects have proven disappointing or even disillusioning, many others continue to provide inspiration.

This growing familiarity with Eastern thought and practices is why we believe it is time to reissue *Pathway*. The information it contains on the transformational energy of dreams and mandalas will now be able to reach many more people than before.

Quite auspiciously, another sign that the concepts in this book are more appreciated today took place last summer, when the Dalai Lama sent four monks of his lineage from Tibet to New York. There, in a special room in the American Museum of Natural History, they created an eight-foot-square sand painting of the Kalachakra mandala. This particular mandala concerns the nature of time and the establishment of peace on Earth.

Thousands of people filed past and viewed this work in creation during the six weeks it took to complete. At the final ceremony, the design was swept up into a glass urn, taken to the Hudson River, and poured in with the appropriate blessings. There are plans to repeat this mandalic ceremony on the West Coast in the near future.[11]

The Blending of Paths

The approach I set forth in *Pathway* is not a simple acceptance of any one Eastern spiritual doctrine. It is an application of fundamental concepts that can fit easily into any dreamer's specific religious practice. I profoundly believe there are many paths to truth, to the higher self, and the ultimate in life. All paths contain some elements of this Great Truth.

We grow, not by simply adopting the garment of another religious system, but by fashioning and fitting the sound material in it and shaping it to bring out the best we are capable of becoming. I concur with Jung's belief that: "It is from the depths of our own psychic life that new spiritual forms will arise. . . ."[12] He felt that the various images of religion have come to be things of the outer world, rather than expressions of our inner life. By looking to the living images that evolve from within, we can create our spirituality afresh.

Assertiveness in Dreaming: The Rise and Fall of the Senoi

Two different but interwoven dream techniques are important to the dreamwork you will encounter in this book. Hopefully, you will begin testing these methods for yourself: the Senoi dream approach, and lucid dreaming. Little was known about lucid dreaming when *Pathway* was first published, and Senoi dreaming was quite new in the public mind—popularized in large measure by my first book, *Creative Dreaming*.

The Senoi, sometimes called the Temiar-Senoi, are a primitive group of people. They number about 12,000, and live in the mountainous jungles of Malaysia. The three basic principles of what is called Senoi dream theory are:

1. Always *confront and conquer* danger in a dream. If you are attacked by a hostile dream figure, fight back; don't try to run or hide. Call on dream friends for help if needed, but defend yourself until they arrive.

2. Always *move toward pleasurable experiences* in dreams. If you are having a sensuous experience, increase it. If you are flying or engaging in other pleasurable dream experiences, relax and enjoy them.

3. Always *give your dreams a positive outcome.* Extract a creative product from the dream, such as a "gift" from your dream figure—a poem, song, dance, design, painting, or creative insight—something beautiful or useful to remember the dream by, and to share with the waking world.

I first became familiar with these intriguing premises during a five-month trip my husband and I took around the world in 1972. Joe Kamiya, a colleague from San Francisco, whom we met at a psychology convention in Tokyo, told us about a Malaysian tribal people. This tribe supposedly maintained a peaceful way of life because of certain dream practices. Since Malaysia was part of our itinerary anyway, I was eager to investigate this new approach and began researching everything I could find about the Senoi.

Most of the information available to me at the time had been written by Kilton Stewart. Born in Utah, Stewart had received his Ph.D. from the London School of Economics in 1948, based in part on his fieldwork with the Senoi.[13] He had been an assistant to Herbert "Pat" Noone, a British anthropologist who was working as a Government Field Ethnographer, gathering basic anthropological data on the Senoi. Stewart assisted Noone for a few weeks in 1934, and again for a couple of months in 1938, collecting data for his thesis.

As I stated in *Creative Dreaming*, I drew largely on Stewart's published accounts of his work. I read every paper I could locate written by him on the Senoi's unusual dream practices, including his dissertation. While in Kuala Lumpur, the capital of the Federation of Malaya, I arranged to meet and speak with a few Senoi who were at a hospital at nearby Gombak. Of course, I was speaking in English to a Malay physician who translated my questions into the aboriginal tongue and the answers back into English for me. While much information may have been lost in this exchange, I found it puzzling that what the Senoi told me did not totally endorse the practices described by Stewart.

Nevertheless, it was clear that dreams did play a prominent role in the Senoi culture, and that they did influence daily life. At the time, I thought these particular Senoi might have been distorted by their exposure to Western culture.

Kilton Stewart claimed that the Senoi's methods of defusing conflict in dreams made them a peaceful people in the midst of warlike tribes. I met two researchers at the University of Singapore who had worked with the Senoi,[14] and they confirmed the nonaggressive nature of these people, as well as some of the other features of their life as described by Stewart. But just like my Senoi informants, they did not corroborate all of his comments.

However, when I attempted to apply the principles I was reading about to my own dream life and discussed these concepts with my husband, both our dreams began to change. Back in the States, in our new home in San Francisco, I began sharing my enthusiasm about Senoi practices with a class of students I was teaching. They soon began reporting astounding changes in their dreams as well, as I've described in *Creative Dreaming*.

Appeal of the Senoi Dream Theory

Up to this point, Stewart's material had been buried in obscure journals. His first article about the Senoi, which appeared in 1951,[15] drew little attention, and a book he had written was out of print.[16] But with the publication of *Creative Dreaming* in 1974, the public's interest in Senoi dream practices skyrocketed. I was besieged with requests for information and for television, radio, and newspaper interviews. Soon, *Creative Dreaming* was a bestseller.

There was a controversial side to all of this as well. The great rush of popularity of Senoi dream theory produced renewed research into Senoi life, and a number of critical analyses of Stewart's work began to appear in print. None of the countless researchers who tried to verify his material came up with concrete proof that all of Stewart's claims were accurate—especially in relation to the teaching of dream techniques to children, and the demanding of gifts from conquered dream figures.

While certain claims may indeed have been exaggerated by Stewart, most of the critics will admit that the Senoi are, in fact, relatively nonaggressive; that they do give dreams a central role in their culture, and that they derive songs and patterns from their dreams.[17]

Was Stewart a fanciful storyteller? Was he simply inaccurate in his reporting? Had there been significant changes in the practices Stewart described? Did he overexaggerate to suit his own purposes? Is "Senoi dream theory" really "Stewart dream theory"? I doubt that we will ever know the answers. But, for me, it seems fruitless to continue speculating on the pros and cons. The principles attributed to the Senoi are effective.

My own experience in assisting people to deal with their frightening dream figures suggests that it is helpful to begin with fighting back. I call this "confronting and conquering" danger in your dreams. This rule is similar to the psychological principle of "desensitization" to a feared object. It is a kind of "assertiveness training" that behavior therapists use. Success with confrontation proves to the dreamer that his or her action makes a difference in the dream; confidence is boosted. Once successful confrontation occurs, the dreamer is able to apply more subtle means of interacting with the dream figure, including questioning it.

One of my colleagues, Pierre Étévenon, who is troubled by the idea of combating hostile dream figures, prefers to surround them with golden light. The crucial point, it seems to me, is not so much *which* action is taken toward the hostile dream figure—whether we eradicate them, challenge them, stare them into submission, reconcile with them, or love them—but that *some* action is taken. By taking positive action within the dream, rather than collapsing in fear, dreamers learn that they can make a difference in their dream life and hence in their waking life.

Let us leave the Senoi rest in peace. Call the dream principles Stewart's if you like. Call them behavior therapy of dreaming if you prefer, or assertiveness in dreaming. But since we know the psychological principles upon which they're based are highly effective, *let's use them*. We don't need to wait until every critic agrees to find out whether these techniques work for us or not. Try facing the enemies in your dreams with confidence and courage. You have nothing to lose but your fear!

Lucid Dreaming

As you work with your dreams, you may find yourself becoming "lucid"—being aware that you are dreaming during a dream. Lucid dreaming allows the dreamer a power and freedom that he or she never experiences in waking life, including the magical ability to fly. Dreamers who become lucid sometimes experience, as I did, extrasensory perceptions. You may wish to sharpen your lucid dreaming skills by following some of the suggestions given toward the end of this Introduction.

Many of the monumental figures and goddesses I encountered in my dream world emerged in lucid dreams. Perhaps this was one of the reasons some people had trouble grasping *Pathway*. However, over the past ten years, lucid dreaming has become a household word, and the field is flourishing.

Descriptions of people becoming aware that they are dreaming during a dream date back to ancient Greece. Aristotle, in the fourth century B.C., referred to "something in consciousness which declares that what then presents itself is but a dream."[18] Countless others have related this exciting phenomenon as they dreamed it.

Yet, these descriptions were dismissed as mere anecdotes. Small wonder that my own encounters with lucid dreaming, reported in my first two books, were not accepted as credible either. Sleep researchers commented that such experiences must be imaginings, the product of the drowsy mind in a hypnagogic state, hallucinations, or "mini-awakenings;" they could not possibly occur during dream states. We know now that they do.

The most important single development regarding dreams in recent times is, beyond doubt, the demonstration that lucid dreaming is real dreaming. Stephen LaBerge of the Stanford University Sleep Clinic crushed the skepticism. For the first time he was able to show that lucid dreaming does indeed take place within the dream state.

In 1978, initially using himself and a few lucid-dreaming friends, he carried out the definitive experiment. Subjects made eye-movement signals during lucid dreams that were measured on a polygraph in the sleep laboratory. At last, researchers had concrete evidence that lucid dreaming occurred during rapid eye movement (REM) sleep.

LaBerge initially had difficulty getting his findings published. But when his popular book, *Lucid Dreaming*,[19] came out in 1985, the topic took off. Lucid dreaming groups began forming like wildfire all across the country. The press picked up the subject and wrote about it avidly. Television and radio media probed and pondered the implications of this peculiar state of consciousness. An event first mentioned by Aristotle became hot copy in the modern world because it had been scientifically measured.

Where will all this interest in lucid dreaming lead? We don't know the answer yet. Currently, LaBerge has developed prototypes of infrared goggles that signal to the dreamer when a dream has begun by means of an electrode that emits a pulsing red light. Using this "Dream Light," thousands of people may soon be able to dream lucidly. More than ever, we now need a framework and a working set of values to sail these uncharted inner seas in the vastness of our sleeping minds.

Learning from My Dreams

What have I done since *Pathway* was written? To speak of this, I must speak of disillusion—not with my life, nor my lover, nor my work, but with my meditation teacher. He was not mercenary as some gurus have been, nor was he unethical or evil, as others have become. He was simply all too human and flawed.

When I wrote this book, I was beginning the practice of an esoteric form of ancient Chinese Taoist meditation, and I rapidly found myself getting remarkable results. In fact, the swiftness of the changes in my body alarmed me. This led me to seek and find an expert who was skilled in Taoist meditation. This teacher was extremely helpful to me in a time of need, and I began to study with him and his followers in regular group sessions.

This relationship continued beyond the publication of

Pathway. I was surprised to find I had developed a close psychic connection with him in my dreams, perhaps because he was so reticent about his personal life. He would appear at class and then vanish. One day, I showed up for class and found the other students practicing alone. No one knew where our teacher was, or when he would return.

A few weeks later, when I was in Hawaii on a business trip with my husband, I had what turned out to be an amazing dream:

> The telephone rings. My daughter answers it, then hands it to me, saying it is my meditation teacher.
> "Hello, Pat, how are you?" he says, his voice shaking with emotion.
> I reply, "I'm fine. How are you?"
> "Not so good. I really miss to see you," he says in his broken English.
> I'm astonished by how distressed he sounds. He says something about being at the tennis courts near my house and that he's been thinking of me.
> "Can you see me?" he asks. I go get my date book, pondering when we can talk privately.

When I awoke, I dismissed this dream as speculation about my teacher's emotional state, and as my wish to reconnect with him. However, when I arrived for the next class, I found the doors bolted and no one around. What had happened?

A few days later, my housekeeper, who had once accompanied me to a class session, said, "Guess who I just saw at the bus stop—your meditation teacher." Later that week, instead of driving my usual route to the market, I had a sudden impulse to drive by the bus stop—and there he was.

As I drove him to his destination, I asked him where he

was living now. I was stunned when he said it was on the same street where I live, about a block away *near the tennis court!* This was exactly what my dream had told me, and there was absolutely no way that I could have known this information consciously.

For about a year after this event, he came to my home every week to give me private lessons in meditation, and work with a group of my friends. Yet, gradually, I began to notice inconsistencies and untruths in what he said and did. I found it more and more difficult to accept his guidance. While I was grateful for all that he had taught me, I sensed that I had reached his limits.

"When the student is ready, the teacher will appear," runs an ancient saying. But, teachers can only accompany us partway along the journey. We must each find our final destination alone. Ultimately, we must become our own teachers. Still, this parting of ways is often very difficult. The conflict between my gratitude for my teacher's initial help and disappointment over his flaws ignited an internal war.

During this time of inner struggle, the women in my dreams grew stronger. Eventually, I was able to see that I was being forced to create within myself what I had needed all along—a central core of strength. While I still valued what I learned from my teacher, I now had to acknowledge my own power and wisdom. I had found the courage to create my own pathway.

From the safe harbor of a loved and loving life with my man, I ventured elsewhere to test the waters. I honed my skill in painting. Although I reduced the intense level of meditation I had been pursuing, I continued to practice. I discovered what crystals stimulate the vibrational energy within my body, what foods enhance it, and what circumstances dull or bring it to a peak. More than ever, my body and my dreams became my finest teachers. If we but listen, there is a central self that never deceives.

My wider sense of freedom led me to other areas of dreams that I wanted to understand better. How does dreaming develop from childhood? I wanted to identify common childhood dreams and their composition; and to explore how the dreams of boys and girls are similar and how they are different. To answer these questions, I researched and wrote *Your Child's Dreams*.[20]

Next, because I felt there was no book that explored the phases of a woman's life as seen through dream spectacles, I focused on women's dreams. I wrote *Women's Bodies, Women's Dreams*,[21] pinpointing the recurrent dream symbols that appear with each new life passage, and what they mean.

At the moment, I am writing *Dream Well*,[22] a book that discusses the seven steps of physical healing that appear in our dreams. Working with people who've undergone physical trauma, I'm showing how they can accelerate their return to health by using their dream imagery.

After forty years, I still write and draw my dreams. My dream diary continues to be the most centering and instructive activity of my existence. *Your* dream diary may become so for you.

Learning from Your Dreams

Since you are about to embark on a momentous journey of your own, I offer here a few useful techniques on lucid dreaming and mandala making to help you chart your voyage.

Many dreamers find that just working on their dreams over a

period of time seems to stimulate lucidity and psychic ability. If you want to get started on lucid dreaming now, here's a summary of suggestions to use before, during and after dreams.

Before Dreaming

1. *Set goal.* Plan what you will do when you become lucid in a dream. Will you fly? Make love with the partner of your choice? Rehearse some skills? Ask your dream characters what they represent? Travel to a predetermined place? Try to contact another dreamer? Experiment with ESP? Ask to learn whatever you most need? Your first goal may simply be to have a lucid dream. It often helps to write your intention down in your journal before you go to sleep. This serves as a suggestion to yourself.

2. *Remember goal.* Remind yourself of your lucid dream goal during the day by putting it into a short phrase that you repeat like a chant or mantra as you drift off into sleep. For instance, "Tonight I fly." If you awaken during the night, repeat your phrase over and over until you fall asleep again.

3. *Visualize goal.* Picture yourself remembering your goal during a dream. Imagine what it will look like and feel like.

During Dreaming

1. *Changes in sensation.* Be alert for:
   a. The feeling of wind blowing in your face or a cool draft.

b. A tingling of your skin. This often involves the image of light rain or drizzle.

c. A sound or vibration, like a combined buzzing-tingling or a buzzing light.

d. A patch, crack, or hole of light that appears—sometimes as a window.

e. The sense that a dream story is beginning again (what I call "doubleness," rather like a waking *déjà vu*).

f. An intense staring or focusing of your eyes (what I call "fixedness").

g. Rhythmic movements, such as dancing, spinning, swimming, or pelvic thrusting.

h. A shift in consciousness within the dream—a sense that you are "going to sleep," "waking up," "going into a trance," feeling "lightheaded," or feeling "tired."

i. Suspension in the air—such as flying, floating, or levitating.

2. *Dream mirrors.* Pay special attention if you find yourself looking into a reflecting surface, such as a mirror, window glass, or pool. This is often a symbol for self-reflection and may mark the commencement of lucidity.

3. *Dreamlike elements.* Notice any incongruities, frightening or bizarre elements in the dream story. Test the reality of the dream. Recognize those two giant horses in the sky as dream creatures. Some dreamers find it useful to question themselves during the day ("Is this a dream?") and test their answer.

4. *Analysis of ongoing dream.* Are you having the same old frightening dream again? Are you suggesting to yourself what some dream image symbolizes? Recognize it for a dream.

5. *Maintain emotional balance.* Once you are lucid within a dream, stay calm. Keep a balance between becoming so emotional that you awaken, or so unfocused that you forget you're dreaming. Perform your goal or just let the dream play out while you watch, unafraid and conscious.

After Dreaming

1. *Review pre-lucid moments.* When you have a non-lucid dream, re-examine it for the points when you might have realized that you were dreaming.

2. *Visualize being lucid in the next dream.* When you awaken from an ordinary dream, picture yourself recognizing the next dream as a dream.

3. *Give waking form to any impressive lucid dream images.* "Artifacts" from dreams will help you comprehend the meaning of their symbolism and remind you of their message. Paint or draw your special dream images or find pictures that recapture the feeling they gave you. Put this dream artifact where you can see it until you feel you have absorbed the message of the dream figure.

Creating Your Dream Mandala

In this book, I construct my dream mandala step by step, from the outermost rim to the sacred center. As you read, you will probably be thinking about what images would go into your own mandala. You may wish to construct your personal mandala as you progress through the book, finding parallels for my dream images in your own. If so, here are some suggestions to get you started:

1. *Identify frightening dream images.* This first step is easy. Simply look for the frightening or horrifying images in your dreams. Although you'd probably rather not think about these, they are the very figures that can be transformed into your strengths. Their power to terrify has the same degree of force as their power to teach. Their energy can become your personal vigor.

   Don't restrict your thinking to the wild animals, evil villains, or inhuman threats that endanger your dreams. Also consider the places in your dreams that seem especially ominous. Do you dream of being back in a childhood home that you hated, as I did? Is there a setting where bad things happen to you in your dreams? This spot, unappealing as it is, contains energy that can be freed for positive growth. As you read about the elements in the mandala, temporarily assign some of your negative dream figures to the places that seem appropriate to you. You might want to make photocopies of the blank mandala form that appears in the Appendix and make notes in pencil—in case you later encounter more apt dream images to place in it.

2. *Identify helpful dream figures.* What are the images that assist you in overcoming your dream fears? What figures or things help you cope with the frightening animals, things, people, and places in your dreams? Among some adults, as well as most children, savior characters may be stereotyped heroes and heroines, such as Superman or Wonder Woman. Dreamers sometimes choose religious figures to save or protect them in their dreams, for example, Christ, God, a saint, a guru, or a goddess of mercy. Some dreamers utter prayers or chant mantras when they are in dream danger. Other dreamers may call on their mate or even the family dog. Still other dreamers encounter some idiosyncratic dream figure that comes to their rescue. This may be a talking animal, a person with magical powers, or a fantastic weapon or instrument that protects the dreamer. Regardless of its form, notice it and cherish it. Helpful dream images will emerge as dreamers begin the process of facing their fears and calling for help.

3. *Identify dream figures associated with competition.* Most dreamers have a characteristic way of expressing competition or pride in their dreams. This may take the form of a fight or duel, a singing or dancing contest, or a race.

4. *Identify dream figures associated with cooperation.* What images appear when you are participating in a group in your dreams? Are you singing in a chorus? Dancing in a circle? Sharing food? Look for the dream situations that seem to express loving cooperation with others.

5. *Identify dream figures that are associated with passion.*
   Are your dream lovers strangers or known persons?
   Do they represent themselves, or some quality that
   you need to incorporate? Is there a pun on the dream
   lover's name? One woman who dreamed of making
   love to a man named Art was actually missing her
   art activities that she had suspended, rather than
   yearning for the particular person. How do you
   picture yourself in dreams when you feel passionate or
   lustful? Are you dressed seductively? Do you wear
   red or some other color? Is your hair style different?
   All these have symbolic meaning.

    Whenever we are dreaming, our genitals, along with
   the whole central nervous system, are activated.
   Scientists have recently documented that women and
   men alike are experiencing sexual arousal while they
   dream.[23] It's not surprising that so many dreams have
   sexual content, direct or disguised. This is a natural
   part of dreaming. What form does it take in your
   imagery?

6. *Identify dream figures associated with genuine loving.*
   What shapes do your dreams take when you are in
   love? How do these differ from lustful dreams or
   dreams of romantic yearning? Are you given gifts of
   jewels or flowers? Delicious drinks or appetizing food?

7. *Identify dream figures associated with greed or
   overdoing.* What shapes does your dreaming mind
   conjure when you have been overeating, overworking,
   or overdoing in some other activity? Do you dream
   of hundreds of tiny pigs or one huge one? Do you see
   neglected gardens overgrown with weeds? Do your

dreams depict construction crews working to the point of exhaustion?

8. *Identify dream figures associated with balance.* Do you see healthy, blooming plants? Do you dream of riding a bicycle successfully over rough terrain? Are you able to whiz across the ice performing tricky steps with ease? What shapes appear in your dreams when your life is going smoothly?

9. *Identify dream figures associated with ignorance.* Are there lost children in your dreams? Has a baby been abandoned? Are there homeless men or starving women? Are animals wounded, hurt, or dying? How do the missing elements in your life appear in your dreams?

10. *Identify dream figures associated with growing knowledge.* Is a new born babe in your dream? Is there a brilliant baby or child? Do you discover rooms you never knew existed or new areas in a familiar city? Do you meet a wise old man? Do you encounter a priestess or goddess? Meet a mysterious guide? These are the "archetypes," the powerful figures that emerge as we begin to better understand ourselves and our dreams. At times these may be highly idiosyncratic—strange combinations of animals, plants, and people. At other times they may take the form of magical patterns or designs. All bespeak the beginning of new aspects of the self.

11. *Observe the special characteristics of your lucid dreams.* What happens to you when you become aware that you're dreaming? What sensations do you experience? See how these compare with the characteristics

listed under "Lucid Dreaming." What sort of figures appear before and after you are lucid? What changes do you observe? We have much to learn about lucid dreaming, so each dreamer has something to contribute.

12. *Construct your dream mandala.* All the images and sensations you have identified will have a place in your mandala. You'll be reading about how I constructed my mandala step by step. How do your images seem to fit the framework? You may wish to make tentative decisions as you read the book and complete your mandala later, or construct it as you go along. Further suggestions appear in the Appendix.

Giving your powerful, positive dream images waking form helps retain what you learn from them. Make or find images that capture the feeling of each special dream. Adjust the basic mandala framework to meet your own needs and interests. A woman dreamer who is a dancer used her dream images in a dance around an imaginary mandala. You may make a simple, temporary mandala or produce a permanent one, such as a small woven rug. The important thing is to become involved in the process, so that you discover the secrets contained within your images as you work with them.

Jung tells us, "There is no linear evolution; there is only a circumambulation of the self." By identifying your special dream images, rendering them in waking form, and placing them into your dream mandala, you are doing more than expressing yourself in a personal piece of art. In effect, you are re-creating yourself, image by image, color by color, until

your true pattern takes form. May your journey along this
path lead you to light.

San Francisco
St. Patrick's Day, 1989

NOTES

1. Patricia Garfield, *Pathway to Ecstasy: The Way of the Dream Mandala* (New York: Holt, Rinehart & Winston, 1979).

2. Patricia Garfield, *Creative Dreaming* (New York: Simon & Schuster, 1974).

3. C. G. Jung, *Memories, Dreams, Reflections* (New York: Vintage Fountain Books, 1963).

4. At the suggestion to Stephon Kaplan-Williams, he, Jeremy Taylor, Gayle Delaney, Stephan LaBerge, John Van Damm and I met in the fall of 1982 to co-found the A.S.D.

5. Founded by Dr. Stephen LaBerge, the Lucidity Institute conducts training programs in lucid dreaming and publishes a quarterly newsletter. For information, write to: Lucidity Institute, P. O. Box 2364, Stanford, California 94309.

6. Sylvia Brinton Perera, *Descent to the Goddess* (Toronto: Inner City Books, 1981).

7. Jean Shinoda Bolen, *Goddesses in Everywoman: A New Psychology of Women* (New York: Harper & Row, 1984).

8. Plato, *The Apology of Socrates*, in *Harvard Classics* (New York: P. F. Collier & Son, 1937): 26.

9. Shirley MacLaine, *Out on a Limb* (New York: Bantam, 1983).

10. Gelsey Kirkland with Greg Lawrence, *Dancing on My Grave* (New York: Jove, 1986).

11. Barbara Shor. Personal communication, September, 19, 1988. This event was carried out in association with the Samaya Foundation, New York City.

12. C. G. Jung, *Modern Man in Search of a Soul* (New York: Harcourt, Brace & Co., undated): 250.

13. Kilton Stewart, "Magico–Religious Beliefs and Practices in Primitive Society—A Sociological Interpretation of Their Therapeutic Aspects" (London School of Economics, 1948). There is much fascinating material in Stewart's dissertation. If he invented large portions of it, as has been suggested, he was indeed a skilled novelist. On the other hand, it may have been accurate at the time it was recorded.

14. Ivan Polunin and British anthropologist Geoffrey Benjamin, both then at the University of Singapore.

15. Kilton Stewart, "Dream Theory in Malaya," *Complex* (New York, 1951). Reprinted in *Altered States of Consciousness*, ed. Charles Tart (New York: Doubleday, 1972).

16. Kilton Stewart, *Pygmies and Dream Giants* (New York: W. W. Norton, 1954).

17. "Temiar Dream Songs from Malaya," recorded under the direction of H. D. Noone and E. D. Robertson (Ethnic Folkways Library, album FE4460, New York: Folkways Records, 1955).

18. Aristotle, *On Dreams*, from *Great Books of the Western World*, Vol. 8, ed. R. M. Hutchings (Chicago: Encyclopedia Britannica, 1952).

19. Stephen LaBerge, *Lucid Dreaming* (Los Angeles: Jeremy P. Tarcher, Inc., 1985). See this book for a history of LaBerge's work on lucid dreaming.

20. Patricia Garfield, *Your Child's Dreams* (New York: Ballantine, 1984).

21. Patricia Garfield, *Women's Bodies, Women's Dreams* (New York: Ballantine, 1988).

22. Patricia Garfield, *Dream Well* (New York: Simon & Schuster, in press).

23. For data on male sexual arousal in dreams, see C. Fisher, J. Gross & J. Zuch, "Cycle of Penile Erection Synchronous with Dreaming (REM) Sleep," *Archives of General Psychiatry, 12* (1965): 29–45. For data on female sexual arousal in dreams, see C. Fisher, H. D. Cohen, R. C. Schiavi, D. Davis, B. Furman, K. Ward, A. Edwards & J. Cunningham, "Patterns of Female Sexual Arousal During Sleep and Waking: Vaginal Thermo–Conductance Studies," *Archives of Sexual Behavior, 12*, no. 2 (1983): 97–122.

The dream of yesternight I now relate,
Exactly in the manner it was dreamt;
Be pleased . . . to vouchsafe thine ear awhile.

—Milarepa to his guru, Marpa
circa A.D. 1060

1 INTRODUCTION

There is a silent evolution taking place within us. Imperceptibly, dream by dream, in the dark of the night, we gradually transform ourselves into the new self that we will be tomorrow. Even as we are not aware of our own physical beginnings, of the merging of sperm and egg, of our embryonic development and differentiation, so we have little awareness of the ceaseless changes at work in our sleeping minds. Unknowingly, we evolve ourselves in our dreams.

The Dream Mandala* is a way of charting this process of inner evolution. A system I have devised for organizing and utilizing dream symbolism, it is a personal path to enlightenment founded upon the symbolic images of our dreams. It draws from the universal human concepts in Tibetan sacred art. Setting our individual dream images within the timeless, classic framework of the man-

* *Mandala*, a Sanskrit word, is pronounced with the accent on the first syllable with the first *a* sounded like the *u* in *circus* (*mŭn*·duh·luh).

1

dala, we are able to construct a plan for self-discovery: the Dream Mandala becomes a map of our inner world. It can reveal where we are at the present moment of our lives; it can guide our travel forward.

The figures of our nightly dreams have evocative resonance because they are already connected to our emotions. They are many-sided, multidimensional symbols of our living experience. They have the power to transform us, to the degree that we are able to penetrate, understand, and interpret them. These images of our dreams are not like pictures in a book nor carved idols on an altar; they are essences emerging from the depths of our psyche. They are crystallizations born of the raw material of our living and given shape by our imagination. They are our creations.

These most intimate of images can evoke universal forces. When understood, the fragile, momentary forms of our dreams are expressions of eternal laws or patterns. The shifting shapes that we may glimpse in a dream only once can actually reconnect us to the current of vital energy that moves all life, if we but recognize their nature and their place in the organization of our personal mandalas. In a very real sense, we create every night our own gods who can guide us along the pathway to ecstasy.

Mandalas are meaningful, organized structures, not merely concentric drawings or decorative formal designs. They convey, in a pictographic way, whole philosophic systems, entire bodies of knowledge. Every detail within a mandala is symbolically significant. However, the elementary framework of a Tibetan mandala is simple: three protective circles surround a square temple with four gates; within the temple is an inner sanctum where the deities are arrayed in four quarters of the space around the inmost center, where dwells the holiest image of all. In the present book, we shall take the journey from the outermost circle to the Sacred Center.

The Way of the Dream Mandala, I have discovered, can lead to altered states of consciousness, to lucid dreams, to out-of-the-body experiences, to orgiastic ecstasy, to healing states, and to mystic experiences. Finding ourselves is a forever-unfinished journey. The route one takes may lead, as it did for me, across cultures and time and through extraterrestial spaces. But it begins for each of us when we lie down to sleep tonight. . . .

2 THE GREAT STEERING WHEEL

The day is bright and beautiful. I'm driving my car down a street in San Francisco, where I live. It's an ordinary city scene on an ordinary sunny, windy day, and I'm thinking ordinary thoughts about some arrangements I must make for a contractor to inspect a house we want to buy (all current events). I whiz along the street, feeling the wind blowing hard. At that moment, for some unknown reason, I realize that it's *not* an ordinary day, place, or feeling: *I am in a dream*. Still driving, I command, "Up!" and my body lifts from the ground. The car is gone. I now whiz through the air as I lie on my stomach about ten or fifteen feet above the earth. I'm no longer driving but I still grasp the upper part of the steering wheel, which has become huge, a great circle. I hold the top rim, and the lower part rests on my thighs, above the knees. I feel the sun and the wind. I see the pavement clearly as I sail along. Everything is sharp, bright. It's a glorious sensation. I ask myself, "Are you happy?" and I know

that I am. "And you know that you're dreaming?" and I know that I am. I start to wonder what to do with this lovely lucidity as I zip through the air with the sun and wind in my face. However, the scene fades, like a light dimming, and suddenly I'm awake in bed.
("The Great Steering Wheel," May 29, 1974)

I had this dream more than four years ago. Yet I remember the wondrous glow, the sensations of reality, of joy and power that this dream flight gave me. The pleasurable feelings saturated the following day. This was not ordinary dreaming.

True, in symbolic terms, "The Great Steering Wheel" dream was ordinary enough, and understandable. At the time I had this dream, I was (as I am now) living with my beloved husband in a splendid city. My days were full and mostly happy; I felt able to resolve whatever problems confronted me. Furthermore, my career was advancing. I had just finished writing my first book* and was busy with plans for its forthcoming publication. As a symbolic expression of satisfaction with the way I was "steering" myself through life, this dream is straightforward indeed.

However, the *feeling* of this dream was something special. It bordered on the magical. I had often flown in my dreams; yet this dream was a *conscious* flight. I went "Up!" by deliberate choice. I flew at will and drank the flight through every pore as intensely as if the happening were a highly charged waking event. Just as I was about to explore this fantastic space further, the light faded and I woke.

How to continue that flight? How to get back to that real-unreal world? How to find once more the conscious-unconscious state? *How?* It was a mystery I set out to solve. And did . . . somewhat. I did not know then that it was life's mystery itself I was seeking to

* Patricia Garfield, *Creative Dreaming* (New York: Simon and Schuster, 1974; Ballantine, 1976).

unravel. Or that I must find myself in the search in order to carry it forward.

When I had "The Great Steering Wheel" dream, I was just beginning to taste the heady power of conscious dreaming—the *lucid dream*, in which the dreamer becomes aware that he or she is dreaming *during* the dream experience.[1] I had no idea into what unknown worlds it would lead me, what remarkable adventures. I had not yet learned how to sustain my lucid dreams, how to control or develop them, and how to project from them. I had no conception of what mysterious, frightening-majestic heights my dream flying would take me to. I did not know then how to travel in sleep to other worlds. The more I learn the way, the more I know I must seek, for there is no bottom, no top, and no end to this astonishing, sometimes fearful, exciting adventure. The finding is in the seeking.

These strange worlds may be within me rather than outside, but regardless of their locale, they are quite real. My quest to find the way, my discoveries as I went, my warnings to those who would set foot on the same path, my experiences, my fears, and my sense of what is yet to come—all will be described in the chapters that follow.

First, let me glance back at the little-girl self whose dreams started me in this direction so many years ago.

If "The Great Steering Wheel" dream was far less complex than the dreams and astral trips that would presently follow, it was well beyond my dreams as a child. Alone, in the dark, in a narrow wooden bed, I slept heaped round with my dear dolls—a tall Snow White, a petite Sonja Henie, a baby doll with checkered pinafore, a little-boy doll named Butch with blue rompers and red hair, a grown-up doll named Mary, among others. And in my early childhood there was a recurrent dream: I flew high in the air in a tiny plane. How terrifying when it began to fall—down, down, round and around. My stomach sinking, my heart pounding, I would fall with the plane in a heavy thud onto the floor by my bed. A familiar thud indeed. Over the years, in many homes, in many beds, children replay variations of the same dream, often without the accompaniment of an actual fall from bed. But if the falling dream is a common one, it may still be significant that it is the first dream I remember; especially since my dreams as an older child, when I was about eight, also dealt with flight.

These were unusual dreams; at least they left an unusual impact. As a result of several dreams of flying I began to have the curious suspicion that I really could fly while awake. I was not certain of it, or else I'd not likely be here. But it was a haunting idea made all the more eerie by the conviction that to prove it I must throw myself off some high place. On occasion I'd be tempted to test this obsessive thought by jumping from my front porch or a rock pediment. Not at all discouraged by my failure to fly under those circumstances, I reasoned that I must have faith and jump from a really high perch, such as the roof of a car or a garage, to be able to fly. In order to fly I had to *believe* that I could. (This is true, but only in the dream state.) Fortunately, rationality prevailed. Gradually and reluctantly I gave up the belief that I could fly while awake. I contented myself, instead, with such activities as hanging my head upside down while lying sideways on a bed and imagining myself walking on the ceiling. Or whirling until dizzy and falling into a heap.

Despite these concerns about whether or not I could fly, and a shy and mildly anxious approach to life, I was a relatively well adjusted child. Always slender, I was not yet the skinny teenager who would suffer so much from small breasts and a face pit-marked by the storms of adolescence. My long brown hair with reddish lights reached to my waist, and neighbors cautioned my mother that it would sap my strength. People praised my large hazel-green eyes and long, slender fingers, and I was pleased to be considered pretty and smart (though inwardly yearning to be beautiful and brilliant); and so life went along tolerably well.

School was satisfying, but the most fun was after school hours. Then, deep in solo fantasy, I played among the fragrant lilies of the valley that lined the side of our tree-shaded house. The plants became a jungle-forest for the adventures of the tiny dolls I had made, using pipe cleaners for bodies and thread for hair. Or I would hurry home after classes to huddle close to the radio for the latest episode of "Superman" and decode Captain Midnight's daily message by means of my secret-code ring. Or sit with girl friends transforming little silk and velvet scraps into garments for our storybook dolls. Or play hide-and-seek in the twilight with the neighborhood children and feel the delicious excitement-fear of hunt-and-chase.

There were two special joys during these childhood years, one from each parent. My mother, who was always an avid reader, had a gift for storytelling. This was a marvelously portable talent. Whenever we had long waits—at a bus stop or in a hospital clinic—she would weave endlessly some further adventures of the Five Little Peppers or other favorites of mine; sometimes she invented characters and plots to soothe my restless wiggles. The stories she told me continued into my dreams. And from my dreams grew new stories. Before the conflicting emotions of adolescence battered the relationship between mother and daughter, I could immerse myself in the magic of her tales.

My father provided another, more tangible, magic. He was a skilled craftsman with an artistic flair who loved making things. For the most special birthday I ever had, at age ten, he made the happiest of childhood presents—my very own marionette theater. The stage was large, with long brown velvet drapes to hide the operators, and a green crepe curtain that raised and lowered. The footlights were made from Christmas-tree bulbs that could be switched on and off. The backdrops were beautifully painted poster-board scenes—a forest, a village street, a palace room—whatever a fairy tale required. In front of the backdrops were perfectly scaled canopied beds or rustic tables. And the marionettes were my dolls magically come to life. Now they could walk and dance and play out parts together. My father carved their heads of wood, adding detailed features with plastic wood and paint. He put their bodies together from dowel rods and carved scraps. Each detail represented some clever use of a household item—an old music box became an organ-grinder's organ; a curtain ring was the ring in the nose of a bull. Strung together, dressed and painted, they were a whole population, and I, their mistress. Now I could play out my dreams on a waking stage; my mother's stories took on concrete form.

The range of characters delighted me: Koko the Clown and his younger brother, in white suits with red polka dots; the King of Stumpingham, the Queen, the Prince, the Princess; an elflike Robin Goodfellow with pointed, feathered cap; two fairies with blue gauze-and-tinsel wings that flapped; Tony the mustached organ-grinder, who could crank out a tune on his music box; Rosalita, his tap-dancing wife; their monkey in a red jacket; a "pistol-packin' Mama" (from the song of that name) who could push her flower cart and fire live caps from her pistol by the pull of a wire; a Scheherazade who could sinuously roll her bejeweled torso and arms; a Santa Claus who could mount and ride his tail-wagging reindeer; Ferdinand the Bull; and many, many others added over the years.

It was for me a fairyland come to life. True, we ended up only giving shows for churches and schools and other children's birthday parties; and my father would get cross if I let strings sag, or suspended a marionette in midair, or, worst of all sins, dropped a control stick onto the stage. Yet the magic held, and by subtle movements of sticks and strings I could create another world. Perhaps all of this was preparation. Maybe that riotous childhood imagination was needed many years later to help me discover the subtle internal movements connecting me to further worlds. (But I have yet to learn how to operate reliably the controls for that performance.)

This relatively happy time ended when we moved to a different house, a hated house. I was then twelve years old. Perhaps my unhappy state would have emerged in any case with the onset of adolescence, but I always associate it with the ancient, crumbling, dank place that became our home and seemed to invade my inner life.

The relationships with my parents crumbled, too, as did their own in the next few years, and I still recall a specific dream fragment that heralded the feelings to come. My favorite doll, Mary, became, in my dream, somehow very cruel and mean to me. I hated and feared her. When I woke I could no longer look upon that doll, much less play with her with pleasure. I set her aside and exiled her to the attic. At last, repelled by her crackled face and creaking limbs, I discarded her altogether. Of course, I did not think then of the symbolism of Mary, the mother, and of *my* mother and my increasingly hostile feelings about her at that time. Nor did I know either that one cannot conquer fear by avoiding it, that both in waking life and in dreams the only way to overcome fear is to face it and transform it. There were many fears I tried to escape from—and failed—in the next few years of my life before the joy and magic of the winged fairy marionettes returned, with a personal security that grew in part out of my dream life.

Moreover, in a foolish moment of young adulthood when I had the job of clearing out that dilapidated home after my parents' separation, I let a large cardboard box packed with my father's magical marionettes be carted away with the boxes of discarded goods. On second thought, at the last minute, I pulled three only from the top, as mementos. They sit now on my bookcase—Koko the Clown, still smiling, leaning against a tattered Scheherazade, curiously symbolic of my parents' relationship, with a battered Ferdinand the Bull at their feet. I could not have foreseen how I would achingly wish to repossess all of those dancing dolls. Nor how the memory of my father, dead some years later, would linger about their painted features, so like mirrors of our family. I cannot revoke the act of giving them away or reclaim the lost box of childhood, but the memories are indelible. In my dreams the dolls dance once more and my father's smile is radiant and the joy of my childhood is lit again.

3 THE OUTERMOST RIM
OF THE DREAM MANDALA

Each of us must find a means to "steer" himself or herself through life, as I was doing in "The Great Steering Wheel" dream. For we are all involved in a great adventure. In our own ways, we struggle to find ourselves—who we are and what the meaning of our lives is.

My way of finding myself began with ordinary dreaming. I suffered over the usual nightmares: I fell through the air, and I was pursued by ferocious creatures. I chuckled at the fantastic pictures my dreams concocted from waking stories; I conversed with fairies and romped with giants during my sleep. Because my mother was interested in dreams and often discussed her readings of Freud and Jung at the dinner table, I became curious to see whether my own dreams contained important self-knowledge. I had always been a vivid dreamer and was intrigued by the thought that these chaotic dream images were messages to myself. At age fourteen I began to record my dreams—on scraps of paper from a junior-high-school class notebook, on the back of a letter from a girl friend—I wrote them anywhere and worked with their symbolism. It gave me a sense of well-being, even when the dreams were frightening, to understand how I felt at a deeper level. I never suspected that they would become a focus of my life's work.

I have kept the dream record continuously for the last twenty-nine years. Despite many life changes—a first marriage, a baby, completing a Ph.D. program in clinical psychology, getting divorced, remarrying, living abroad, and extensive travel—I always managed to find the time to scribble down and review the latest dream show. Working with my dreams gave such comfort and inspiration that I refused to give it up.

Eventually, I heard of the Senoi, a primitive tribe living in Malaysia, who teach their children how to dream. I was skeptical as well as curious. Like most Westerners, it had never occurred to me that it was possible to get ready to dream. You worked with dreams *after* they took place, not before. I began to investigate the Senoi, was able to visit them briefly, and interviewed researchers who had lived with them. I experimented with their techniques and found them to be astonishingly effective. Suddenly it became possible to turn and face my dream monsters instead of fleeing from them. As I confronted and conquered the enemies in my dreams, the activities of my sleeping nights changed and a feeling of greater confidence carried over to the waking state.

Wondering whether other peoples direct their dreams, too, I began to study the role of dreams in many cultures. I gathered the results of these investigations into the book I called *Creative Dreaming*.[1] I taught the techniques to my students at California State University, Sonoma, and later in the University of California Extension system. Students' dreams and their lives began to change as mine had. It was truly possible to prepare to dream, and to become an active participant in one's own dreams instead of remaining a passive victim of them.

Meanwhile, I had been experiencing yet another level of dream consciousness. More and more I found myself having lucid dreams—dreams in which you become aware that you are dreaming *during* the dream. In this incredible state, anything becomes possible: flying at will, orgasm with partners of choice, calling forth creative ideas, projecting oneself into distant lands, visiting with long-dead people, and so on. Then, after months of lucid dreaming, I found myself automatically, on occasion, experiencing what people call out-of-the-body projections.

As my experiences in these altered states of consciousness, lucid dreaming and out-of-the-body trips (if that is what they are) gathered force, I needed to make sense of them. It no longer seemed to matter to me whether these worlds are within or without, whether they are in a physical location or in a different state of consciousness. They are a universal human experience and, as such, are real. A pattern was emerging that was crucial to capture and share. I thrashed about in my mind for an understandable way to translate these experiences. Dreams are so visual, their translation should be visual, too. Not words, not lists, not charts, but pictorial symbols that would convey the essence of the experience.

I devised, at last, the Way of the Dream Mandala, a kind of paraphrase, not a duplication, of the original Tibetan pattern upon which it is based. The Dream Mandala, personalized with one's own dream images, becomes a chart for self-discovery. It gives a sighting on the self—the beautiful, ever-shifting, growing bit of life force that is us.

Since ancient times men and women have been doing just this; they have gathered whole systems of knowledge and rendered them into graphic mandala form. I first began to sense the universality of the mandala pattern a few years ago. On a hot summer's holiday in Mexico City, I marveled at the great circular sunstone calendar wherein the Aztecs had chiseled their knowledge of the patterns of time. In the cool drizzle of an autumn afternoon, I stood on Salisbury Plain in England, in the center of a ring of great monoliths where the priests and priestesses of Stonehenge had laid out some long-lost ritual.

In museums, I examined photographs and drawings of sand paintings that the American Indians used to describe their medical philosophy and provide a magic treatment circle for a patient for a moment in time before the sand was swept away. With a hesitant finger, I traced the wisdom of the cosmos that the ancient Chinese had cast into a bronze mandala that graced the back of a mirror for the nobility. In New Delhi, I gazed long at the vibrant colored images of gods and sacred beasts on scrolls framed in lustrous silk brocade that the Hindu and Tibetan Buddhists had made to express their sacred rites and symbols from their Tantric texts. I met the same figures again in brilliant array on lamasery walls on a misty hilltop in Chiengmai, Thailand. I wandered down the tiled walkways and gazed in awe at the intricate mosaic patterns with which the Moslems made their religious beliefs visible in the Blue Mosque in Istanbul. I sat with the warm sunshine streaming through the rose window at the Cathedral of Notre Dame in Paris, the jeweled colors glowing like my state of mind as I contemplated them.

In the living cell, observed through a microscope in a biologist's laboratory, I watched life pulsing. And the basic structure was the same. More and more the impression was accumulating. Whether the content was the elegant flow of dividing chromosomes or the gathering of a body of religious beliefs, *the structure was the same.* All of these mandalas organized a body of knowledge. That knowledge can be reproduced by those who are able to read the picture language, by those who can decode its symbols.

Using the Tibetan system as a provisional guide, we can decode some of the emerging patterns of our inner psychology. The word *mandala* is an ancient Sanskrit label for a "circle" or "group" that is organized symmetrically around its center. It was Jung who brought the concept of mandalas to the Western world. He presented the idea simply as a magic circle that symbolically represents the striving for unity of self. He published several paintings made by his patients—they were basically circles divided into four parts with a center—as well as descriptions of similar mandalas that he made for himself.

In the Tibetan and Hindu sense, however, the concept of a mandala is far more complex than this.[2] Mandalas summarize a philosophy. They refer, in both Hindu and Tibetan Tantric Buddhism, to drawings of a group of deities represented diagrammatically in a circle *according to their relationships.* In picture form, the mandala tells the story of the pathway through various levels of consciousness to mystic union with the source of life. The mandala expresses a doctrine and serves as a guide, a secret meditation circle, to use in developing the mystic union—all transformed into graphic symbols. The arrangement of the images in the mandala shows the route to spiritual transcendence. It is a pattern that one can learn to use to guide one's own mystic experience.

It would be foolish, if not impossible, to try to convey all the complexities and subtleties of Buddhist Tantric philosophy and their depiction in sacred art forms. Such a task would take us many years, and we might never learn to relate the Tibetan images to ourselves, to make a translation. We can, however, share the universal frame: I have used it to record my own dream imagery, and to follow the path to transcendental experiences.

We can place certain key figures from our dreams within the framework of the Tibetan mandalas because the gods and goddesses of the Buddhist iconography are not "out there" in "heaven." They are not embodied spirits to worship from afar, but symbols of self—symbolic forms of human states of consciousness. As close as our flashes of hatred, as real as our waves of pity, they personify our feelings. But, although they are imaginary constructions, they are no less powerful. Their impact is dramatic. We can spend a lifetime serving a god of greed, a goddess of vanity, or a goddess of love and compassion. By giving names and faces to these gods and goddesses, who may appear to us in a variety of guises in our dreams, we can better cope with the states of mind they represent. But always we

must release them back to the mass of swirling life energy (to the "void," as the Buddhists would say) whence they came. We must not become obsessed with them. They are not objects; they are states of mind. They are within us.

These gods and goddesses are like the figures of our dreams. Indeed they may be precisely that. They emerge. We "recognize" them as aspects of ourselves. We may admire or detest them. And we release them, to dream of other figures, and to continue our growth. But first they must give us the gift of self-understanding they contain.

Jung once remarked, "It is from the depths of our own psychic life that new spiritual forms will arise."[3] By inclining our ear to the incessant tapping of our dream code and transcribing its messages, we can tune in to our psychic growth. The Way of the Dream Mandala is a path to enlightenment. It is a journey signposted, for me, by the symbols from my own dream record.

In Tibetan art, the outermost circle of a mandala marks the

Facing page:
Tibetan Buddhist Mandala. *This is an example of a typical Tibetan Buddhist mandala of the simplest form. The five "Meditation Buddhas" appear as figures in the central portion. The dots between the figures represent various attendants and minor deities. In some versions there are no dots; in others there are more or less than here. (Based mainly on mandalas in the collection of The Society for Asian Art.)*

The Outermost Perimeter of a Tibetan Buddhist Mandala—the Ring of Flames. *This outer circle consists of stylized flames in five alternating colors.*

boundary to another state of consciousness. For us to move into this different state of consciousness we must cross the threshold. The border surrounds and protects the mystery, the holy place. What is enclosed is our consciousness in a special, a changed, form. When we are able to cross the boundary, we move toward the Sacred Center. *In Tibetan art, this outermost perimeter is invariably a ring of multicolored flames at the edge of the mandala.* The fire is meant to dispel intruders and to burn away our ordinary consciousness before we can enter, purified.

For myself the outermost perimeter of the Dream Mandala was the great steering wheel, which I substituted for the traditional ring of flames. I have mentioned that on one level "The Great Steering Wheel" dream was a straightforward expression of satisfaction with the way I was "steering" through life at that moment. On another level, however, the great steering wheel was in itself a kind of huge mandala on which I, as if on a magic carpet of old, flew to another world where conscious mind and fantasy dreaming are joined. It is a

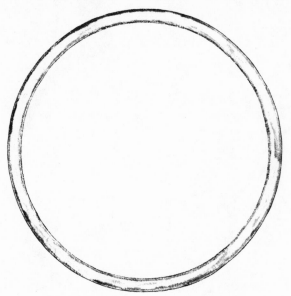

The Great Steering Wheel—*the outermost perimeter of my personal Dream Mandala.*

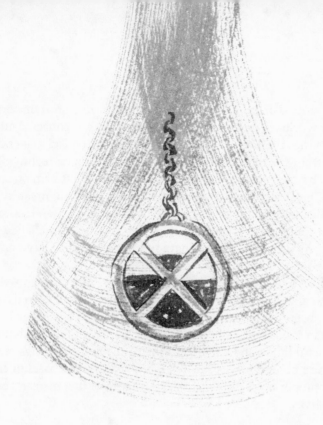

The Hypnotic Wheel—*dream image symbolizing the method I used to reach an altered state of consciousness.*

world of glowing colors and sharply etched shapes. There, fully conscious in a state of lucid dreaming, I can wander among my visions and all things become possible. Because the sense of flying steers me to the altered state I wish to produce, the great steering wheel seems appropriate for my mandala border. It takes me within the boundary. My Dream Mandala summarizes for me the state of lucid dreaming.

Circular forms may be minute or vast. In another dream at the same period as that of "The Great Steering Wheel," I was shown a small wheel, about an inch in diameter. It was rendered in silver, with four spokes dividing sections that were filled in varying amounts with a dark substance. A person held the wheel by a chain while it swung to and fro, to and fro, putting the watching woman—

myself—into a trance. This small circular form also transported me to other worlds. The great steering wheel altered consciousness by literal flying; the little hypnotic wheel altered consciousness by a kind of flying within the head, a lightheaded trance feeling. Both wheels changed consciousness for me within the dream state.

The great steering wheel marks the border. The mystery, the secret, lies within. Inside the circle of my Dream Mandala, my joys, my pains, and my regrets have their destined position. They tell the story of my past. They illuminate my present. They have given me a route to new adventure.

Painful experiences can provide impetus to future growth. We seldom realize it while we are suffering them, but the trials of our past can become our greatest assets. The hated house that I moved into when I was twelve became such a transforming symbol for me. So, too, childhood and adolescent pleasures and sufferings recalled in dreams are pivotal pieces in the giant pattern to be assembled. Seen in their proper perspective, these fragments of dreams can transfigure our lives.

4 THE HOUSE ON
WILLOW GROVE AVENUE

I am in the attic of an old, crumbling house. It is hard to find my way because of the darkness and great masses of piled junk. Everywhere I turn are boxes of trash, crates, and old, discarded household equipment. I pick up a box to clear a space and am shocked to find that it is coated with thick gray dust, which clings to my hands. Now I feel the light, sticky touch of spider webs across my face. Shuddering, I try to push them away with the back of my hand. I struggle frantically to shove aside the trunk in front of me, and behold with horror a mass of swarming, crawling bugs, shining in the dark. They were hidden until now. I wake in terror.

("The Mess in the Attic," a composite of selected dreams between 1946 and 1950)

This dream from adolescent years, a composite of the many that plagued me on the same subject, expresses some of the horror that the house on Willow Grove Avenue generated in me. It reflects the internal horror that built up during my teenage years.

The house was old, perhaps 125 years, a tall and narrow stone relic of the Civil War period. In the front yard stood a pump. There were three fireplaces, one above the other—a large one in what became our cellar, a medium one in the front living room, and a small one in my bedroom. Visitors admired these and the beamed ceilings. But to me it was old, old, cold, and crumbling. No matter how one cleaned the wooden floor, great clumps of gray dust gathered in the cracks. In winter or in brilliant summer, the two-foot-thick stone walls held the chill and led me to imagine damp dungeons. I was only comfortable at the dinner table, where my chair was directly in front of the heating outlet and warming blasts from the coal furnace enveloped my skinny legs. Or else deep under piles of fleecy bed covers.

But then, possessed of keen hearing, I could hear all the terrifying sounds of the night. Each scrape of the windowpanes as the black-walnut trees groaned against them brought new alarm. From time to time a vagrant squirrel scampered under the eaves to roam the attic above my head. In later years I lived there briefly with my first husband after my parents' divorce. The house was really falling apart then. A swarm of wasps built their nest in the attic, blocking all visitors to that area, and by means of some unknown-to-us hole managed to reach the single bathroom, where one was always in danger of wasp stings. We went to the toilet armed with bug spray. There, while washing one morning, I was stung on the breast by a wasp that flew up my nightgown. But these repugnant conditions came later, along with the invasion of cat-sized rats in the cellar. The adolescent anxieties in that house were sufficient. My father toiled to move earth, build stone walls and gardens, and patch the holes, but the house remained a horror to me.

I was ashamed to bring my friends to this wreck of a place, so different from their homes. It was far away from the street of my hide-and-seek playmates, up steep hills, and, to my childish view, very ugly. No matter that there were cozy fires and marshmallow parties. No matter that my pale little brother grew stronger and rosy-cheeked from romping in the large yard, or that we had flowers and fields to look upon. For me, the house was hideous and my social life a shambles.

Although there were woods to one side of the house on Willow Grove Avenue and fields across the way, to the other side and behind it in cavernous holes was Sine's limestone quarry. Orange-and-black trucks ceaselessly hauled the white rock that was chewed into powder and spat out by a monster grinder. Day by day the dragon mouths bit off larger chunks of rock until our house and trees clung precariously to the property line on that side. In an unpredictable rhythm, the dynamite blasting came, boom after boom, loosening the rocks before it. Our whole house shook with each tremor. I felt as though there were no peaceful place on earth.

Perhaps it was the trauma of the change, or the increasing tension between my parents, or my own fears grown large, or a predisposition from infantile whooping cough, or the gray-white dust of the quarry, or all together—whatever the reason, my mother swears that on the first day I saw that house, I lay down and began to wheeze.

Thus began many years of torment with asthma, miserable nights of gasping for breath, agonized waiting for morning while Mother read to distract me until the drugstore was open and we could get medicine, or until we could trek to the doctor for emergency shots of adrenaline. The discomfort was not constant, but it was an oft-recurring plague until I was well into my twenties and well away from that house.

Things grew worse on every front. I'll not dwell on the painful skinniness that evolved, the boys who taunted me with "Toothpick!" or called even my still-small breasts "Fake!" or the hated girl who wanted to count my vertebrae and stuck pins into me in civics class, or my poorly cared-for teeth that began to decay like the house, or my agonized loneliness at not being elected to the junior-high-school sorority.

My face reflected my inner pain. Deep purple pustules filled and erupted endlessly, increasing my everyday turmoil. Once, as I entered one of the long line of doctors' offices of that time, a little child asked his mother, "Does that lady have measles?" I shriveled and wished I were dead. Those people who said, "You would really be beautiful if your skin were clear," gave no comfort. That impossibility only heightened the torture.

The most painful part of this period was the sense of isolation. When the school buses assembled outside Thomas Williams Junior High School to cart their peg-panted, felt-skirted, dickey-bloused, bobby-soxed passengers home, I was relegated to a different route. No longer hurrying home joyfully to play out fantasies alone or with girl friends; slow-footed, heavy-hearted, I reluctantly returned to the cold house on the hill.

The physical distance imposed an additional burden. The two great social events of junior high school were the formation of sororities and fraternities and the beginning of instruction in ball-room dancing. I've mentioned being excluded completely from the sorority. It was a matter of tearful nights and days. And endless comforting by two staunch girl friends of storybook-doll days, who continually promised that on the next voting I could not possibly be blackballed. But dancing classes were open to everyone each Friday night through the school year. What desolation when I learned that the location of our new house required my attending the nearer of the two dance classes. It was almost entirely populated by students from the rival junior high school.

So I found myself almost alone in two worlds: feeling isolated and adrift among my own classmates during the week; and, on Friday nights, dressed in red corduroy and black patent pumps, staring solemnly at the dance floor more often than not as others fox-trotted by. And the rehash of last Friday's dance class was the prime topic of discussion first thing on Monday morning, leaving me feeling further and further alone and more and more different.

I turned inward. I wrote poems. I attended church (at least there I felt part of a social setting). I read a great deal, although schoolwork no longer gave me pleasure, and I wavered on the thin edge of sanity.

All was not despair, however. There were some sustaining forces. I was fourteen when I began to date a little, and despite conflicts over whether or not kissing on the first date was immoral, and though I suppressed sexual thoughts in accordance with my traditional Methodist upbringing, there were compensations. Still too skinny, still broken out in facial bumps, still too tall for most of the slower-growing boys, I began to find I had a certain charm for some of them.

About this time, too, I began to record my dreams. I had no precognition of my future work, simply an interest that grew out of my mother's description of her widespread psychological readings and my own always-vivid dream life. I remember the first dream I tried to analyze, the skeptical approach with which I free-associated to the dream symbols, and the flash of pleasure that came with insight into the meaning of the dream. Earlier that week, I had gone on a first date with a boy from school, a rare event. Eager not to appear as shy as I was, and to impress him with my lovability, I had behaved boldly. It startled him into retreat and led him to comment to others on how forward I was.

In the dream that followed—the first that I tried to analyze—one of the images was that of a governor. I sought to understand its symbolism by writing down a long list of my associations to the term. For several minutes, I could not see any sense to it. How silly; it doesn't mean anything. Then, I glanced back to the head of the list. With a start I saw that the very first association I'd written was "Governor: grants pardons." But of course, that's what I wanted desperately, a pardon, another chance with that particular boy. Thus I realized that my dreams were a means to understanding myself, not simply a curiosity, but a key. I kept a running record of any striking dreams and felt a catharsis from working with them.

The ups and downs of the remaining adolescent years were roller-coaster-like. I suffered and agonized still. Yet the brighter moments increased. The sensitive skin calmed a bit. I had a steady date with the boy who was to become my first husband. I had some skill in art. I began to feel joy in learning again. In particular, I discovered the value of one's own unique characteristics.

From childhood I had the sort of hands that prompted people to ask, "Do you play the piano?" Since I didn't and thought perhaps I should, I felt embarrassed. I trembled when the sixth-grade arithmetic teacher with the flashing glasses stated accusingly, "Someone in this room has long fingers!" How could I have known she meant that someone was stealing and not that she had noticed that I possessed a body fault? I diligently filed my nails short and tried to make my hands look like my classmates', feeling slightly deformed to be so different. It wasn't until the end of high school that I let the nails grow. Suddenly everyone began to exclaim, "Why, your hands are beautiful!" Soon I was modeling them—doing television commercials, finger-walking through the yellow pages for the cameras, and being handcuffed for a detective-magazine cover. For modeling, long-and-slender was desirable. Now I began to feel different for good reasons.

I graduated from high school, spent a few months in a drama school, took a job as a social-service worker, then as a secretary, and, at twenty-one, married the boy I'd dated steadily since I was sixteen. The problems came and went, the misery ebbed and flowed. At the best times I dreamt of beautiful jewelry, rings and pins. At the worst times I dreamt of uptorn, dying trees with masses of tangled roots. I rarely flew in my dreams.[1]

As my mother aged and struggled to cope with her own life problems, her ever-lively imagination took on alarming proportions. She began to suspect unknown people of poisoning her food or of following her, and in other ways clearly exhibited paranoid behavior.

To my young adult eyes this was more than a menopausal crisis reaction that would pass. It was, it seemed to me then, distorted and grotesque thinking grown out of too much fantasy. Imagination was dangerous and I was done with it. My mother's behavior aroused fears for myself. How much was I like her? How secure was my own sanity? I determined to be a totally different person. I disavowed any further connection with waking tale-spinning and suppressed any stray snippets that wandered into my mind. Only the way of science seemed sane.

Married, and in a new setting, I felt that I had escaped from the house of horrors. Indeed, some of the suffering was over, but, like all of us, I carried the shadow of the past within me.

The house on Willow Grove Avenue became a recurrent symbol in my dream life. It was some twenty years later that I came to recognize the significance of my dream visits to that spot. I did not realize how necessary it was for me to explore again and again the thick dirt and gray quarry dust, the ugliness and coldness of the place. At first I did not grasp the implication of my dream chores when I found myself sorting through the junk accumulated in the dream attic or cellar—the endless distributing into piles of things to throw away, to give away, or to keep. Only when I began to discover in my dreams something of value midst the trash and the dirt—a brilliant blue vase, an old painting I didn't know was there—did I begin to suspect the quiet evolution taking place within me. There, among the worthless objects, hidden by the junk, I would find again and again in my dreams *something*, something of value, something precious, something worth keeping. And the satisfaction of that discovery was beyond words. I believe it is a discovery that each person must experience for himself or herself—the worst parts of our life contain something of value. We must dig through the dirt and ugliness to find them. If we throw it all away we lose something precious, irreplaceable. We must find the beauty within our house of horrors to be complete. Our dreams can remold us.

I had learned a great deal by the time I uncovered the riches buried in the house on Willow Grove Avenue, but I still did not know how to go there by will, how to evoke the treasure by request, how to feel my father's arms hold me once more. I did not know the hidden wealth in my mother's tales, nor the strength of healthy imagination. I did not yet have the power of conscious dreaming. It was necessary first to develop a variety of skills in the waking state before I could believe in flying and magic once more.

5 THE TEMPLE WALLS OF THE DREAM MANDALA

Among the dream symbols that we beget nightly, we find words and images—chants and gods of our own—that are potent with meaning for us. These symbols are already connected to our deep-seated emotions. They stimulate our imagination without preconditioning because they are *formed by* our imagination. Devotional symbols without an experiential background have little emotional appeal and therefore are impotent. Gods foreign to us are castrated gods, whereas our own dream figures easily move us to passion. We can learn to concentrate the forces that these figures generate, to direct and release them. First, however, we must locate the symbol that moves us.

For me, the house on Willow Grove Avenue is such a dream symbol. It is heavily laden with emotion. In waking life, the adolescent years that I spent within its cold stone walls were a continuous source of misery. Its recurrent presence in my dreams was likely to be the setting of some anxiety-producing dream experience. That house seemed to me to be a totally negative part of life that I would gladly turn aside from.

Yet the years passed since I had lived there—ten, then twenty—and still I found myself returning in dreams to that unhappy dwelling. As I have mentioned, I began to notice that the content of such dreams was shifting. Although the structure was still old, cold, moldering, and messy, my activities there seemed to be ones of sorting things out. This was sometimes a literal packing into boxes and shipping away of masses of junk; sometimes it was a bringing of order by better arrangement; sometimes a fixing up and redecorating. I would be in the attic, or the cellar, or the garden, or my bedroom, or the main living quarters, but somehow I was making things better. The most impressive part of these dreams, as I've said, was the constant discovery of a thing of beauty midst the trash that I had almost overlooked. As if to demonstrate the assertion that this dream image is connected to powerful emotions, my eyes well up with tears as I write those words, "a thing of beauty midst the trash that I had almost overlooked." To others it may appear simply a trite phrase. It moves me profoundly. And in my mind's eye I see flashes of objects uncovered in these housecleaning dreams—the blue vase of great beauty, the magnificent painting, the jewels covered by ashes—that I hadn't realized were there. These objects as such did not exist in the house, so their presence in my dreams had to be symbolic. The more these prizes emerged, the more I was prompted to reconsider the house on Willow Grove Avenue. What does that house mean to me? Why do I find such things there? What does it signify?

At last the repetitive dream messages and my reflecting upon them brought me to a new awareness: there was something of value in that place, in that very spot of so much adolescent pain, that I had overlooked. The power of imagination that had once so fascinated and then frightened me had been buried in the mess of those times. I had exiled my fantasy from waking life, just as I had exiled to the attic the doll that had frightened me in a dream.

The treasures that I had overlooked were direct gifts from my parents: the artistic skill of my father (which most notably took the form of marionettes) and the story-weaving skill of my mother. As a troubled adolescent, I had needed to set these parts of myself aside and concentrate on making a marriage, and then, later, on book learning, on memorizing sets of facts, and on achievement in educational and material terms. Yet now I needed to go back and unearth these treasures and integrate them into my present life. They were never really gone—only suppressed, held at a distance. I had rejected the fantasy world they represented; it flourished untamed in the landscape of my dreams. Perhaps I sensed its importance by recording my dreams over all those years, so that it was never totally out of sight. Finally, I recognized my love for fantasy-making when it surfaced once again in my waking world.

It happened a few years ago, when, after long training in writing research papers for college classes, plowing through a lengthy dissertation, and writing professional papers, I had produced a book on dreams that was intended for students in the classes that I was teaching. When I showed it to textbook publishers, however, they viewed it as too popular in style. Trade-book publishers, on the other hand, thought it too academic. Finally one of them offered a contract with the proviso that I would transform the manuscript into a totally popular form. Faced with the alternative of not getting the ideas into print at all, I set about converting the manuscript into the most appealing and interesting form I could devise. It took a while to get into a storytelling mode again after so much training in writing reports, but at last the ideas began to flow. Picture after picture, scene after scene welled up into the waking state. And I found that I loved it! For now the fantasy-making served a purpose. It worked for me instead of against me. Stories emerged by the dozens, and I loved creating them. Work ceased to be drudgery and became pleasure. And after scarcely drawing since grade school, when I'd won a local art scholarship, I even began to sketch again. I knew that I was home. The powerful imagination that was my inheritance from childhood came out to play. I had uncovered the treasure that was buried inside the house on Willow Grove Avenue.

Naturally, the cold stone walls of that once formidable house became the temple walls of my Dream Mandala. It would have been a great personal loss had my dreams not led me to enter those walls again and again until I heard the message. What vital part of every person might not lie buried in the pains of his or her past? Should we not walk deliberately toward the sorrows of times gone by and find the gems locked inside? They may be the most precious things we possess.

In Tibetan sacred art, the temple walls come immediately after the three protective outer circles. Our view of the temple in a mandala is an aerial one. As though we were looking directly down from the sky, we see the walls constructed thickly like a fortress's. Both outer and inner walls are subdivided into five colored bands. Embedded within the wide outer portions of the walls are victorious and propitious symbols of Buddha. The walls are hung with necklaces and jeweled fringe befitting a royal palace.

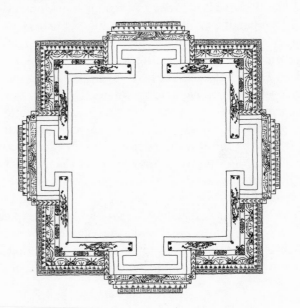

The Temple Walls of a Tibetan Buddhist Mandala. *These walls, divided into colored bands and hung with jewels, surround and protect the sacred figures.*

Built upon the top of a sacred mountain, the temple seems to hover in the air. There are four gates to enter the divine citadel—or holy city, as some prefer to think of it. These gates are depicted flat, as though lying back, in the form of a T. Over the gates rises a kind of triumphal arch composed of several little roofs, one on top of the other, and each one shorter than the one under it. (The number of roofs varies; in some mandalas there are four, in others eleven.) On top of the arch rests a disc called the Wheel of the Law. Above the wheel is an umbrella, symbol of royalty, and from its sides issue ornamental streamers. To the right and left of the wheel are two gazelles, recalling the preaching of Buddha's first sermon in the deer park.

The Wheel of the Law—*Tibetan Buddhist symbol representing the teachings of Buddha.*

The symbol of the Wheel of the Law particularly intrigued me. This emblem represents universal and spiritual law and its ethical application in personal life. It symbolizes the doctrine of Buddha that leads from a mundane existence to the center of liberation. Each spoke signifies a desirable form of behavior. In some mandalas it is rendered with twelve spokes; more often it is shown with eight spokes. To me, it looks amazingly like the four-spoked hypnotic wheel that appeared in my dreams before I had even heard of Tibetan Buddhism.

Each of the four gates is guarded by a fierce deity. This wrathful guardian directs his vengeance toward intruders. His purpose is not to torture the follower, but to lend his power to help followers conquer their egos.

One enters the mandala by way of the eastern gate and passes the terrible guardian at his post. Within the inner sanctuary the visionary splendor unfolds. The divine figures will emanate from the Buddha at the very center and array themselves around him. This is the home of the deities.

Here, in my personal Dream Mandala, I sketched the thick stone walls of the house on Willow Grove Avenue. For me, these walls, although hardly comprising a divine temple or holy city, delineate an area of personal power. A spot once fearful and repulsive,

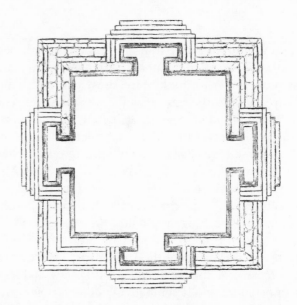

The Walls of the House on Willow Grove Avenue. *In my Dream Mandala, I have replaced the temple walls by my waking and dream image of the stone walls of my adolescent home.*

it has become transformed into a place of personal strength. Within its enclosure, I can invoke my own dream deities and hear their responses. I added the small hypnotic wheel to my Dream Mandala, in place of the customary Wheel of the Law.

The temple walls take on many forms in dreams. Some participants in my dream workshops relate finding themselves in dreams trapped in corridors or lost in the endless rooms of vast buildings. Others return in dreams, as I did, to houses familiar to them in childhood. A friend of mine often sees herself in dreams in the home of a favorite grandmother, looking again at the fantastic paintings and hand-carved furniture in its rooms. One workshop participant had recurrent nightmares as a girl of sinking in a sea of tapioca pudding in the basement of her childhood home. Another, a young man, had terrifying nightmare rides in a trolley driven by a demonic-looking aunt; she drove the trolley off its tracks into a dark and dangerous section of town where he was menaced by gorillas peeking in the windows.

Any enclosure that rouses strong feeling in our dreams—airplanes, cars, ships, fences, grottoes, as well as buildings—can be the space of mystery where we can connect with the universal forces that live within us. If I had not had frequent nightmares about the house on Willow Grove Avenue, I would have selected a castle to form the temple walls of my Dream Mandala, for the fairy tales I absorbed as a child were often constructed anew in my dreamscapes.

The crucial aspect is the marking off of an area of strong emotion.[1] The power that lies within the boundary can become directly accessible to the dreamer. Disciples of Tibetan Buddhism enter the gate of the temple in their imaginations during meditation and literally during an initiation.[2] So, too, do we in our dreams. The temple walls, whatever their form, surround a space of magic for the person whose emotions are aroused and who knows how to deal with the potent forces therein.

The images from our dreams that we shall encounter within the temple walls, whether they make us shudder with anxiety or fill us with awe and love, attach us to our deepest selves. Small wonder that they can transform us when we relate to them. Even images that are foreign to our emotions can have a powerful effect in the proper setting.

My personal experience of Buddhism is limited, although I have done a fair amount of research on the topic, visited a few monasteries, and, in the course of extended travel, seen a goodly number of Buddhas—the Emerald Buddha, the Reclining Buddha, the Great Buddha, etc.—at various shrines. Yet during a weekend seminar with Tarthang Tulku Rinpoche[3] at the Nyingma Institute in Berkeley, I found some of the Buddhist ritual surprisingly effective. At the conclusion of a full day of various meditation and relaxation exercises, I and about a hundred other participants turned our prayer cushions in the direction of the setting sun. Our gaze was protected by translucent red curtains that covered the windows of the meditation room. As the sun set, the room filled with a blazing red light. Meanwhile, we were all taking deep breaths and chanting repeatedly, "Ahhh," each at his or her own rate and tonal level.

All shifting of bodies and painful rearranging of legs ceased. We inhaled the incense, stared into the red light, and chanted. After a while, the room began to reverberate with overtones. The air pulsed and was palpable with our voices as we were bathed in the rosy glow. I lost awareness of the passage of time until the high, clear bell chimed to signal that we were to stop. We turned back to the Rinpoche and unwound our legs. Stretching, I looked at my watch. I was astonished to see that almost an hour had gone by! For people unaccustomed to lengthy meditation, as most of us were, it was an impressive event. We were given no explanation of the procedure, but I knew from my reading that, facing west, we were invoking the visionary deities whose symbolic color is red.[4] It was a remarkably moving experience, even without emotional connection to images of Tibetan deities. More effective yet is the experience of re-evoking, or relating to, the powerful emotional images of our dreams.

Within the temple walls of our Dream Mandalas dwell *our* deities. I have spoken of a parallel between the temple walls of the Dream Mandala and the enclosures that mark off our own sacred spaces in dreams. These dream enclosures—houses, towers, ships—also often represent our own bodies.

I firmly believe that we must always make our own current associations to each dream symbol—as when we dream of a particular house—and give preference to these personal associations over classic dream theories. However, it is also useful to look at dream houses from the classic view that they represent the dreamer's body or personality. Some theorists see dream houses as extensions of the dreamer's general life situation, relationships, or psyche. Others, like Freud, see them as the physical body of the dreamer, with the parts of the house representing various limbs and organs of the dreamer—for example, doors as body openings. Once, as an adolescent, when I dreamt of a house on fire there was no question in my mind when I woke that the dream referred to my aroused sexual condition of the moment. My body, as my dream house, was "on fire." After another dream, in which I watched a tall skyscraper being erected, I knew clearly on awakening that the dream was a reference to a prominent "erection" on a young man I was dating.

Our dream enclosures, then, can take on many dimensions of meaning. The house on Willow Grove Avenue was a symbol in waking life associated with a period of adolescent turmoil, conflict with parents, struggle with self, physical and mental distress, search for identity, and coping with emerging sexuality. In my dreams it played a similar role, now taking on one aspect of misery, now another, as something in my daily life, far removed from that place and time, reminded me of the former struggle and returned me to its site in dream life.

There were many levels of meaning, too, in the finding of something worthwhile in the dreams of the house on Willow Grove Avenue. The rediscovery of my powerful imagination, symbolized by the treasure, was one level of meaning. Looking at the house as a symbol of my body, rather than of a conflictual time in general, I believe another meaning emerges. The uncovered treasure—the vase, the jewels, the painting—becomes the discovery of the joyful, loving sexuality that blossomed for me in later years.

Within the temple walls of the Dream Mandala lie many treasures. Awakened sexuality carried me forward on the path to enlightenment as I encountered my dream deities. My body itself became a living temple.

6 THE TEMPLE DANCER

Dad and I are both performing in some kind of play at school. I wear my hair in long pigtails tied with red ribbons. Dad whispers to me to dance out a few steps with him. We do so. He grabs my hand and runs across the stage. I know that my role calls for me to laugh freely, but I feel afraid that I won't be able to do it right. Then I hear myself laughing aloud just as I should. Dad, still holding my hand, swings me high into the air. He lets go, and as I sail through the air I have a queer feeling in the pit of my stomach, like when riding in a fast-moving elevator. I tell myself that I mustn't think about it. Then one of the boys from school catches me, and the audience bursts into applause. I know the performance is a success, and I wake with the applause resounding in my ears.
("The School Play," July 1949)

This dream from my fifteenth year was an unusual one. At that time I rarely experienced physical sensations in my dreams like sailing through the air. Of course, I did not then recognize the sexual connotations of the swinging and the flight. Psychoanalysts would make much of the Electra aspects of sexual attraction to my father. It was many years indeed before I allowed myself to think about "the queer feeling" in the pit of my stomach and was able to laugh freely and sail freely into a bursting of any kind, applause or orgasm. I was much too careful for that.

I was raised to be a "good" girl, to be dependent and yielding. Tears were a permissible form of resistance, but my parents regarded any show of anger as intolerable. Rebellious thoughts were choked down (contributing no doubt to my asthmatic attacks) and my tendency was to accept in turn my parents', my teachers', and my peers' view of the world. It took many years before I was able to realize that I could be right when many others disagreed or that I could independently contrive a better way than the ones given me. Struggling to keep my intense feeling in total control, I trod a rigid, careful path through life.

One bright Sunday afternoon in my teenage years, my family was gathered on our stone-paved terrace, each puttering with individual chores. In the distance, very faintly, I could hear a cry. "What was that? Did you hear that?" I asked. One after another listened and heard nothing. It was a soft sound, almost like wind. "You're imagining it" was the consensus. Yet I *could* hear something. And leaving them at work, I wandered down the road, into the fields, listening for the soft sound. Now it grew louder and I was more sure of myself. Running through the tall grasses, looking sharply, I saw at last a limp bundle of a child of two years or so, in sunsuit and bonnet. Her face was streaked with dirt and tears, and her sobs were near exhaustion. I scooped her up and carried her back to my house. There followed much excitement, calling of police, and the return to home of the little girl who'd wandered away from one of the rich houses on the other side of the hill and become lost in the fields across from our house. I was pleased to have helped; but what impressed my teenage self most was the fact that I had been right when all others thought I was wrong. It was the first time I can remember believing myself over others. Until then I had always tended to accept that I must be the one who was wrong in the face of others' certainty.

This single experience did not alter my passive ways, but years later, when I was twenty-two and gave birth to my own daughter, the realization that I could trust my own perceptions was greatly reinforced. Highly sensitive to pain, I had decided the best way to cope with childbearing was to learn as much about it as possible. When I'd asked my mother whether it was more uncomfortable to have a baby than to have a menstrual period, she scoffingly replied, "Is an elephant bigger than a mouse?" My sister-in-law, a nurse, said all-knowingly, "Don't let *anyone* tell you having a baby doesn't hurt!" I wanted to be prepared. Accordingly, I took a natural-childbirth course, read Grantly Dick Read, and exercised my pelvic muscles diligently.

There was a gap of nearly three months between the end of my childbirth-training course and my delivery date. (I knew the exact date of conception because my husband had been away at army basic-training camp. He had visited on specific weekends; on one of these I became pregnant.) My labor began at six o'clock one dark morning with floods of amniotic fluid. It was ten days early so I could hardly believe it was real.[1] On the way to the hospital with the strange stretching sensation occurring every two minutes I was convinced that I must be in false labor. When we discovered that the George Washington Bridge, on the road between Fort Belvoir, Virginia, and the hospital in the District of Columbia, was raised to let a ship pass, my husband panicked. I felt unconcerned. However, by the time we were able to proceed, and reached the hospital to go through admission and I was prepped and shaved, I had become uncomfortable. There was no relief from the down-pulling sensation, a constant ache, and I felt nauseated.

The nursing aide, busy with preparing the enema, said with mild disdain, "This is your *first* baby, isn't it?" suggesting I was quite a sissy to be edgy already. With discomfort I waddled carefully to the labor room. My doctor popped in on his way to change clothes, and when I said, "Hey, this is getting uncomfortable; the panting doesn't help," he shook his head regretfully and replied, "Well, it's not good to have so long between the end of the course and delivery." He went to change. I lay uneasily gripping my husband's hand and thinking, "If this is going to get worse and go on for hours, no wonder people take medication!" I'd never had a baby before, and the doctors and nurses should know. Memories of visiting the ward, part of our course, and hearing women screaming for help flooded into my mind.

Back in whites, my doctor examined me and gasped in shock, "My God, you're fully dilated and the head's in the pelvis!" A great flurry followed with shouts to ready the delivery room, calling staff to come look at the "woman from the course who's been here since ten-thirty. She's fully dilated and not a peep out of her!" Wheeled to the delivery room where crowds of curious staff and attendants gathered, I grew stage-shy for a few minutes. I was warned it wasn't good to keep the baby's head in that position for long, so I pushed harder, and then proceeded to deliver my baby easily at twelve-thirty, a record six and a half hours' labor for a first child. The only anesthetic was a local shot of Xylocaine to do the episiotomy, and the only real pain came from the stitches to sew it up. My greatest difficulty was to stop pushing as the baby began to emerge. This time, with my own beautiful child in my arms, I knew I had to listen to myself first, what my body felt, what my senses conveyed to me. The most knowledgeable professional can only know from the outside. I can know from the inside. I can trust myself.

It was during this pregnancy that, bored with housework, I'd started college in earnest. I'd played with a couple of home-economics courses before marriage, but now I took on a regular program. I was ready to learn. My first marriage had taken me away from the horror house of adolescence to a dull routine. I'd thought I could invest joyfully in housekeeping, but being the wife of an army officer in a barrackslike flat left me bored. With eagerness I delved into the courses offered to servicemen and their families. My mind responded and I was off to my first intellectual adventure.

The next several years mingled child-raising and homemaking and intense studying and restless seeking. I was miserable and joyous in turn, yet found a solidity in my undergraduate college work. I finished at the head of my class with all sorts of honors in addition to my baccalaureate degree, so fierce was my desire to know. I could memorize almost anything to perfection. But it had to be factual, statistically valid, proven. I wanted to assimilate it all, to understand. I distrusted the loose, the poetic, the fantastic. Convinced that the way of imagination was dangerous, I turned to science. Only science, with clear experimental controls, was acceptable to me. Art, drama, literature were pleasant enough as entertainment, but not concrete or solid enough. I'm sure those in other sciences—math, physics, etc.—would regard clinical psychology as a loose and inadequate body of knowledge itself, but to me it was reason, clarity, sanity. I embraced it and excelled at it.

This need for control extended to every level of my being. Indeed, it was a rigidity that penetrated my body as well. Athletics in general were avoided as much as possible. I shrank in terror from volleyballs aimed in my direction. Frequent constipation was part of the fear-tight body picture. I had long been in conflict over my sexual feelings. A deeply sensuous person, I love to be held and touched, yet my religious upbringing restricted this pleasure to very limited conditions.

Like many of my generation I was torn between natural impulse and ethical judgments. As a young girl before marriage I had a built-in turn-off switch. I could kiss, even on occasion pet, but there was an undefined limit where good girls must stop. So far, and no further. This was a well-learned response, and, dizzy with embracing, lightheaded with passion, wet with desire, I would always obediently stop. When the proper conditions of engagement and then marriage were met, I still could not go beyond my switch-off point. I could make love, of course, but not fully, not with my total self. Nor could I achieve orgasm. I remained continually hanging, suspended on edge, aroused but not satisfied, disappointed again and again.

There was an accompanying fear of loss of control whenever I hovered on the edge. To burst into orgasm was equivalent to coming apart, dissolving into nonbeing. There was a sensation of being overpowered. I could not trust the wild, abandoned state of orgasm. It was too much, unbearable, and better left alone. I experienced only a half-dozen orgasms with intercouse in thirteen years of marriage and almost came to the conclusion that sex was hardly worth the bother. Because my body was so tight, my emotions were volatile and it was some relief to dissolve into weeping.

My dreams reflected this tension. At first they were preoccupied with the moral conflict over engaging in sex. Once on an early teenage date I ended up with an aroused boy in a van at a beach party. When I stopped, he was unwilling or unable to do so. To my amazement, he proceeded to spurt into orgasm as I watched. That night I dreamt of walking through dripping sewers, clearly conveying my attitude of disgust toward the situation. Other times, simple petting sessions with my fiancé led to dreams of dirtied wedding gowns and bruised lilies.

Later, when I was in the married state, my continual arousal and frustration with sex were clearly represented in my dreams. Even now, if I am deprived for short periods of time, "starving creatures" populate my dreams. Disheveled caged birds who haven't been fed in weeks or neglected, hungry pussycats symbolically call my attention to my state.

It was not until conditions were really right, until I was more at one with myself and felt truly safe with a skilled and beloved man, that I felt free to come apart and knew I would still survive. Orgasm became a consistent and near-daily part of my existence.

And my dreams mirrored directly the waking change. When sexuality is portrayed symbolically it is usually in positive terms such as rubbing sweet-scented oils into my skin, or dressing in lush furs and silky gowns, or being given armfuls of fragrant flowers. More often, sexuality is expressed directly. Dream characters often and easily engage in sex and experience orgasm. I accepted the premise that all dream lovers should be encouraged to experience orgasm and should be asked for a gift to remember them by—each lover being an aspect of myself that needed to be integrated.[2] My dream lovers increased, as did passionate feelings at all levels.

In fact, I discovered yet another level of sexuality. When I finally learned to become conscious during dreaming, I began experiencing dream orgasms of profound intensity. With a totality of self that is only sometimes felt in the waking state, I found myself bursting into soul- and body-shaking explosions.

At first I thought these frequent dream orgasms were a result of having been nonorgasmic for so long. I surmised it was some kind of personality need to assure myself that I could still experience orgasm at will.

However, the orgasmic response was so consistent, a near-inseparable part of a conscious dream, that a different surmise took over. I thought that I was choosing to have yet another orgasm because, when one can choose to perform any behavior, as one can in a lucid dream, orgasm is a pleasant choice. I knew that flying was often the activity of choice for lucid dreamers, as well as frequently preceding or accompanying the awareness of dreaming. Perhaps I chose orgasm as I chose to fly.

Finally, a different conclusion forced itself. My present hypothesis is this: *Orgasm is a natural part of lucid dreaming.* My own experience convinces me that conscious dreaming *is* orgasmic. Too many of my students have reported similar ecstatic experiences during lucid dreams to attribute the phenomena to my individual peculiarity. There is a kind of mystic experience involved, a mini-enlightenment, when one realizes one is dreaming and can prolong the state. I believe it quite possible that in lucid dreaming we are stimulating an area of the brain, or a chain of responses, that is associated with ecstatic states of all sorts. Sensations of flying, sexual heights, acute pleasurable awareness, and a sense of oneness are all natural outcomes of a prolonged lucid dream.

In my early experiences of conscious dreaming I woke immediately prior to, during, or after orgasm. Now I've learned to stay within that special space moments longer and explore it further.

I've come a long way from the skinny adolescent whose body was fear-frozen. Changed, too, is the inhibited college woman whom classmates described as a "cool cat." My body is more a part of me and responds flexibly to my intent. It can ripple freely with passion; it can relax out the tension that clutches my shoulders and neck; it has been stretched and loosened with yoga and Tai Chi Chuan. Recently, I uncovered another activity that has made further changes.

I have always been responsive to rhythm (though I have no ear for musical tones). Drums excite me and moving to folk dances with their heavy beat is pure joy. Although I have never until recently had formal dance training—ballroom-dancing lessons in junior high hardly count—I have taken an occasional modern-dance or folk-dance or water-ballet course, and my dreams have been consistently full of dancing throughout the years. In my dreams I watch marvelous performances, or I am the dancer weaving incredible movements and rhythms. I *experience* dancing.

In one particularly strange-feeling dream, I was a dancer and I was simultaneously my ancestor who was a temple dancer. There is undoubtedly a dream pun here in that I am a graduate of Temple University, but there is more. In the dream I felt being myself and felt being my ancestor temple dancer at the same time. I *experienced* the two realities. In another dream where I was dancing, I began to sing:

> This is the dance that my grandma used to do—
> Long, long ago; long, long ago.
> This is the way that my grandma used to go—
> Long, long ago; long, long ago.

Whether these dreams inspired me or whether it was the mere fact that I wanted to slim my stomach to look good for personal appearances for my book-publicity tour, I cannot say for sure, but I proceeded to begin the study of belly dancing. I had no intention to perform, simply to exercise and experience.

Now, after more than three years of study, my body continues to loosen. When I began, like all beginners, I found that my hips were tight and could only move in conventional Western ways. Within months they began to sway further and differently. The ligaments stretch slowly but eventually become flexible, and the movements flow and swing widely. Months of neck stretching and circling, shoulder swiveling, rib-cage sliding, and belly rolling upward and downward set their own body rhythms going.

Once in an early lesson the teacher instructed, "Put your weight on the right foot." To my astonishment, I found my weight was *already* on the right foot. I began to notice that at rest I always stood with my weight shifted forward and to the right. Indeed, my whole right side was more rigid than my left. When I made a "forward figure eight" with my hips, a standard belly-dance movement, my hips swung far to the left side, but they were much more restricted swinging to the right. I sensed myself always ready to move, to do, and thus the right side of me was always slightly tense, ready to act. Once aware, I could shift back to a centered, balanced position. With directed practice, my right side loosened and came more into balance. I still have to remind myself to relax that side, to shift to center, but my thighs grow strong and support me well and the body swings easily right or left to the beat of the Middle Eastern rhythms.

The changes belly dancing wrought in other areas of bodily activity were profound. My once-restricted asthmatic lungs expand with deep breathing during the three or four intense weekly sessions. The sweat pours off and my formerly always-chilled body becomes resistant to cold. Now other people complain of the cold, whereas I feel warmed from an inner source. Long walks that formerly found me dropping behind leave me steady and ache-free while others complain. No doubt the constant exercise has made cardiovascular changes and changes in metabolism, but it seems as though there is an inner energy and a strength that is more than strength of limb.

I was not surprised to find my waking dancing increased my dreams of dancing, but I was amused to discover the new use I put it to. On a recent dream flight, instead of my usual swimming-style flying—pushing off from the floor and moving in breaststroke fashion—or gliding, or sailing on air currents, I merely gave a shimmy of my hips. And like a motor, the movement easily propelled me through the air in a dance-style flying.

And so over the years I have learned that I can trust my body. I can allow myself to loosen on every level. My body needed the strength and freedom, the flexibility I found before I dared let my mind range beyond the known scientific, beyond what is taught and statistically supported. Now I venture to free the mind, too. I can let my body sway easily to the rhythms within and without. Once I pulled the strings to dance the marionettes. Now I let the rhythm flow and I dance myself, freely, easily, imaginatively, orgasmically, in my own life space. And that life space grows larger every night.

7 THE EASTERN QUARTER OF THE DREAM MANDALA
Chief Deity: The Mirror Gazer

The dancers who have fluttered through my dreams for the past twenty-nine years are a varicolored troupe. Some are primitive women, savage and wild, moving with abandon. Others are ancient priestesses garbed in flowing robes. Often I am among them, swirling, for instance, in a silky, silver-gray hooded gown to the heavy throb of drums. At times I am the sole performer; at other times I am one of many women and men who move in lines and patterns with inordinate skill. Occasionally, the dancing creatures are animals. Once, as a young girl, I came across a photograph in *Life* magazine of a cat standing on its hind legs. I gasped in shock. It was so like a childhood dream of mine about a dancing cat that I clipped it out and saved it. Capturing the *feeling* of that particular dream, the faded picture still stirs similar sensations as I contemplate it. Another dancing animal was a "snowbird," an all-white creature with thousands of legs who glided over the ice in intricate patterns.

Dreams of dancing, whether I am an observer or a participant, are always pleasant for me. Perhaps that is why I never thought much about them for a long time. Unlike the frightening dreams of the house on Willow Grove Avenue, dreams of dancing did not *demand* attention, perhaps because dancing is so much a part of my waking existence. Assuming that the rhythmic movements had some sexual connotation, I simply enjoyed the dream of dancing whenever it occurred.

The dream of "The Temple Dancer," however, startled me into a new view of dancing. As I've said, this dream simultaneously depicted me as myself and as my ancestor temple dancer. Perhaps it was the curious sensation of experiencing two realities at once that directed my attention to the role of dancing in my dreams.

I began to notice that rhythmic movements were often associated with the onset of lucid dreams. Dancing in waking life produces a delightful euphoria; I feel radiant and happy when I dance. Even when physically tired, if I hear danceable music, especially with a folk or an ethnic beat, I have a near compulsion to dance, and if I yield to it and begin to dance, weariness is swept away in the pleasure of motion. I love intricate, complex movements that I can master and then allow my body to dance of its own volition, slipping into what I have learned more recently is a very mild trance state. Dancing in dreams gives me the same sense of lightness that waking dancing does.

As I observed dancing dreams more carefully, I realized why they often appear prior to lucid dreaming: when I am about to become conscious in a dream I get a strange feeling in my head. Suddenly, within the dream, I will "feel tired" and may even lie down to sleep. Or I will have the impression that I have been asleep and have just awakened. In some dreams I feel I am in a trance. Spinning around and around in a dream, like dancing, also produces the peculiar feeling—a lightheaded exhilaration—that is the frequent precursor of conscious dreaming.

This feeling of lightheadedness was depicted in striking fashion in a recent dream. In it, I was a dancer watching other dancers.

The Lightheaded Dancer—*dream deity of the Eastern Quarter of the Dream Mandala.*

There were close-up views of the dancers, perhaps photographs. I carefully examined one of these, a crystal-clear image of the heads of two dancers who were upside down. Their headgear was marvelous —a kind of helmet formed from spots of light. When I awoke, this image charmed me. To show an upside-down dancer whose head was literally covered with light seemed an apt way to express a feeling of *lightheadedness.* Her upside-down condition reminded me of my childhood activity of hanging my head over the side of a bed. The dream picture was a graphic expression of the physical feeling of lightheadedness.

I made a sketch of the Lightheaded Dancer to record the state of mind that she represented. I thought, as I drew, about the relationship she bore to the Temple Dancer and to all of her sisters (and a few brothers) who have danced through my dreams all these years. The act of drawing this dream image became a meditation for me. I understood her significance better as I sketched—the state of mind she depicted, the understanding light she shed on the dream around her, how she was a visual image of an internal state, and how light-headedness in many forms is a forerunner of conscious dreaming.

I drew several versions of the lightheaded lady, each becoming more expressive of the feeling I have had in dreams. Holding this feeling in mind while I drew, I could recapture more and more of it and transfer it onto the paper, giving me a waking remembrance, an artifact brought back from dreams. The Lightheaded Dancer is indelibly etched in my memory now. By rendering her with feeling, I have fixed her as clearly in my imagination as she was in my dream. When I contemplate the finished drawing, or the crisp mental image I have of it, I can recapture some of the original sensation when I desire it. I realized that the Lightheaded Dancer is a dream deity for me because she is attached to an important feeling: the sense of lightheadedness that emerges as I become lucid in a dream.

The Lightheaded Dancer was only one of a new kind of dream character that was appearing in my dreams. Instead of figures that threatened me and produced fear, instead of figures that frustrated me and produced anger, I found myself encountering more and more often dream characters that evoked a sense of wonder, as she did. Fascinated, I would find myself in dreams examining some intriguing image, talking with it, or listening to its teachings. I felt my role in dreams shifting further.

Here, again, I was faced with "facts" that seemed to contradict my own internal experience. Even as I had heard the lost child crying in the fields when no one else believed me, I heard my dreams changing despite the claims of experts that an individual's dreams do not change.

Calvin Hall, for example, the American psychologist who has collected thousands of dreams, says that dream content does not change to any extent in the same dreamer despite long passage of time and change in life circumstances.[1] I decided to test my impression that dream content does change. My own records could be used and statistical measures applied to them.

Taking the first fifty dreams in my diary, from my fifteenth year, in 1949, and the first fifty dreams from my forty-second year, in 1976, I compared the two sets on several measures. I discovered that, on some measures, Hall's claim was accurate: despite the twenty-seven years separating the two sets of dreams, there were several consistencies.[2] However, on other measures, there were dramatic differences between the two sets of dreams. In the early set of dreams, when I was fourteen, the emotions that I expressed were usually passive: I often felt frightened, worried, apologetic, left out, or sad, and, in general, withdrew from or avoided fearful images as much as possible in my dreams. In the later set, when I was forty-one, I rarely felt this way. More often, I was annoyed, resentful, cranky, or furious at bothersome images in my dreams; I actively approached the troublesome figure to scold it or challenge it, often with an awareness that I was dreaming. The shift from withdrawal to active coping with threat was important. My role as victim in my dreams had become sharply reduced (as it had in waking life, as well). In addition, a kind of positive emotion that I labeled *wonder* appeared. I felt entranced and I marveled at the fantasies I witnessed. There were several other changes that I verified.[3]

I see in these dream changes an important pattern: *there is a movement from dreams of fear to dreams of anger to dreams of wonder.* This is a generalization, of course, and even today I may be momentarily shaken by a frightening dream. But this is now rare. The change in dream content has taken many years to evolve and is still evolving; it is more a shift of emphasis. The pattern—from fear to anger to wonder—is pronounced and unmistakable. It is a pattern of growth, I believe, that all of us may develop.

Thus, we have levels of interactions in our dreams: *at the first level, we are total victims of our dream figures.* What the Tibetans call "wrathful deities" hold absolute dominion. In earlier days, if I had made a Dream Mandala based on the Tibetan model, I would have placed my nightmare figures—the teasing boys, the gangs of men, the spiders, the biting dogs—into the Eastern Quarter of the mandala, where figures relating to fear are traditionally placed. I was projecting my energy onto "outer" figures: it was *they* who were hateful; I was an innocent victim. These are the dreams of fear.

At the second level, we are active participants in our dream struggles. The wrathful deities' dictatorial rule is challenged. We rebel; we enlist aid; we become wrathful ourselves. The energy of the horrific figure becomes active in us. Now the energy of the Eastern Quarter takes shapes of hate and fury.

Psychologically, anger is a more adaptive response than depression.[4] Withdrawal is as poor an adaptation in the dream state as it is in the waking state. When we flee from the dreaded figures that pursue us in our dreams, we leave them to return another night, without solving the problems they represent. We express the fear that these figures evoke without connecting ourselves to the tremendous energy that they can provide. We are running away from our own potential strength.

When my dreams began to take form as a struggle against the threatening figures in them, I fought off a gang of would-be rapists with a spray can; I defeated a man who tried to strike me with a white rock; and, in another dream, I fiercely ordered a snarling dog to behave and he obeyed me. If I had made a Dream Mandala in the days of these dreams, I would have put these images into the Eastern Quarter. I was coping more effectively. I was counteraggressive to protect myself. These are the dreams of anger.

At the third level of interaction, we are conscious and peaceful participants in our dream adventures. The wrath of the images dissolves and is replaced by benevolence. By absorbing more of the figures' energy into ourselves, our dreams take on a wondrous quality —crystal clear, brilliantly colored, filled with light and bliss. The shifting images of our conscious dreams are reflected as in a mirror, without hate or anger *in* the figures or fear or hatred *toward* the figures. Recognizing them for what they are—projections of ourselves —we can let them exist without being distressed by them. We may tame them, talk to them, exchange with and learn from them, but we need not hate or fear them. Not suppressing negative feelings, we are moving *beyond* them.

The current focus of my dreams is at the level of the wonder of conscious dreaming; it was with these images that I built my Dream Mandala. I feel superconscious and expanded. I fly, or become giant-sized, or shrink to a pinpoint. I flood with passion; I marvel at strange sights. I am beyond fear and hate in myself or others. These are the dreams of wonder.

At the fourth level of interaction, we move into a full-blown mystical, ecstatic experience within the dream. Forms disappear and all is radiance. We are part of a single life force. I glimpse the brilliance of this level fleetingly, at one with the universe. These are the dream experiences of light.

The dream figures that I placed in the Eastern Quarter of my personal Dream Mandala, then, are those that I encounter with wonder at the onset of lucid dreaming. In the same way that the initiate in Tibetan Buddhism enters the mandala in his or her imagination by the eastern gate and meets the first deity and his attendants, I encounter a certain type of imagery at the onset of a lucid dream. These figures, like the Lightheaded Dancer, are my deities of the Eastern Quarter.

The initial sensations in a dream that becomes lucid are bodily changes, like the lightheadedness I have mentioned.

Closely allied with lightheadedness in the initial stage of a lucid dream is *an experience of intense visual focusing, a staring with total absorption.* I named this characteristic *fixedness* while I was experiencing it during a particularly vivid lucid dream. Circles of energy were radiating in my cheeks. Outside of my body, images were swirling before me. Both at once, inside and outside, were whirls of activity, yet I was absolutely fixed. It was a most strange sensation, of which I can reproduce a pale imitation in the waking state by recalling how those pulsating miniature whirlpool spots in my cheeks felt during that dream. I also drew a sketch of this experience while

The Woman of Fixedness—*dream deity of the Eastern Quarter of the Dream Mandala.*

re-creating as much of the internal feeling as I could muster.[5] By contemplating the finished picture I am able to recapture some of the sensation when I desire it.

Lightheadedness and fixedness are thus early signals of the onset of a lucid dream state for me. There are two other characteristics to mention that often accompany these bodily changes. One is a peculiar dream event that I have termed *doubleness*. Doubleness is similar to, but not exactly the same as, a sense of *déjà vu* in the waking state. Immediately prior to the beginning of lucidity I often notice that something is beginning again. In one dream, a movie that I had just seen was about to start over; in another, a story that had ended was about to repeat. In yet another dream, the dream of "Fixedness," there were several rounds, not simply one repetition, of the same dream activities—I ate in a restaurant, I flew, I landed in a restaurant, I flew, and I landed, again and again. In one instance I noticed how many people had look-alikes; each had a twin. Sometimes I can determine that the symbol has actually occurred before in the same dream or in a previous one; at other times doubleness seems to be only the feeling that some scene, activity, or symbol has occurred before, and the present dream appearance is a recurrence.

Doubleness is closely allied with the final characteristic I've observed in the initial phase of lucid dreams: seeing myself in a mirror. In this case, the "double" is literal. I am myself and I see myself. Sometimes I merely catch a glimpse of my reflection as I pass a glass door. At other times I examine my image with great intensity, looking at the color and shape and condition of my eyes. I arrange my hair, and so on.

These images are astonishingly clear. They may not resemble my present condition, differing in hair or eye color, or style or age, but there is no question that they are myself, and I gaze into their depths with wonder. For this reason, I have termed this type of image the Mirror Gazer. If I have not already become fully lucid by the time I see myself in a mirror in a dream, I will almost invariably, as I gaze into the dream mirror, realize then that I am dreaming. Occultists would suggest that such images are astral projections and that the "reflection" that I see is not a mirror image but the double, the astral-body form itself. All I can say for certain at this stage is that many of my lucid dreams are preceded or triggered by the image of the Mirror Gazer.

These peaceful figures that emerged for me as I experienced dreaming that was beyond fear and anger were, I found, uncannily appropriate to Tibetan mandalas, where *the ruler of the Eastern Quarter is the conqueror of hate and anger.* Tibetans have named this conquering lord Aksobhya.*

In their sacred art, he is most often rendered in blue because he is associated with the element of water.[6] Like our own dream figures, he takes many forms. He is usually seen in his "peaceful" aspect, in which he looks very much like a Buddha, dressed in simple monk's attire. Sometimes Aksobhya appears robed as a king rather than a monk. At other times, he appears united with his sexual partner, the All-Seeing One. (These figures linked in sexual intercourse are referred to as *yab-yum* form: the male is the *yab*, "father"; the

---

* pronounced Ahk·shō·bē·ă

Aksobhya—*chief deity of the Eastern Quarter of Tibetan Buddhist mandalas.*

female, the *yum,* "mother." Their sexual union represents *his* type of energy interacting with *her* type of wisdom.) He may also appear in a wrathful form, a horrific image, decorated with human skulls and flayed skins; he then represents energy clouded by passion. His consort, too, may appear with him in wrathful form, clinging to his neck and offering him a shell filled with blood, while her body is locked in intercourse with him.

Whatever shape Aksobhya assumes, he is known as the Unshakable. He is a pictorial embodiment of an aspect of our personality: the wisdom that conquers anger. If we think of this deity of the Eastern Quarter as an energy that can take on many forms, we will have little trouble recognizing him in our own dreams. All figures of our dreams that are irascible, angry, or hateful can be considered to be wrathful forms of Aksobhya.

The female student of mine who was terrified by a gigantic rooster (a dream pun on the word *cock*?) that pursued her, and woke just as its claw was digging into her back, was having such a wrathful image. A workshop participant, a mature man, had another wrathful deity in his dream: an octopuslike creature who engulfed him in its many arms and began to devour him. Nightmare figures such as these and the dreamer's desperate attempts to escape them are common nightly events. They are our version of the deity of the Eastern Quarter in wrathful form.

When we are operating at the second level of dream interaction, and meet threat with anger, we become wrathful ourselves. Once when I was greatly frustrated by the waking-life presence of a senile relative, I, in a dream, bit her on her hairy chin. That was myself, in my wrathful form, or Aksobhya, if you will, in his wrathful form, manifesting himself in my dream. When the energy that appears in the Eastern Quarter is expressed neurotically, it takes on the form of anger; the same energy that shapes the wrath can be transmuted into peaceful forms.

The anger that is cloudy, turbulent, and aggressive is also brilliant, powerful, and energetic. When we recognize that positive qualities are part of the same passion, we can transmute the negative aspects into the positive. Tibetan Buddhists call this transformation *the wisdom of the mirror*. Because the Eastern Quarter of the mandala is associated with the element of water, cloudy, turbulent water represents anger. However, the water can become clear and unruffled, representing the sharp, precise, clear reflectiveness of mirrorlike wisdom.

The Mirror Gazer—*chief deity of the Eastern Quarter of my Dream Mandala.*

When we are operating on the third level of dream interaction, beyond fear and anger, we see in our dreams our versions of the peaceful forms of Aksobhya, the conqueror of hate and anger. At this higher level, we need not become disturbed at all. According to Tibetan Buddhists, the enlightened person reflects with the impartiality of a mirror the nature of all things and of self. The enlightened being is an observer, unaffected by the images the mind reflects. This is not to say that compassion or action are undesirable; indeed, these qualities are encouraged in other quarters. But one aspect of higher consciousness is an introspective attitude, an inner stillness and peace that observes all that is around one and within one, yet remains undisturbed. Since the deities are manifestations of our own thoughts and feelings, we must penetrate the terror they produce in order to understand it. If we do so, the power of the terrible figure can become our own strength and fearlessness. Then the wondrous figures of conscious dreams emerge.

It seemed remarkably apt to me that my analysis of lucid dreams exposed an image that fit so perfectly. My Mirror Gazer became for me the dream deity representing the wisdom of the mirror that is beyond fear and anger and hate. The wisdom that reflects what exists, without disturbance on the part of the viewer, is represented for me in her. I sketched the Mirror Gazer as well.

For me, the Mirror Gazer is the chief deity of the Eastern Quarter, corresponding to Aksobhya. She is the All-Seeing One, who is conscious of dreaming. She is the Lady of the Double Image. I placed the mirror, her symbol, in the Eastern Quarter of my Dream Mandala. Her attendants are the Lightheaded Dancer, who radiates, and the Woman of Fixedness, who, like Aksobhya, is unshakable. I have rendered them in blue like the element of water associated with this quarter. They appear in the final version merely as dots, as Aksobhya's attendants often do.

These "deities" do not always come forth in the lucid state, but

The Eastern Quarter of my Dream Mandala—*the mirror.*

usually at least one of them will emerge. A lightheadedness, a fixedness, or a doubleness will take shape from the continuous flow of shifting, dancing dream pictures to become a version of the Lightheaded Dancer, the Woman of Fixedness, or the Mirror Gazer. I catch hold of these special figures and give them waking form because they teach me of the psychological and probably physiological states through which I move. I assign them to my personal Dream Mandala as substitutes for the chief deity and attendants of the Eastern Quarter. I will release them as new images crystallize. They are not gods; they are pictures of states of mind. As we grow, new images will come forth from the mass of life energy to symbolize our current states and replace those that were our earlier selves.

Eventually we may all reach the fourth level of dream interaction—beyond form. The myriad figures of our dreams are varied expressions of the single life force.

This energy of our dream images, capable as it is of assuming any form, has endless potential. In its ceaseless dance, a huge field of life energy concentrates for a moment of our night's sleep into a small space, a kind of "knot" of energy, a dream figure. Then it dissolves and reshapes on other nights into other guises. The patterns are without limit. Beyond them lies the formless source of life itself. Through our dreams, we can move forward on the path to full enlightenment.

8 THE BIG GAMBLE

I am riding in a car beside a young girl who is driving. (She is the daughter of a friend of mine, and the ultimate spoiled child.) The girl is handling the steering wheel in a wild way. Greatly alarmed that her reckless driving will crash us both, I reach for the ignition key to turn off the motor. I think I succeed. . . .

Later the same night, I am in a gigantic department store, rather like Gimbels in Philadelphia, but even larger. I keep thinking that the name is Gambels—in fact, the name of a gasoline service station that we use. In the store's immense space, I wander from department to department, looking at various things, some of them purses with oriental designs. Downstairs, there is a great central section with columns and arches, suggesting the rotunda in a museum, and a large storage room. I continue to explore.

Finally, I am in an upper level of the huge store, where I sit with a girl friend from college. We are discussing a course that

she is taking in linguistics. She tells me the meaning of words is based on mathematics and that by using this system one can make predictions of the future.
("The Big Gamble," November 13, 1970)

This sequence of dreams from the same night a few years ago represents my anxiety over an important decision. Before I describe the specific situation that stimulated them, I can say that these dreams made me realize that the decision I had made seemed reckless, a gamble (symbolized by the Gimbels-Gambels store) that would profoundly affect my future and might lead to a crash.

That decision was the latest and perhaps the most far-reaching of a series of gambles I had decided to take. As I see it now, this gamble helped prepare me for the greatest adventure of all, which was yet to come. It had been preceded by several other risk-taking actions. For those of us who have led inhibited lives, it seems that part of the move to personal freedom involves developing a willingness to take risks. Recognizing the danger, feeling the fear, we learn to move bravely ahead into the unknown. We may make mistakes, but we become able to act and to accept the consequences of our actions, right or wrong; we accept the responsibility for our decisions.

The thirteen years of my first marriage were filled with struggle —emotional and economic. I had tried to perform the stereotyped role of a wife. My husband, whom I had dated exclusively from the age of sixteen, tried, too, to make our marriage succeed. Our financial problems were not all that different from those of any other young couple starting out. Yet, given our own unresolved emotional difficulties, our inexperience of the world, and our undeveloped selves, tight finances added to our difficulty in helping one another to live happily.

The bright moments during that marriage mostly had to do with my lovely, growing daughter—as a suckling baby who paused to giggle intimately; as an eager child who cuddled close to hear a favorite story; as a young girl who joined me and her handsome father, a splendid dancer, to learn a new folk-dance step.

My great joy during those years was in the few hours of academic classes I managed each week. I started college with courses that George Washington University gave at reduced rates to service personnel and their families on the post at Fort Belvoir, Virginia. By then, I was twenty-two and pregnant. Although at first I felt unsure and awkward squeezing my thickening midsection behind a student armchair, I was ready to learn. More than ready—starving.

With a passion, I poured myself into the world of the mind. (I'd never worked terribly hard in junior or senior high school; the reputation of having too high grades might have hampered an already dismal social life.) Now, no book was too difficult, no amount of reading too much. Books on every subject were piled at every convenient reading spot in the house. And I devoured four, five, six at once. There was a book for the time when I was soaking in the bathtub (not too heavy in weight or tone and capable of sustaining wetness), one for studying at a desk (the textbook, read with pen in hand), one for the purse (lightweight, light subject, for reading on trains, at bus stops, and other distracting spots), one for in bed (not too heavy to prop up and absorbable while sleepy)—those were the bare minimum. I gobbled them eagerly. A book addict. I hunted for something that would fill the sense of emptiness. I was partially successful.

Meanwhile, my husband completed his army tour and we returned to Philadelphia, where I continued my education at Temple University. Philosophy courses and discussions with colleagues began to undermine the values I had always accepted. Once I dreamt that statues of ancient gods carved into a rocky mountain face were becoming loose and shaky; they might topple. Awake, my "gods" were *very* shaky. The foundations of the only life-style I had known were challenged by exposure to different ideas in college. Disturbed and unhappy, I started psychotherapy at the university medical center, a step made possible only by student rates, and found it sustained me through difficult times. Therapy itself became a mind-stretching process.

By 1968, my first marriage was over. I faced the fact that my husband and I had become quite different people, with different interests and different lives to lead. With some agonizing and trepidation on the part of both of us, we divorced. I was thirty-four. In truth, I was divorcing more than a person. I was divorcing a way of life. It was not a bad way; it was just not my way.

There was no assurance that the move to divorce was right for me. In fact, my own experience of men had long suggested that the world was populated with two types of males: the dull faithfuls and the charming rats. Zal changed my mind.

Zal—from Zalmon, for Solomon, my wise old man. I believe that people with unusual names are either crushed under their weight or else grow strong enough to support them. Zal is such a one who became as unusual as his name.

When I met him, older than I by fifteen years, wiser by many, he was a bit world-weary. He had already had several careers—journalist, editor, navy lieutenant in battle zones of World War II, progressive politician, super businessman—and now he was a clinical psychologist. Never having loved completely, he was ready for love. He was ready to look inward. He was ready to find me.

We stood eye to eye in the Ph.D. program where we met. In any other setting I would surely have been intimidated by his cosmopolitan air—his strength of purpose and integrity, his boundless endurance, his powerful and persuasive speech. I would have been too shy to be myself. Yet, by then, school was *my* world; being a star student, my specialty. We shared as equals the struggles and triumphs of examinations, experiments, and reports. We grew to know each other well.

Despite our apparent differences—I, a timorous small-town girl tentatively reaching out, quick to retreat in tears or depression; he, a bold and sophisticated adventurer, ready to flash in fury when frustrated, optimistic and assured—despite all this, we soon realized how good we were for one another. What I saw as weakness in myself, Zal saw as gentleness, a tender spirit, what he wanted in himself. What he perceived as a tendency to dominate and to be irascible in himself, I perceived as strength, self-confidence, what I wanted in myself. By the process of loving one another, I absorbed some of Zal's strength; he absorbed some of my gentleness. Together we became more than ourselves—our own *yab-yum*.

We wrap each other round with love. Zal used not to believe in love at all; once convinced, he became totally committed. His devotion helped me to give myself fully for the first time. Sometimes when we are making love, I cannot feel the skin that separates our bellies, only the energy force flowing between us, so close is the oneness. Sometimes when we are holding hands, I cannot feel where my hand stops and his begins, only a warm glow at the end of my arm. I no longer feel vulnerable and lost when I burst into orgasm, but well loved and home.

Thus the partner I chose when I remarried was quite different from the one I had selected when I was sixteen. Of course, I had developed into a different person, one that was more my real self. There were further changes to come. Casting my lot with Zal was a major life risk, but, knowing him, I felt the odds were on my side.

I had presupposed the delicious nature of our relationship, even before it had hardly begun, from a dream. In the dream, Zal asked if I would like him to fix me a drink. I, who find the taste of alcohol bitter and medicinal, and never drank even wine in those days, replied, "Yes, if it tastes good."

Life with Zal tasted mighty good. After our marriage, another world opened for me. Evenings became filled with theater, opera, dinner parties, and talk of politics, ideas, and philosophies. My days working at a local college, busy with the teaching I had grown to love, were punctuated with exotic, romantic, and mind-opening travel to Jamaica, Mexico, England, and France. Zal brought with him a full and exciting outer world just as I was ready to step into it. And I brought to him a full and rich inner world just at the moment he was seeking that. I had gambled that life with Zal would be good; it was and it is.

The next unknown I found myself facing was even more far-reaching. During the first two years of our marriage, Zal had become involved in politics again. A former business colleague, Milton Shapp, had persuaded him to run his second gubernatorial campaign. After a successful campaign, with Shapp as governor, Zal accepted a top-level cabinet post for a brief time, helped fill cabinet positions, and launched the administration. Our lives became inundated with political activities. I began to see Zal more on television or in the newspaper than across the dinner table. When he was at home, the phone rang incessantly with one crisis after another so that conversation became impossible. It was not a life for lovers. We conferred at length, considered the situation from all angles, and made a monumental decision: we would move to England.

The night we reached our decision, I had the series of dreams described above, "The Big Gamble." By then, I knew my dream language well enough to recognize that if a spoiled and willful child is driving a car I am in, I feel that the spoiled part of me is more in control. In dreams, the figure controlling the car is always significant. Perhaps the decision to move was a wild and reckless one and I had better turn it off, as I tried to do in the dream by reaching for the ignition key. This series of dreams told me that at least part of me felt that our decision to move was a gigantic gamble on our future. But change almost always involves risk. We were off to try our lives in London.

There were times I thought we had lost everything on this particular turn of the wheel. Life in a foreign country taxed my adaptive powers. But when we take a chance and lose on one level, we can still gain on another level. In the end, I found that living abroad was an experience in which I had grown.

Mostly I was plain uncomfortable for the fifteen months that we lived in London. There was something similar between the old, crumbly house of my teens and the antiquated way things functioned in England. Certainly both places were ancient and damp. The chilly drizzle, or relentless downpour, so different from the sunshine of our earlier summer holiday there, soaked into my bones. I marketed daily to fill the fridge, designed to hold a carton of milk and two tomatoes; I struggled to untangle the bewildering world of sexually incompatible electric-appliance plugs and outlets; I rigged up a temporary shower (showers being American devices) in the tub, with a rubber hose tied to the spigot with string; I bundled up when oil heat was rationed; I hiked to our seventh-floor "luxury" flat when electricity was rationed and the lift was inoperative; I occasionally cooked by candlelight and banked or shopped by kerosene lamp during the power rationing. I could hardly believe it was 1971; it seemed more like frontier times, and I, a pioneer woman facing the wilderness. All in all, it was rather like camping. In winter.

My negative feelings about England had less to do with the qualities of the country than with my responses to them. Even with Zal beside me, I felt homesick and alien. My young daughter, Cheryl, then fourteen, had been miserable, and we finally had to send her back to the States. In my dreams, I struggled with the sense of loss her absence gave me, as well as my feelings of frustration as I tried to sort out life problems anew.

Zal and I had originally considered making our move to London permanent. He would have been happy to remain; I definitely wanted to return. Our being there was a gamble and I felt that we had lost. Zal, as always, sought to satisfy my needs, and we determined to go back to the States. Once I was a visitor again and not a permanent resident, I was able to enjoy England anew. The theater, the parks, the museums, the countryside all glowed again as they had when we were visitors.

I began to realize that London had bestowed an extraordinary gift. Because I was not permitted to work there, at a time of massive British unemployment, I was forced to find another professional activity. It seemed a perfect time to try myself as a writer. I could write in spurts, and carry an unfinished manuscript along on our frequent trips to the Continent. I started with an article on dreams, which was later published in a professional journal.[1]

Focusing intently on dreams, the interest I had sustained since I was fourteen, led to a flowering of dream awareness. I found my dreams were doing more than expressing feeling and reflecting my struggles to cope with daily problems. A kind of mythological theme began to appear frequently during my nights: in one such dream, I was doing a spring dance to the gods in soft, hot mud, which bubbled and rumbled beneath my bare feet. My dreams began to convey a deeper significance. More and more I became aware that I was dreaming during a dream. I felt the excitement of an inner world expanding.

I noticed that in my dream language, London, in general, became a symbol for physical discomfort and outdated modes of behavior. The weather in London, in particular, took on a separate symbolic meaning. My ordinary dreams that transformed into magical lucid dreams often started in a setting like London—I would find myself in a gloomy, cool, and drizzly place just prior to emergence into the sunny light and vivid color of lucid dreaming. Without knowing it, I was beginning to learn the secrets of the Dream Mandala.

Twenty years or more had had to pass between my adolescent suffering in the house on Willow Grove Avenue and the realization that there was a treasure contained in it that I had overlooked. It took less than one year to recognize that, amid the trials of life in London, I had discovered a level of dream consciousness that connected me to another level of living. The worst of things can lead to the best of things . . . and so turns out not to be the worst of things, after all. This gamble, too, although it yielded some discomfort on one level, provided reward on another. Beyond the land of gloom and drizzle there is sunshine. And then . . . yet another unknown.

My life, then, has been a series of risks. Over and over I have found myself confronting some unknown—and seemingly dangerous

—situation. As I look back over the past twenty years, these risks, these gambles, seem stretched out like a staircase behind me. Each step has appeared, at the time I ventured to take it, to be a daring move into dizzying heights.

I had had a simple high-school education; after a gap of some years, I decided to go to college. I had married at twenty-one; I divorced at thirty-four. I had been constricted and conventional; I became more expressive and liberal. I had wanted to understand myself; I underwent ten years of intensive therapy. I had been afraid of orgasm; I grew to love it. I had always withheld portions of myself; I committed myself fully to Zal. I had known only a provincial lifestyle; I discovered a cosmopolitan world in living abroad and at home with Zal.

Every major life decision has carried with it a similar sense of tremendous risk, as though I were moving off a precipice into empty space. Each time, I debated with myself at length, gathered my courage, and plunged ahead.

Then, once more, a new unknown loomed into view. I had confined my inner life to dreams. Recently, I began to find that it was extending to psychic levels. As with all the unknowns that preceded it, the one facing me seems the most dangerous . . . and the most exciting.

The incidents that signaled the development of this new phase were small in themselves, but monumentally impressive to me. For instance, once, about three years ago, Zal had invited an out-of-town associate and his wife to spend the night in our home. The following morning, we sat chatting at the breakfast table with the couple, whom we scarcely knew. Soon a man they had identified simply as a "friend" arrived to pick them up. As the stranger climbed the long flight of stairs up to our flat, I observed that he wore the clerical collar and garb of a Catholic priest. When he reached the top of the stairs, however, the man wore a regular sport shirt and jacket. I stared at him in amazement because I had *seen* the clothing of a priest. I was utterly confounded when our guests proceeded to introduce the man as the priest who had married them. Somehow, in some way, I had perceived that he was a priest and literally *seen* him, for a moment, as such.

Another of this strange type of "perceiving" that I began to experience occurred when I was watching a television show. The program was one in which Milton Shapp was appearing along with several other presidential candidates for the 1976 election. Zal had gone back to Pennsylvania to assist Shapp in his campaign, so, home alone, I was curious to see how things were going and the impression that Shapp would give in this network appearance. As the various candidates gave short talks, I was astonished to observe that, as Jimmy Carter spoke, I "saw" him as President, even as I had "seen" the priest. This was not a vague impression that Carter might become President, but an experience of viewing him *as* such. At the time of the show, during the early stages of the campaign, there was absolutely no reason to suspect that Carter had any more chance of success than the other candidates. Yet I was not surprised when eventually he won the election; I had *seen* him as President.

This type of "perceiving," I found, was operating in my dream state as well. One night, for example, I dreamt that I signed a contract to write a book with an ice skater—hardly a typical dream for me. I had the notion that the skater was Dick Button. The following day I received a letter from a student asking me to serve on her Ph.D. committee. Although this kind of letter is not rare for me to receive, it included references to her being a U.S. gold-medal winner in ice skating. Curious, in light of my dream, I agreed to meet the student. When we talked in person, she told me that her Ph.D. project was to write a book on dreams and that, in fact, she had skated with Dick Button! Reluctant to go against such a prescient dream, I consented to assist in the project.

During this same period of time, at the conclusion of a speech I had given at a large conference, a heavyset man with a gray beard came up to introduce himself. "I came here only to meet you," he said. "I'm a psychic. And so are you—you just don't know it yet!" I had not mentioned one word about these more unusual experiences, simply given a straightforward talk on dreams. These mystifying events combined to give me a most uneasy feeling.

The world of the paranormal, it seems, is opening before my eyes, dreaming or awake. Asleep, I will project into outer (or inner) space, and "learn" something by unknown means. Awake, I will "know" and "see" things that others do not. At times it is alarming and even terrifying. At other times it is exhilarating and ecstatic.

This, then, is a new risk. It is an internal journey that I must take in large part alone. If I proceed, there is no guarantee of safety or success. Yet every time that I have felt this way before, and took the risk, my life grew wider and deeper and richer. Sometimes the rewards came quickly, as in college studies; sometimes they took longer, as in realizing the value of experiencing life abroad. This unknown—this mystic, psychic, spiritual world—is probably not all that different from the other unknowns I have already confronted, each seemingly the worst at the moment it presented itself.

The adventure of living is in stepping over the threshold into the next beyond. A timid but persistent explorer, I take a deep breath, and prepare for the next big gamble.

9 THE SECOND CIRCLE
OF THE DREAM MANDALA

As I experienced lucid dreaming more often, I found that this strange kind of psychic "perception" increased; so too did occasional sensations of lifting out of my body. Trying to understand what was happening to me, I examined my lucid dreams even more carefully. I discovered that, regardless of its content, each dream had a basic internal pattern that was the same as that of other lucid dreams.

This process of becoming lucid can be illustrated more clearly step by step, using one dream. Notice, in particular, the outstanding role of water in this dream:

I am with Zal in London on a cold, raw day. We are walking around an elegant yet dangerous section of town. I notice newspapers in coin machines. Then we are standing across the street from a modern art museum and decide to go in to explore it. As we enter, I pause to notice something written in the cement sidewalk: the word *PADDEUS*. I think that perhaps it stands for Paddington Station.

Now Zal seems to be ahead of me in the crowd. He wears a cap that is slouched back on his head. A guard stops him and admonishes him to fix it. He ignores the guard, and a bystander volunteers, "You'd better listen, he could throw you out." I'm not sure what Zal does. A woman with long brown hair in front of me carries a shoulder bag. The guard says, "No purses." Since I have none, I pass on through.

Before and behind us is a huge crowd. Suddenly we all seem to be caught up in a swift current of water that comes rushing into the corridor. The water fills the space rapidly and we are whisked down the hall, people and fish and water swirling on all sides around us. The current is strange because it is so clear. I can hardly see it, yet I know it is there. Spinning about, we are swept faster and faster. . . .

(Opening scene, "Paddeus," December 31, 1973)

The clarity of the water in this opening scene may be symbolic of the clarity of the lucid state that followed. Partly because water is cool and partly because being swept through water is similar to the sensation of flying, its presence was important. I gave the sensation of cold in this dream no special attention at the time it occurred because it had actually rained all day and I had felt cold. Only later did I discover it was one of the crucial elements in the emerging pattern of lucid dreams. Eventually, the opening portion of this dream helped me to realize that swimming or being swept away in water is analogous to flying or being swept away by air currents. Flying or swimming movements, or both, often precede lucid dreams.

Like so many of its predecessors, this lucid dream deeply refreshed and revived me for the problems of the day. Although it remains to be explained why, people universally seem to find lucid dreams refreshing. I had no time to work with the symbolism when this dream occurred, but when I examined it later I was struck by the strange word *Paddeus.* It sounded remarkably like *Patty-us,* easily a reference to my own name. It was as though I were being told, by the writing on the sidewalk, that all the parts of the dream were part of me. I am *Patty* myself, but I am also *us*, all of the dream population.

Some of the other symbolism seemed obvious—the passing of a special entrance, being let through by the "guard," and being swept away in a strange current to the new and different experience that followed:

The scene shifts and now I am lying in bed with Zal on my left (as I actually am). It's dark, as though I have just awakened in the middle of the night, yet I know that I am dreaming. I feel very peculiar—as though I am in a trance. I decide to test whether I can move out of my body. The idea frightens me (as it actually does), but I allow myself to try it. Immediately I feel "myself" rising from the bed, lifting straight up from my body as though I am floating on my back in a swimming pool. I remain in that position, hovering above my physical body, without looking down. The sensations are strikingly real. I am very excited. I hear and feel the blood throbbing loudly in my ears. Accompanying it is a *sound-feel*, a kind of whirring-vibration that continues so long as I am "out." Then I seem to float back down into my physical body and the whirring-tingling ceases.

I look around the darkened room. Seeing a window with light sky beyond it, I say to myself, "Well, look out of it!" The window itself seems to move from spot to spot on the wall. I attempt to steady it with an outstretched hand. When the window is still, I can see that outside of it there is a city skyline with a dome and a cross. . . .
(Middle scene, "Paddeus," December 31, 1973)

The trancelike state that occurred in this portion of the dream is related to my later image of the Lightheaded Dancer, both in the peculiar lightheaded sensation and in the patch of light outside the window—both typical lucid-dream phenomena. This dream became even more unusual as it continued and reached a climax:

Suddenly, I become aware that a man is in bed with us, lashing out in attack. He is dark-skinned and dark-haired, perhaps Indonesian. He wears olive-khaki clothes, as though he might be a jungle fighter. His crisply outlined image strikes at me.

My mind is struggling to hold on to the idea that I am dreaming. I try frantically to think of the word *lucid* but I cannot recall it. I say to myself, "Simultaneous! Remember, 'simultaneous'! You can do anything." The man and I wrestle, thrashing from side to side on the bed. For seconds at a time, I am losing and I forget that I am dreaming. At these moments, the fight is as though it were a real and desperate one with my life at stake. Yet the realization that I am dreaming always returns and, with it, the knowledge that I can change what is happening. The mental struggle to hold on to dream consciousness seems to be portrayed in literal, physical terms.

Finally, at one moment when the awareness of dreaming is strong and the idea that I can do anything in a dream holds, I find that I am clutching a table knife. With a great thrust, I plunge the knife into the man's now-bared buttocks. I see the blood gush up and tell myself, "It's all right, you're dreaming." Then he is gone.

I have a strange physical reaction. All of my muscles, especially in my face, twitch and jerk. The whole body goes into spasms, out of control. It resembles a strong orgasm, but is more intense and more like what I imagine an epileptic fit would be. The spasmodic sensations finish and I lie relaxed.

Lazily, I stretch and lift up an arm that almost collides with Zal as he moves in his sleep, but we pass. I decide that I had better wake up and write all of this down before I lose the detail. I wake, feeling deliciously refreshed. It seems as though all the tension I experienced earlier has been discharged. I feel marvelous.

(Final scene, "Paddeus," December 31, 1973)

This dream of "Paddeus and the Jungle Fighter" occurred about a year after Zal and I had returned from our London venture. We were well settled into our new life in San Francisco. It was generally a period of great happiness and content for me. However, the day preceding the night of this particular dream was a tiring one; I had spent several hours interviewing replacements for my secretary, who was moving to another city. My bedtime mood was irritable and tense. The "Paddeus" dream brought total release.

By now, as I have said, I have experienced hundreds of lucid dreams. All have definite characteristics and a basic, organized pattern of events. Lucid dreaming, I found, is an almost sure path to out-of-the-body experiences. I don't know why, but it seems to be related to psychic "perception," too.

The typical lucid dream begins with an initial change in consciousness. An intense body movement in air or water—such as being swept away in the water current in the "Paddeus" dream—is followed by a different state of mind, as it was with the trancelike effect in "Paddeus." A sensation of coolness often accompanies or precedes the lightheaded feeling—in the "Paddeus" dream, for example, I was immersed in cool water. *Next, in the typical lucid dream, I am likely to have a vivid sensation of rising in the air.* This lifting up is sometimes simultaneous with a whirring sound and a vibration feeling that travels through my dream body, as happened in "Paddeus." The lifting sensation or active flying builds to a crescendo. I may decide to plummet back to earth, or I reach a peak in the air and arch backward or go into airborne spins. In any case, *there is a physical climax—a sexual orgasm, a visual burst of light and color, or (as in "Paddeus") a total body spasm.* At this point, my typical lucid dream often ends (though it may not) and I wake feeling wonderfully refreshed.

Since lucid dreaming began to flourish for me in England—the waking land of gloom and drizzle—it was logical that the coolness I felt when lucidity began should be explained by the image of rain in my dreams. The rain is usually depicted as a light drizzle, although sometimes it is a downpour. Other lucid dreams have contained imagery of my walking through sprinkles of snow, or being in cool night air, or feeling a fresh, cool breeze, and so on. Sometimes in lucid dreams I am immersed in flowing water—as in "Paddeus"—and at other times the sensation of coolness is justified by images of my diving into deep pools of water.

It was a long time before I recognized that rain, water, or a sense of coolness was a frequent precursor to my lucid dream states and, especially, to out-of-the-body experiences. This delay in recognition occurred because my dream images seemed, in themselves, to give logical explanations for the rain and coolness. Because London and San Francisco *are* often raw and chilly, I didn't realize how significant it is when I see myself in a dream in these places or I feel cool during a dream. A sensation of coolness is one of the first clues that my consciousness is about to alter.

Spurred by my own experiences to examine the literature on this topic, I found that many lucid dreamers and out-of-the-body travelers have also noticed and recorded perceptions of coolness that precede altered states of consciousness. Robert Crookall, for example, in his massive collection of cases of astral projection, reports numerous observations of coolness at the onset of the astral-projection experience.[1]

Because for me the sensation of coolness plays such a pivotal role in marking the boundary between ordinary dream consciousness and the extraordinary state of lucid dreaming, I decided to insert raindrops into the second circle of my personal Dream Mandala. I had previously filled the first circle of my Dream Mandala with the great steering wheel, my personal symbol for flying from one state of consciousness to an altered one. The rain in the second circle represents an extension of my altered consciousness.

In the Tibetan system, this second circle is a black ring filled with drawings of diamond scepters (*vajras*) placed end to end upon it like jewels. These diamond scepters symbolize, as does the single scepter that Aksobhya holds, wisdom that is as hard and sharp as a diamond. Invincible, shining, and clear, the diamond scepter cuts through erroneous conceptions. At a certain state of enlightenment, a disciple is said to have attained a "diamond body," suggesting that he or she is strong enough to sustain any psychic force. Enlightenment, once won, is never lost; like the diamond, it is unchangeable. According to an outstanding authority on the mandala, the circle of *vajra* represents reaching the threshold of reality.[2] When the disciple crosses it in meditation, he or she is passing from the clouded experience of everyday life to the diamond-clear reality of illumination.

Drizzly rain in the second circle of my Dream Mandala may seem a poor substitution for a girdle of diamond scepters. Yet, for me, it serves the same function. Rain and coolness signal the passing of a threshold to changed consciousness.

Below:
A Vajra—*the Diamond Scepter symbol used by Tibetan Buddhists.*

Right:
The Second Circle of a Tibetan Buddhist Mandala—*the Ring of Diamond Scepters (Vajras).*

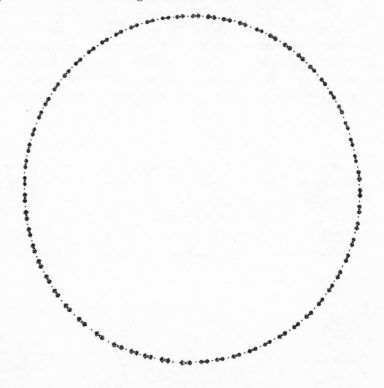

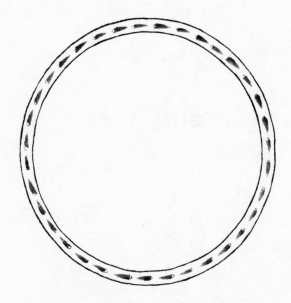

The Ring of Raindrops—*the second circle of my Dream Mandala.*

As I hovered on this threshold between ordinary and altered states of consciousness, I began to wonder whether facing *this* unknown was not too great a risk after all. The region looked dark and fathomless. I stepped over the threshold with trepidation.

10 THE BLUEBIRD TREE

 In the course of a long nonlucid dream, I am with a group of people (business associates and a friend) on our way to visit a publisher. We are going to discuss a children's book that I have written. As we stop to chat at a street corner, and they ask me some questions, I realize that I have left some important papers at home that will provide answers. I say to the others, "Wait here. I'll be back in ten minutes." I turn and, hurrying, run lightly down the sidewalk in bare feet. I reach an iron gate at the entrance to the narrow, pretty alley where I live in this dream. I open the gate. As I close it, I think how, while I am gone, my friend might talk about her involvement with some strange things. She seems to want to be helpful, however, and will surely use judgment. With the iron gate shut behind me, I look across the alleyway and am thunderstruck at the sight.

There stands a great tree. It is magnificent. In place of leaves, it bears beautiful pale-blue feathers. The entire tree is covered with these lovely fluffy feather-leaves, and midst the branches sing hundreds of tiny bluebirds. With a sense of revelation, I know that I am dreaming. The scene floods with more intense color. I watch in wonder. Suddenly one of the tiny bluebirds alights on the forefinger of my left hand. Spellbound, I caress his feathery breast with my right forefinger. He looks a little like a parakeet. "Oh, you pretty. . . ." I start to say "kitty" and smile at myself. I begin wondering what to do with this precious lucid state, but now I feel overcome by a wave of exhaustion. My ears begin the familiar ringing, my head feels floaty and dizzy (the Lightheaded Dancer). I must rest.

I lie down on the ground on my right side and close my eyes. The whirring-buzzing sound grows louder, drowning out everything. This time it does not stay centered in the head, but moves around my body and travels to my bottom. Like a point of buzzing light, it traces a pattern around and around the cheeks of my buttocks. It's a lovely sensation. I know that I am dreaming and that I can have *anything* happen. I wonder whether I am partially awake, because I see a crack of bright light in the sky that might be daylight (it was not, for the room was in total blackness when I finally awoke). I watch the light.

Through the swirling in my head and the feel of delicious buzzing, I struggle to decide what to experience. Clearly I will go into orgasm soon. It seems a shame to spend lucidity on yet another orgasm, but it is coming close. Should I try to see the children's book? Should I. . . .

Unexpectedly, there is a sharp movement, as though of the earth beneath me (it is Zal shifting in our bed). The dream snaps to ordinary. The whirring stops. I am no longer me, lying lucid in a dream wondering what to do. Instead, I see a small boy who lies on his right side in a crib. His mother, a large, plump woman, has just startled him awake by opening the door. "Oh, did I wake you? I'm sorry," she says apologetically. He looks up at her. She sets a small dish on the bedside table. "Here's your

choice for dinner," she says. "What would you like?" He is to look at the dish and make a selection. I awake.
("The Bluebird Tree," October 30, 1974)

The joy I felt, inspired by the magnificent blue-bird tree and the tiny creature who flew down from it to perch on my finger, was extraordinary, near ecstatic. I had been able to recognize the dreamlike quality of the tree during the dream and so precipitate the exciting altered state of consciousness that I always seek to recapture.

As in most lucid dreams, symbolism was still operating. I "passed a gate" and discovered a thing of grandeur—an experience of bliss. The bluebirds and the feather-leaves most probably symbolized my sense of great good fortune. So much had been going well when I had this dream. Zal and I had left England and adventured for five full months eastward across the globe to return to a beautiful new home in San Francisco. My daughter, Cheryl, was living with us again. I was teaching once more and writing and being published. The "bluebirds of happiness," an association from the Maeterlinck play, were abundant.

The specific day I had "The Bluebird Tree" dream I was somewhat shaken. We were back East briefly on one of Zal's political consulting trips. I had been running around doing errands in a rental car and had a minor accident in the rush-hour traffic on the expressway. A large truck had ripped off a right-hand rearview mirror as we passed at close quarters. Although the damage was small, my serenity was jarred. As I drove around the suburbs from shop to shop the remainder of the day, I felt a bit jittery. Even so, I found myself admiring the glorious fall foliage. In particular I was struck by a line of majestic sycamores whose leaves were all bright yellow-orange. The branches were still thick with these yellow-orange leaves and beneath them fluttered more leaves like a rain of petals onto the ground below. Later I met Zal and we made our way to the Pennsylvania capitol. He was especially understanding and soothing about the accident.

The vivid waking impression of the yellow-clad trees was transformed in my dream of that night to the bluebird tree.[1] Other waking imagery that influenced this dream went further back in time—to a parakeet pet who was a lovely shade of pale blue with a black droplet necklace. My memory records are clearer on parakeets than on views of bluebirds, explaining the bird's parakeetlike appearance up close; memories of my several kittens are also vivid. Our dreams, it seems, weave themselves from many sources—events and even colors of our immediate day, events of our past—all combined with a symbolic expression of our current view of our life situation.

Beyond the immediate symbolism, however, was more of that mysterious realm I had become determined to penetrate. I had learned that the sense of weariness I felt in the dream was often a component of lucid dreams. The altered state of consciousness is frequently depicted by a literal shift in consciousness in the dream, by "going to sleep" in my dreams, or falling into a trance. As this "Bluebird Tree" dream became lucid, I lay down to rest. As it became ordinary, when my husband shifted in bed, a little boy was startled awake. It seems that in my dreams, when a dream figure "goes to sleep" I become conscious, and when a dream figure "wakes up" I go into unconscious dreaming. Also there seems to be operating in me a kind of body awareness while I sleep. I was in fact sleeping on my right side throughout "The Bluebird Tree" dream, as both the small boy and I were doing in the dream state.

The second scene of the mother and boy is almost a symbolic replay of the end of the lucid portion. In the same way as I was wondering what to choose to do, she asks the boy what he would like to choose for dinner. There is also a sensation of change in sound and light—which is typical of becoming lucid, as I've said.

I had had a lot of practice in becoming lucid by the time of "The Bluebird Tree." When I first became lucid in dreams the consciousness was of such brief duration that it seemed unimportant. I had no conception of how valuable these flashes of knowledge of the dream state could be. As so many people do, I would find myself in the midst of a terrifying dream with an enemy closing in, feel that my life was over, and suddenly, seemingly miraculously, realize I was dreaming. I could wake up if I wanted to. With a shudder of relief I'd escape to the waking world. Occasionally I would begin to interpret an ongoing dream. For instance, in one dream I was bitten by a dog. As I lay on the grass with my clothes and hair disheveled, I turned to an onlooker and said wisely, "That's another symbol for sexual attack," as though to assure the person not to worry.

These brief flashes and mild forms of lucidity gave me no clue to how special the state of dream consciousness could become. I used them mostly to wake myself. Once in a while I'd try to prolong an intriguing dream to see what would happen.

In England, as I've mentioned, the skill of lucid dreaming began to emerge more often. Since I began attending to my dreams intensely, and recording every daily tidbit rather than only the dream feasts, my output increased dramatically. Soon I found myself waking in the middle of the night fresh from a dream. I developed a method of recording my dreams in the dark with my eyes closed.[2] (I began it to keep from disturbing Zal's sleep. How serendipitous acts of love can be.) This method of writing makes dream recall more complete; my memory for dream experience improved enormously.

As this habit of dream recall and recording grew by giant steps, I would find myself in a dream seeming to be writing my preceding dream. Something, I knew not what, would clue me that I was still asleep, dreaming I was recording a dream. With a kind of internal wrench I would actually awake in order to make the written record. Snuggled under our down-filled quilt, my body warmly tucked to Zal, my face chilly with the crisp early-morning air and the catlike cry of the peacocks in Holland Park rising to our open-windowed flat, I would grope, eyes closed, for the bedside pen and pad to scribble the latest nocturnal story. Thus the snippets of dream consciousness were still brief, but they occurred with more and more regularity.

Since I had never heard of the concept of lucid dreaming, I regarded these lucid moments as a curiosity, no more. Later, as my voracious reading led me to distant paths and I encountered descriptions of the special state of lucid dreaming, I recognized my frequent, albeit small, sips of the same delicious nectar. Despite the problems of daily living I had to cope with, my being in England helped me launch my dream quest.

Many British people are deeply interested in the occult, in haunted houses, in the supernatural in all its aspects. Thus it was inevitable that at some point I would be led into bookstores that offered a different variety from the mundane books to which I was accustomed. Up winding streets, through narrow, wet lanes, I would go, into old-fashioned, lantern-hung, bottle-glass-fronted shops, where a new kind of literature portentously proclaimed: "Read *me!*" And I did. As I did, I began to reach for the relationship between the dream state, the lucid state, and what people have long called mysterious, occult, or simply inexplicable.

Reading books by continental authors on dreams led me to out-of-the-way paths, even to foreign languages. As my time was freer and the book selection wider and more unusual, I soon found new areas to explore. I wanted to know about dreams related to the cycles of the moon, and so was led to both astronomy and mythology. I learned that many great dreamers were artists, writers, scientists, and theologians, so I was led to accounts of their lives. I had thought I was narrowing choices by focusing on dreams. In a way I was; yet in another way the focus on dreams opened a whole new spectrum of life.

My dream pad and notebook became my constant companians. At home in London, or in the Cotswolds in a chilly, crooked-floored, step-squeaking stone inn, or in the tower room of a castle in the Trossachs of Scotland as the rain poured outside and we huddled close to the crackling fire, my dream pad was always on the bed-side table. Whether I was in Copenhagen on midsummer's-day festival, the longest day of the year with a mere hour of moon-bright darkness, or rocking on the Aegean in our tiny berth on the steam-ship *Romantica* as we sailed toward Delos, or tossing hot and sticky on a dank pad in Marrakesh, or in a canopied bed under a fluffy feather quilt with deep snow outside a *gasthaus* near Stuttgart—the dream pad was always there.

And gradually I saw how my dreams reflected the changing set-tings and the changing emotional climate as Zal and I struggled and loved toward each other in the unfamiliar world we moved through. These dreams, of course, contained scraps of my past. But also, they expressed—with exaggeration—all the problems and pleasures of the moment. I became able to read from my dreams the messages of my heart; I learned the intimate language of my dreams. Beyond their everyday statements, I sensed a mysterious undercurrent.

The combination of widespread reading, a wide-flung personal experience, and wide searching into my dream life led to profound changes, in both my dream state and my waking life.

We closed our flat in London in June of 1972. The final few weeks in England had been sheer delight. In my own characteristically per-verse style I enjoyed them immensely. Prior to our decision to re-turn to the States, it had been terrible: I couldn't bear to live there. Instantly after our decision to leave was made, England was won-derful! I soaked up the television, the theaters, parks, and museums, and admired the peacefulness and the friendliness of the people all over again. At the very least we'd come back to visit. Freed from the sense of a "big gamble," I could enjoy the remainder of our stay, happy to have the experience of living in England but buoyed up by the thought that we were going *home.*

Our general route was upward through the Scandinavian coun-tries, downward through the Soviet Union, across the Middle Eastern countries, to India, then further down through the Far East, to Australia, and, finally, to Tahiti, and then home.

Outwardly, the trip was a fantastic, exotic experience around the world. Inwardly, it launched a fantastic, exotic experience *out* of the world. Both journeys were equally exciting and real.

When I think back on the trip it is like rapidly flipping the pages of a photo album stuffed full with brightly colored snapshots —a montage of images. Some in particular leap out of the pages and rekindle memories.

I can feel myself once more in the temple courtyard of a village in Bali, close to Zal in the light of the full moon. I watch the dancers sway hypnotically to the incessant throbbing of the gamelan gongs. The white-garbed priestess holds aloft the sacred kris (a wavy dagger) and a man runs screaming in a trance. The others catch him, cover his head with an animal mask, and lift him high for all to see. The animal moans of the entranced man, the clanging music, the swirling dancers merge. . . .

I am again standing in a dusty field watching weeping relatives and topknotted, long-nailed priests adorn with flowers the corpse of a young Balinese woman in her coffin. She has died in childbirth. Her physician husband and three small sons, all in white mourning headbands, watch sadly from a nearby platform. Now the lid to her coffin—carved in the shape of a great cow—is replaced. The fire is set. Flames and smoke rise up, enveloping the body and the crowd of mourners. . . .

I fiind myself in the dark in the center of a great horde of swarthy, curly-headed Turks. They are shouting taxi offers that are the equivalent of twenty to fifty dollars. They gesticulate wildly. The bus driver has refused to take us. Zal has left me alone with our few bags to get the police. We seem to be the only foreigners in the country and I feel like meat for hungry sharks. At last Zal reappears with a policeman and we are whisked away through the crowd of angry, waving men, past the sea of squatting, shawled women, to the safety of a cab. It is like a nightmare, but it is very real. . . .

I see a blur of people, ever shifting in size and shape and style, as well as sound. There are the old-looking children of Rome, aged faces in child bodies; there are the tall, slender blonds of Stockholm, who make me feel short for the first time in my life; there are the husky, Slavic, high-cheekboned women of Helsinki and throughout Russia, who make me feel dainty. There are the small, volatile people of Rumania; the dark, mustached, liquid-eyed men of Turkey, looking alternately fierce or melting; there are the friendly-faced, smiling, gentle people of Bali.

In particular, I see the women: skeleton-skinny prostitutes in Bombay, with garish lips and short skirts, standing in front of hovels; the plumply pretty ladies of the night in Amsterdam, sitting in display windows, costumed, under the glow of red light. I see groups of women in Morocco, bent double from the weight of the sticks of firewood they carry in sacks on their backs. I see the husky women unloading baggage in Bulgaria. I sit upstairs with the other women in a synagogue in Jerusalem, hidden from my husband below by elaborate latticework. I look with wonder at the Muslim women of Kashmir, who are permitted out only under a huge tentlike covering with a small grilled window that is said to ruin their eyesight. I marvel at the grace of female dancers in Thailand. Occasionally, I meet a woman activist or intellectual with whom I can exchange ideas.

I find my own social status constantly shifting in a dizzying way. At one moment we are pushed and shoved like cattle in the airport mobs of Bulgaria, deprived of all belongings. Next moment, we are being served by a turbaned porter who crouches outside our bedroom door in the Oberoi Palace Hotel in Srinagar, Kashmir, awaiting our smallest request. Then we are being begged for coins by throngs of skinny, deformed folk calling "memsahib" as we drive in our air-conditioned limousine touring Bombay. I am appalled by the conditions but grateful to be on the other side of the glass from the sickeningly humid 105° heat and the vultures that perch on the trees we pass near the Tower of Silence. The birds are waiting for fresh corpses to be placed in the open tower so they can pick the bones clean.

The scenes and people that passed my outer eyes were incredibly exotic. But it was not only the scenery that changed. The contrasts in my physical health and state of mind from day to day were as different as the icy peak of Grindelwald in Switzerland is from the cavern-cathedral carved into the rocky mountain of the Valley of the Fallen in El Escorial, Spain. My mood blew as dry and hot as the sand that stung and cut our faces in Ouarzazate, Morocco. I grew as tearfully wet as the flash flood in Bangkok where we toured the city in bare feet and with slacks rolled up, sloshing through a foot or more of water, under umbrellas, to see the Emerald Buddha. At times I felt as chilly as the cool mist clinging to the mountaintop of the monastery in Chiengmai where a sign proclaimed NO WOMEN PERMITTED near the sacred relics of Buddha. At other times I felt as soft and sweet as the garland of jasmine put around my neck when I entered the Hindu temple of Krishna in New Delhi. Or as irritable and peckish as the huge black crows cawing in the gardens of our hotel in Delhi. I felt as unstable as I had been upon the elephant that lumbered up the hill on the circular path to the Temple of Kali in the Amber Palace at Jaipur.

The conditions of my health and stamina were as unsettled as my mood. Even Zal, usually Gibraltar Rock–like, succumbed to bouts of hay fever and dysentery. A Viking banquet following a pageant play in Frederikssund, Denmark, left him pale and weak. We made a shaky tour around the magnificent statues in Vigeland Park in Oslo, our next stop, Zal never allowing a bathroom to be far from his sight. India almost unglued us both, but a physician friend with supplies of Mexafoam came to the rescue. It was a roller coaster that exaggerated my usual mood swings and slowly eroded my energy. The plights of travel were a strain, but the experiences were well worth the discomforts.

In fact, I became quite resourceful. In Turkey, I learned how to make my own sanitary napkins. It had never occurred to me that such necessities would be unavailable (and if it had, five months' supply in my small bag would have left no space for clothing). I'd assumed that, like toothpaste, sanitary napkins could be purchased along the route. When I was finally able to communicate my needs, I was given boxes of "cotton wool." By wrapping strips of toilet paper around the loose cotton and pinning the whole contraption to my underpants, I constructed a reasonable equivalent to a pad— though hardly as convenient or comfortable.

When we took the Pan Am flight from Istanbul to Tehran, I felt as though I'd found a tiny microcosm of the United States. I was elated to eat American food once more, and I stuffed all the sanitary pads and tissues I could manage into my purse.

My internal scenery was changing as rapidly as the time zones we crossed, which threw my hormones into turmoil. The nightly dreams did more than reflect my state of health, my mood, my experiences and problems of the day, mixed with imagery of the past. The dream consciousness that had begun to grow steadily in England seemed to flourish in the exotic air I breathed.

Of course, my dreams still expressed "this is where I am." Shortly after Zal and I had quarreled in Delos, I dreamt about a country at war and living in a police state. I saw myself with two firecrackers attached to my head. That made me look like a devil, which is perhaps how I viewed my anger. When we were having a particularly happy time in Kuala Lumpur, I dreamt I met a woman who had two daughters named Harmony and Melody. These tiny girls danced on a keyboard, playing tunes with their toes. When I felt I was managing the emotional bumps better, I dreamt I was riding a bicycle and keeping my balance very well on lumpy ground. I find that riding a bike in a dream suggests that I am even more under control than being the driver of a car because it is more expressive of my direct effort. The bicycle moves and is balanced by the dreamer's own power and skill.

I began to notice physically peculiar dreams such as a dream character hanging upside down or doing a headstand, or I would find myself clinging to the sides of walls or ledges. These dreams seemed to be a precursor of the Lightheaded Dancer. Most striking, however, was the growing appearance of flying dreams. I danced, I glided, spun, leapt, and twirled on ice, but most especially I flew. In my dreams I flew over stranger countries, and saw even stranger sights, than I did while awake.

The greatest change in my dream life occurred when I encountered the Senoi tribe. It was in Tokyo, while we were attending the Twentieth International Congress of Psychology, that Zal and I first learned of the Senoi people of Malaysia. This remarkable primitive tribe literally teaches its children how to dream. It seemed unbelievable to me. With much excitement I set out to learn more about the people who totally eliminated nightmares from their children's dreams. Within the framework of our shortening time schedule, I was, while in Kuala Lumpur, able to arrange to meet some of the Senoi, who were in a hospital at the edge of the jungle where they live, and to speak with them through an interpreter. In Singapore, I talked with researchers who'd lived with them for lengthy periods, and obtained all the literature about them I could find at that time. I grew excited about the possible implications their system might have for understanding and using dreams in our culture.

Although some of the material was contradictory, the basic picture that emerged was one of training, a cultural dream pattern.[3] I pieced together some rules of their system and gave them names: *confront and conquer danger in your dreams; approach the positive elements in your dreams;* and *always end the dream with a positive outcome.* My own dreams began to change immediately, as did Zal's.[4]

Although the dreamer who uses the Senoi system must be at least partially aware that he or she is dreaming in order to apply the rules, the dream consciousness is not total. For instance, in order to turn and face a dream tiger, the dreamer must remember he or she is not supposed to wake up from a dream in fear, is not supposed to run or try to escape frightening dream figures, but must rather confront and conquer them. Applying the rule necessitates being somewhat aware that one is dreaming, but not necessarily stating, "I'm dreaming," and realizing the full impact and possibilities of the situation.

I tried applying the Senoi rules as we headed home. After five months of travel I was aching for one spot to stay in. Although I still felt a surge of excitement as I anticipated what the next new city or country might be like, my body was wearing out. Too many time-zone changes, too many plane trips wreaking havoc with hormonal flow, too many unusual foods, too many bouts with dysentery.

In Bali I started to hemorrhage midcycle. When we reached Australia it was heavier. I bled for days on end. Then I grew feverish. The local doctor prescribed bed rest, feet up, and, several days thereafter, lolling in the sun. Gratefully I crawled under the covers and left the sightseeing to Zal.

I remained in bed for several days, bleeding, and dreaming, among other things, of overflowing sinks. Finally the "overflowing" of my body ceased. Zal and I proceeded to Tahiti for some sunshine and rest.

There in Papeete, swimming, lounging in the sun midst tropical blooms, I began to unwind. I also found myself experiencing, more often than ever before, what I call *dream composing*, a kind of designing of the dream while it's happening; it is a stage that precedes full lucid dreaming. As my life moved toward a peaceful resettling, the power of conscious dreaming gathered force.

I became aware of a new figure in my dream life: a strong, capable woman. Sometimes she was a black woman judo expert, sometimes a superbly skilled opera singer, sometimes a primitive tribal queen. Her shapes and skills took various forms, but she was clearly a newcomer who was slowly edging out the hurt little girls and male heroes that had previously dominated my dream world. Perhaps it was part of the process of becoming liberated in the dream world. It surely symbolized the emerging strength that was forthcoming.

Bodies rested, Zal and I took the last lap of our journey from Tahiti back to the United States. It was hard to believe that all our adventures had been crammed into five short months. Although we had come back briefly three times during the course of our living abroad, this was a real homecoming. In San Francisco we visited a few days with Zal's family. I obtained a job interview at a local college, and, when asked to give a spur-of-the-moment lecture on dreams to a class, I agreed. After it was done I was hired on the spot to teach a course on dreams the following semester. It was truly a coup at a time when academic jobs were so scarce. That night I flew in my dreams with sensations of delight: I sailed up several feet and then threw myself down, stopping a few feet short of the ground, again and again, feeling delicious waves of sensual pleasure.

We went on to Philadelphia to see family and friends and to make arrangements for our widely scattered belongings to be sent to San Francisco, where we had decided to live. I could hardly believe it. We would have a home again. The things we'd left in storage while we were abroad, the things we'd shipped to England and shipped back, the things we'd purchased along our trip and posted home, the things we had with us—all to assemble in one spot. Especially my precious books. I thought I might never set foot outside the door to travel again. In one dream of that period I consulted manuals of directions to find my way in a city. In another, I was in a library searching for The Answer Room. Thus, I was busy daytime and dreamtime preparing for our life ahead.

Cheryl, then sixteen, and I went on to San Francisco ahead of Zal and began our search for a place to live. It was so easy. Everything was beautiful. The buildings were glinting with light and colorful with Mediterranean pinks and yellows. The weather was mild, sunny with a touch of cool, absolutely perfect for me. The apartments and flats had every conceivable convenience, yet the city was sophisticated and exciting. I felt as though I'd found the best of both worlds—the comforts of American living combined with the natural beauty and cultural style of a European city. In my dreams, I flew above sublime coastal views, and temples surrounded by exquisite trees in pink bloom (a symbol from the scene as I rode home from the hospital with my newborn infant); I wore beautiful jewelry; I watched a pulsating, glowing full moon—all reflections of joy.

Awake, I noticed a subtle difference in my taste in housing. No longer did the angular modern style please me as it had in the past. Great glass windows and square stucco walls seemed cold. The Victorian houses held more charm; the Spanish-Mexican haciendas looked warm and inviting. I had changed in England and in those months of travel. Complain as I did, grumbling all the way about how old-fashioned England was and being reminded of the crumbling house on Willow Grove Avenue, I found that now, when I could choose the modern, I no longer wanted it. Perhaps it was my internal acceptance of the house on Willow Grove Avenue, the sense of value that older things can have; perhaps, partly, a sense of my own growing history.

Within a few days, with many attractive choices, we selected a spectacular flat in the Marina district of San Francisco. It was a two-story spread of nine rooms and four full baths, larger than any house I'd lived in. Spanish in style, it had circular archways and wrought-iron porches, heavy wooden doors and trim, hardwood floors, and a staircase with a stained-glass window. There were two fireplaces and three patios. An altogether exciting home. Our things arrived and we set up housekeeping. The windows stood open to fresh sea air, and we had cozy fires, as in London. (But here one could also turn up the heat, run the garbage disposal and dishwasher, and pop a load of laundry in at will.)

The setting was as jewellike as the house. One block from the Bay, we could stroll watching the bobbing sailboats and the Golden Gate. Everywhere were fresh flowers and fresh fruit. Minimum struggle to adjust, no homesickness. Much of the ease of this move was, of course, the result of being familiar with the American way of doing things. I was so glad to be back that whatever problems did arise, I resolved quickly.

We settled into a new social life, met new friends, and visited old friends and family. We set about finding doctors, dentists, lawyers, getting opera seats—activities of resettling. We began the process of living with our youngest teenage daughter again. I took the part-time teaching position I had been offered at a local college and began serious work on my projected book about dreams. Despite small difficulties, I felt altogether happy with our present life. The bluebird tree was the right symbol.

At last in one spot, in my own country, lucid dreams gleamed radiantly during my nights. These came more and more often. They were exciting and delightful experiences and made me yearn to get back to that magical space. But I had also begun to experience an extension of lucid dreams that bordered on the terrifying. I found myself being projected out of my body in the dream state, will it or not. The projection culminated in a truly shocking experience. This was an altogether different situation, one I was not sure I wanted to repeat. And I wasn't sure I could prevent it.

I had returned from an exotic outer world to discover that the world within myself was even more mysterious. But I couldn't "go home" from the world within. I had to learn how to survive in it. I began integrating my lucid-dream experiences and striving to synthesize what I was learning about this remarkable state of consciousness. I had learned from the Senoi how to deal with ordinary nightmares and how to increase pleasure in dreams. I was presently learning how to precipitate lucid dreams and use them for greater understanding and creative projects. Now I must learn how to cope with out-of-the-body experiences in dreams or turn them off altogether. They had become both stunning and alarming. I might know the way to move home and resettle in the outer world, but I did not know the rules of the road in this emerging inner realm of different time and space. It was in this suspended state of mind that "The Bluebird Tree" dream occurred.

The tiny bluebird that lit on my finger in that dream gave me much comfort. It represented more than good luck and happiness in my present situation. It bespoke reassurance of my movement through inner realms. It was a kind of message that approaching the "other" world was safe, that friendly, protecting resources were there, as well as dangerous forces. A few weeks before "The Bluebird Tree" dream I had been badly shaken. I had been "out" in an alarming way and felt the power of forces that seemed beyond my ability to cope with. The bluebird of this dream foretold a presence, a guide, a sense of safe passage. The blue feathered creature I stroked gave me a sense of deep calm. . . .

II THE SOUTHERN QUARTER OF THE DREAM MANDALA
chief Deity: The High Flyer

In a grade-school play, with my classmates decked out as daisies, daffodils, tulips, ducklings, and bunnies, I was the bluebird. My mother had purchased for the occasion a sensational costume—it consisted of a kind of blue gym suit with a matching blue skirt. Pinned to my shoulders and attached to my wrists, as though a cape, the skirt served admirably as wings. I flapped happily across the stage, waving my arms up and down, in and out among the spring flower–animal children. Perhaps this was the beginning of my blue-bird symbolism, for I felt myself to be a most remarkable bluebird.

Birds have been an important symbol throughout my dream life. They seem to signify a stage of spiritual development. In waking life, however, their role had simply been that of pets.

At the time of the grade-school play, for example, I had had a series of parakeets—a pair of green-and-gold lovers, and then a beautiful blue-and-white bird. There were a couple of yellow canaries, too, before the cat family arrived. Years later I bought my own small daughter, Cheryl, a sweet-voiced canary with a black topknot as a birthday gift.

The parakeets were easy to train. They sat on my finger, cocked their heads wisely, and took the tidbits I offered between my teeth; or rode on my shoulder and climbed up my knit cap to watch the world from schoolgirl height. The canaries were more difficult, but I managed to train my daughter's bird, while still inside his cage, to take lettuce from my hand. He would screech and scold, flapping his wings furiously, and finally edge over on the bar to snatch the succulent lettuce from my fingertips. When Cheryl was about eight, she called me in a panic at the office where I was doing my psychology internship. Between sobs she described how the bird had gotten loose in the house. She had been trying to catch him in a paper bag for hours. Arriving home, I easily caught the exhausted creature between my hands as he perched on a bookcase. His heart thumped wildly under the velvety feathers. He died a few months later—probably prematurely aged with heart trouble.

When I was about nineteen, my fiancé won a baby chick in a contest at a country fair we were visiting in Erie. In the car, all the way back to Philadelphia, I held the infant ball of fluff between my cupped hands on my lap, the only position in which he'd peep less miserably. I secreted him in a box in my room at the charity institution in the city where I worked at the time. He loved to sit on my shoulder nestled close to my neck, under my long hair, as in a kind of nest. In the mornings he rode on my slipper when I went down the narrow corridor to the bathroom. Eventually, the directress objected (understandably), and my little friend was sent to live in the suburbs with my parents. Whence he was gobbled by the dog, as I recall.

Butterflies, too (even more delicate than the birds), have figured in this symbolic complex. Once, as a teenager, I caught a monarch butterfly in the garden of the house on Willow Grove Avenue. I was curious to get a closer look at it. When I released it seconds later, my fingertips were covered with a golden powder-dust. The prints of my fingers could still be seen on the poor creature's wings, and it was hampered as it flew away. I felt sorry for that, and much impressed with its delicacy.

Perhaps it was the delicacy I saw in myself that attracted me to these creatures, the ease of inflicting injury by rough handling. In any case, birds have seemed tender creatures to me, needing care and responding to love. They also seem slightly risky—parakeets can nip; chickens can peck. It seemed strange to me that the butterflies of my early dreams could also bite and draw blood. The birds and the butterflies (at least those of my dreams) would attack to protect their vulnerability. Yet these fluttery, easily frightened creatures have a power, if they are free to use it, that is beyond all of ours—the power of flight.

It is this quality, I think, that has led many cultures to picture the soul as a bird. The Egyptian hieroglyph for the vehicle of the soul is *ka*, a creature with the head of a human and the body of a bird.[1] In Christianity, the holy spirit is depicted as a dove. People on the verge of death, from illness or accident, often speak of a sensation of flying. Those who are judged clinically dead and are later revived frequently report flying out of their bodies.[2] Saints mention a sense of levitation during ecstasy. Ability to fly is one of the chief characteristics of a shaman in every culture.[3] Yogis, astral travelers, and mystics of all types universally describe experiences of moving out of their bodies, in a sort of second body, to fly about and adventure. Small wonder that the soul is pictured as a bird who can fly from earth to heaven.

The Soul Bird—*ancient Egyptian symbol for the vehicle of the soul.*

This symbolism is certainly applicable in my dream life. Between my childhood belief that I could actually fly, based on dreams of doing so, and my mid-adult flying dreams, there were years of being earthbound. The more I develop skill in conscious dreaming, the more I find that I can fly again in my dreams. Flying and dream consciousness are inextricably intertwined.

Flying is, in fact, as I have mentioned, an almost certain forerunner of lucid dreaming for me. The lightheaded feeling I have de-

The High Flyer—*chief dream deity of the Southern Quarter of my Dream Mandala.*

scribed is sure to accompany the sense of rising from the ground, if it has not already preceded the takeoff. Once airborne, I am flooded with sensations—often including a whirring-ringing sound, a vibration-feeling that travels through my body, and ripples of sexual passion. This is what happened in "The Bluebird Tree" dream, although in this case I did not actually leave the ground. Merely petting the bird, who could leave the ground, brought on the same sensations. Usually, however, I am flying. The sensations build to a climax of lights, colors, sounds, and passion. I reach a peak and burst. If I am not disturbed, as I was by Zal's movement in bed during "The Bluebird Tree" dream, and if I do not awake from the intensity of feeling, as I did in "The Great Steering Wheel" dream, an explosion is triggered, usually while I am flying.

Thus flying is the second major characteristic of lucid dreaming for me. The first is the change of consciousness I experience in various forms—lightheadedness, fixedness, mirror gazing, etc. I have already placed this initial change of consciousness into the Eastern Quarter of my Dream Mandala. Into the Southern Quarter (the next segment encountered on our clockwise movement through the mandala) I now place my flying images.

I call the chief deity of this Southern Quarter my High Flyer. She is myself, rising above the earthly plane. I drew her in her several aspects—rising from the earth, plummeting back to it, flying swimming-style (she favors the breaststroke, but also paddles while lying on her back), flying-dancing, upright, swooping, hovering, rolling, arching—She Who Moves Through the Air has many modes. Her attendants include the Bluebird and the Butterfly.

These creatures lead the High Flyer—myself—safely through their elements. They are guides of the air. Once when I was pursued by enemies in a dream, I flew away from them, led over fields and hills by a butterfly. In another dream, after having been earthbound for months and having sorely missed flying, I found myself perched on a rooftop with Zal:

The Bluebird—*dream bird of the Southern Quarter of my Dream Mandala.*

He (in his usual supportive role) is encouraging me to take off from the edge with him. I am fearful. "It's been so long since I've flown, I'm not sure I can do it," I say. (This dream is not lucid, so I need a lot of coaxing.) As though to show me it is safe, he dives into the air and flies several yards. Then he seems to be wearing a blue cape that flutters from his shoulders, and before him flies a bluebird. He lands on a lawn, and, taking a stick, he strikes the earth. Great sparks arc up. All this is quite

The Butterfly—*dream creature of the Southern Quarter of my Dream Mandala.*

The Polka Dot Horse—*dream creature of the Southern Quarter of my Dream Mandala.*

convincing to me. In addition, someone is opening a window near the ledge where I sit, so I leap off and, with some shakiness, as though from lack of practice, fly over to join Zal.

In yet another dream, a lucid one in which I was already airborne and whizzing along speedily, I saw on a plain below me a herd of galloping horses:

Overwhelmed by waves of sexual passion, I think it would be fun to ride one of the horses, and I swoop down. Close up, I can see that the face of one of them is orange on the left side and brown with white polka dots on the right. Mane streaking in the wind, he looks magnificent to me, and I ride him joyfully.

Years after "The Polka Dot Horse" dream, I was attending a lecture on magic; bored, I began to sketch that horse as I remembered him. Growing more and more involved in the image, I contemplated his significance for me—how he was related to the flying feeling, how the rhythmic movements of horseback riding are sexual. I noticed how I was concentrating most on drawing the hair of his mane. It was the *flow* of it that was meaningful to me. Suddenly I heard the speaker say, "It's amazing how many women dream of horses." As this statement was a total shift of topic, completely unexpected, and came simultaneously with my absorption in drawing a dream horse, the coincidence startled me. It was as though I had produced the thought in the speaker by my intense concentration on the subject of dream horses (or possibly picked up his intention to speak of it). It was one of many such synchronous events, trivial but impressive, that began happening. The flying Polka Dot Horse was part of the Southern Quarter of my Dream Mandala, too, along with the High Flyer, the Bluebird, and the Butterfly.

For the Tibetan Buddhist, the deity who appears in this Southern Quarter is called Ratna-Sambhava,* the "jewel-born" one. He holds a flaming gem in his left hand as it rests palm upward on his lap. This jewel is sometimes called a "wishing gem," suggesting the possibility that all spiritual desires may be fulfilled, and it represents the "three gifts"—the Buddha, his teachings, and his holy community of monks. Ratna-Sambhava's right hand is held downward, the palm outward, facing toward the viewer, in a gesture of bestowing these gifts.

Yellow is his color, like the warm sun of the South at noon. His element is earth; he appears seated upon a sun-disc throne supported by horses. The fact that Ratna-Sambhava's animal is a horse makes my dream horse with polka dots seem even more appropriate here.

When the energy that Ratna-Sambhava represents is expressed neurotically, it appears as pride, self-seeking, and arrogance. This energy, as with all of the so-called obscuring passions, poisons, or evils, can be transfigured into a special kind of wisdom. In this case,

---

* pronounced Raht·nah·sahm·*bah*·vă

Ratna-Sambhava—*chief deity of the Southern Quarter of Tibetan Buddhist mandalas. Here he is robed as a prince.*

the pride, the self-centered feeling that guides most of our actions, is converted into sympathetic feeling for all that lives. Recognizing ourselves in others, we wish to abstain from hurting them. We comprehend the essential unity of life. Then, our love is not possessive; our compassion is not condescending. It is a warm, human feeling for our equals. This is called the Wisdom of Equality.

Thus, *Ratna-Sambhava, in his warm color, in his gesture of giving, is the embodiment of the conqueror of pride.* Like all the deities of the mandala, Ratna-Sambhava appears in Buddhist iconography in several forms: dressed like a monk, or in kingly raiment, or in *yab-yum* form with his consort, or in wrathful aspect.

The same energy that takes form as Ratna-Sambhava in his many guises appears in our nightly dreams. Here, too, its shapes are varied. Our pride, our self-seeking, our arrogance forms itself into endless pictures. Once again, in order to move toward enlightenment, it is not necessary to suppress this passion, this feeling for ourselves, but to transfigure it, to rechannel it. We need to transmute it into the "Right Knowledge" of a feeling of compassion for all life. Our narrow consciousness needs to become enriched, to widen to a caring for all living beings.

Ratna-Sambhava—*chief deity of the Southern Quarter of Tibetan Buddhist mandalas. Here he is garbed as a monk.*

In my own dreams I still struggle with forms of pride. I have not wholly conquered it. My competitive needs are strong. Having felt myself for so many teenage years to be less attractive, less successful, less rich, and less secure than others, the desire to be outstanding on every front is forceful. One dream of several years ago captured the essence of this feeling succinctly. In it, I was an opera singer in competition with another female singer. As part of the contest, I would sing a line; then she would sing a line. Each time I took my turn, I tried to make my presentation fancier and more impressive than hers. Finally, I burst into an aria of magnificence called "Celia Delwa Fawcett." I repeated the name over and over, ending with a splendid, high, sustained tone. The other singer simply had to admit defeat and withdraw. This dream occurred several years ago when Zal's oldest daughter, Linda, was visiting us for an extended period. It clearly reflected my need for the greater share of his loving attention. In fact, I can barely carry a tune in the waking state, so this was quite a dream performance.

On the one hand, succeeding brilliantly in a dream contest was a valuable preparation for waking experiences. It may well have helped me in performances other than singing that I proceeded to carry out in the waking world, such as expressing myself in writing and giving speeches to large audiences. On the other hand, outperforming others is far from enlightened compassion for all.

I still feel threatened, especially by women who seem to be as well endowed or better endowed than I am. Such a woman appears to me as a rival. If she is attractive but not notably intelligent, well and good. Or intelligent, but unattractive, also fine. But a woman both pretty and clever, perhaps educated and talented, too, who relates well to men—such a woman disturbs my calm. If her temperament is harsh, it is easy to detest her; if she is, instead, sweet natured, I cannot dislike her, but I find that the relationship is marred by internal stirrings of the monster pride.

Despite my own achievements, such as they are, the competitive feelings remain. Only the competitor is at a higher level than she used to be. How to grow past the tag ends of a need to excel all others for fear of being less than them? How to perceive other women as equals and possible friends rather than potential enemies? How to be compassionate without being condescending? It is a problem all of us, male and female alike, must resolve, each in his or her own way.

Other women, too, at least some of them, express similar feelings in their dreams. I was startled recently when a graduate student with whom I worked described a dream in which she heard me singing a beautiful song she had intended to sing herself. But she felt she could not sing as well as I, and went away dejected. This confession touched me and led me to contemplate the importance of reaching out to others as equals. I had not fully appreciated how similar others' feelings were to my own.

On my side, I had been having a similar reaction to her. In fact, her revelation of "The Song" dream was prompted by my having related a dream I had had about her. In it, I was doing an intricate dance *sur les pointes*, twirling under Zal's arm in graceful pirouettes. Although I have some dancing skills in waking life, dancing on my toes is not one of them. The student, in waking life a superior dancer who has studied ballet, stood by silently watching. As I danced faster and faster, I stripped off a cardigan sweater I wore, in order to dance more freely, and as I tossed it aside it accidentally flew into her eyes. I was a bit concerned that it might have hurt her, but I knew perfectly well that she wanted to outdance me. I awoke, relieved. And so it goes, each dreamer feeling threatened by the charms and skills of the other.

Dream forms of pride may be portrayed more subtly than as an open contest. A few months ago, Zal dreamt that he was making a painting. In the foreground was a man with a profile like his mother's. In the background were beautiful warm colors—reds, yellows, and oranges. By some means, perhaps a force, he was able to move the colors in swirls. He was amazed to see that they grew less brilliant, but also less garish, gentler, and less arrogant. He liked them better that way. I saw in this dream of Zal's, and in his associations to its symbols, his own spiritual-artistic force at work, with pride represented by harsh colors. He has, indeed, grown gentler, "less arrogant," with time, his own maturation, and our loving relationship.

Alan Vaughan, the San Francisco psychic and then editor of *Psychic* magazine, told me of a dream in which he saw a large flight balloon, of the old-fashioned kind, with a basket to carry passengers. As it rose higher, a huge and rather terrifying eagle swooped down and dug its claws into the balloon. The eagle was joined by its mate, and soon the balloon was deflated. The two birds transformed into himself and a woman—his wife, Diane. Alan woke with a shaky feeling over the vision of the eagle. In Alan's symbolic language, the balloon represented inflated pride over a particular issue, and the eagles were associated with independence and integrity. Here we have symbols of both pride (in the balloon) and its conqueror (the eagle) in a single dream. These two symbols, placed into the Southern Quarter of a personal Dream Mandala, would recall the dreamer's successful confrontation with pride; the eagle would serve as the deity who is conqueror of pride. Our bird-souls are vital.

The Bluebird, the Butterfly, the Polka Dot Horse, and the High Flyer are my symbols of this reaching out. They rise above earth; they move into realms of radiance. They are within me; they—in varied forms—dwell within others, too. Perhaps this knowledge will help me achieve my own Wisdom of Equality. The leftover lumps of pride may dissolve to make a wide-armed compassion.

Singing contests, dancing contests, puffed-balloon egos, arrogant colors, all speak of the pride represented by Ratna-Sambhava. Each person defending himself or herself against another's charms, skills, wealth, or power. Each dreamer embodies the horrific form of Ratna-Sambhava, swollen with pride, in his own way. Of course, we need to sing our own songs and dance our own dances. But we also need to join with one another in duets and *pas de deux*, in chorales and chorus lines. For we are of one human source, and, reaching outward, we can embrace one another.

Into the Southern Quarter of my personal Dream Mandala, then, I placed the feather, symbol of my High Flyer, hoping she will lead me to rise above pride permanently, as she ranges out to worlds of radiance. The Bluebird—blue, yet partly derived from the waking experience of the yellow-orange leaves—my guide through space, is represented in dot form. So, too, are the Butterfly and the Polka Dot Horse.

The forms of these symbolic dream deities of mine continue to change as I continue to evolve. Even as the house on Willow Grove Avenue changed, their qualities alter with my inner development. At first more often vulnerable and in need of care, lashing out to protect themselves, or flying as a means to escape, they later became guides, inspirations, and ways to encounter higher forces.

In fact, in one strange lucid dream a couple of years ago, I saw the Butterfly as a symbol of an entire new religion. It was a long, complex story about people traveling to the mountains to obtain great knowledge from a wise man who lived at the summit. For a long time he had been cut off from the world, perhaps by snow. The dream contained cool mountain weather (the ring of raindrops), a

The Southern Quarter of my Dream Mandala—*the Feather, Symbol of the High Flyer.*

horse-drawn carriage that had a duplicate (the doubleness), and many other qualities of lucid dreaming. At one point I was chased by an evil man who kept trying to shut doors and trap me. I turned into a butterfly who was able to hide and then escape through the top of an open door. A religion had been thrown into chaos by this, and the people would adopt the butterfly as their emblem. The culmination of the chaotic, complex story came when I, as the butterfly, swooped down near the head of the evil man just as he was about to give a speech. It made his head spin (the lightheadedness). He would have to confess his evil ways and recognize that he could no longer hurt the butterfly because it had become a holy symbol. In waking life, the delicate, sensitive parts of myself symbolized by the Butterfly had become less vulnerable, too, as the butterfly had in the dream. I had learned to use my sensitivity for greater understanding. I think it is the butterfly as a transformed caterpillar that I was responding to in this dream.

Metamorphoses, whether from caterpillar to butterfly, or from person to changed person, are marvels. I had long ago given up the traditional religious forms in which I had been raised. The shaky gods of my collegiate dreams toppled and fell. I lived better than ever without them. Yet, as the years passed, I felt an internal movement, if not toward a formal religion, then toward *something*—a value, a source, a presence within. The gods were dead but the yearning was alive. My dreams seemed to lead me in the direction of something special, an internal experience that was, if not religious, then something very like spiritual in flavor.

I was in a process of metamorphosis, and the Butterfly was still the perfect symbol. This theme reached a culmination in a recent dream I had about undergoing an initiation. It was not lucid, but nearly so, and very powerful. After a long series of ordinary dream events, the ending was so impressive that I quote it in full:

  . . . I have been having a great sword fight with some men, fencing with them as I hover in the air. I finally escape by means of a hole in the roof, squeezing through it. One man who was after me cannot or does not follow. Here, on the other side, everything is changed. I am in a kind of loft, or low-ceilinged attic. I know at once that I am to be initiated. A guru sits to my right, working on some equipment, with his helpers nearby. I notice in particular a butterfly made of turquoise and gold filigree that is quite beautiful. At some point, I hear a voice say, "God is a butterfly."

I go into the next room to gather materials, knowing full well that my task is to construct my own butterfly. There are chalk sticks of beautiful pastel shades. I select several, one of each color—pale yellow, soft blue, a pinky-rose, lavender, and others. I scoop these up with both hands, gently separating them from the chalk dust, and carry them back to the first room. They feel wonderful, like velvet. Again with both hands, I push away the ordinary dust and set down my things. Everyone is watching.

I don't know what to do next. Somehow I understand that discovering what to do is part of the trial. Before me burns a taper under a kind of filmy tent. The taper—of incense?—starts to fall, and I know that this will be considered inauspicious. Quickly I reach over and grasp it. As though to increase my power, I pass the long, burning stick, in a slightly dangerous maneuver, over my head. Now the thin film, rather like a large sheet of plastic food wrap, is in front of me, as though carried by the stick, and it clings a foot or so in front of my face, by static electricity. I look into it and can see my reflection as in a mirror (the Mirror Gazer). I still don't know what to do, only that I must feel my way myself. The guru will not tell me; he and the others continue to watch. I gaze into the crystal-clear image, examining my eyes closely. The light glistens on the surface, making the image shimmer. I begin to feel dizzy. I feel myself starting to lapse into a dream state. I resist for a second, hold on to myself, attempting to fulfill my task of creating a butterfly of my own. Then, deciding that perhaps this *is* the next step in the initiation, I allow myself to relax and I seem to slip under the film.

Now I feel myself to be several things simultaneously (the doubleness—or tripleness): I am still in the loft, the place of initiation; I also see and I am a woman arriving at a house to meet her lover. She-I opens the door and enters. Also at the very same time the woman and the man are making passionate love. I can feel the man's penis thrusting into me from behind and I—the woman feel waves of passion flowing through me. I grow hotter and know that at any second I will be lost in ecstatic orgasm. Again, I momentarily resist so that I can complete my assignment.

Suddenly I have the great realization that *this* is the initiation: I am the person who is to be born of this couple. *I can only make the butterfly by becoming the butterfly.* I must enter the womb-cocoon and grow. I will be born from this womb and live; *my life is my butterfly.* The initiation and the guru will be gone, as though in a forgotten dream. Yet, in actual fact, the life I will live then will be the dream; and when I die, I will return to the reality that is this place. So, understanding that I must be born again from this womb to create my butterfly, I allow myself to become totally lost in the passion. I feel myself existing between the tip of the penis and the mouth of the womb; I let myself melt into the thrusting movements. The bliss builds. I am about to be conceived . . . this very instant . . . I awake. ("The Butterfly Initiation," May 2, 1977)

What an exquisite, strange aftertaste this dream left. Am I living that life now? Will I return someday to that loft and be *really* alive once more? I shake myself and say instead: "Look at the richness of the symbols. See how the chalk dust is the powder-dust of my caught butterfly. Look at the striving to understand by gazing deep within the reflected image of myself." How reminiscent of the Chinese sage Chuang-tzu's dream that he was a butterfly and, on awakening, his wondering whether he was a man who dreamt he was a butterfly or a butterfly who dreams he is a man.[4] Like Jung's dream, too, in which he dreamt of discovering a yogi who was dreaming of Jung and so creating his existence.[5] And also like Borges's story of the man in "The Circular Ruins" who dreamt himself another man, creating him bit by bit, night after night, until he became flesh.[6] I am familiar with all these accounts and tales, and other similar ones. They might easily have provided the material for my "Butterfly Initiation" dream. And yet . . . and yet. . . .

At any rate, the dream butterflies, the birds, and the flying continue to evolve. I am glad that the symbolism is in process of metamorphosis, because at one stage it had taken on a sinister shape. . . .

12 THE LURE OF THE RUBY BIRD

I lie on my back in the darkened room in my bed at home. I am half asleep and will be completely unconscious within seconds. The thought crosses my drowsy mind to test whether I can feel any "vibrations." Instantly, my body is aglow with a strong tingling-buzz. A whooshing-whirring sound such as I often hear in lucid dreams fills my ears. I say to myself, remembering the book on astral projection I read a few days ago, "Oh, yes, I *knew* I knew what he was talking about."[1]

Very gently, I attempt to move the legs of my "astral body." At first I sense a resistance; then my whole "second self" seems to lift up and out. I feel myself floating a couple of feet above my sleeping body. Since it is said to be frightening to look back and see your physical body, I am careful not to do so, even though I reason that my astral sight will not yet be developed enough to see in the semidark. I remain facing upward, hanging horizontally in the air. Even as I experience an intense desire to

113

float away, I remind myself that one is supposed to stay close to the physical body during the first few projections. "Go back!" I tell myself. Immediately, I feel the astral body lower and then click into alignment with the physical. I feel absolutely fine. I even congratulate myself, thinking, "You see, it's not so scary after all. It's easy. Just go slowly and all will be well." I rouse myself from the sleeping state and look at the clock. It is 10:00 A.M. I close my eyes and start to drift off once more. . . .

Pleased and reassured that projection is safe, I decide to retest my ability to leave my body. There's plenty of time. The whirring-vibrations are still flowing throughout my body. Again I will myself to rise. Again I float upward. Suddenly I am caught up, as though in a great gust of wind, and feel myself hurtled away into space. I know perfectly well that my body is sound asleep in my bed in the San Francisco flat, but "I," my conscious self, is being swirled away to other spheres. I have so many weird adventures that my mind cannot hold them— blurred memories of fleeting scenes and colors merge together. Then I seem to become unconscious briefly. Next I fall, for a moment, into ordinary dreaming. . . .

I am in a department store with my elderly mother-in-law and a baby. All of us are waiting for an elevator to go up to the toy department, perhaps to see a Christmas display. Then Mama disappears with another woman, to go to the ladies' room. I follow them, up and down ramps, up and down, up and down. Mama, who has trouble walking, will have difficulty with this route, I think.

Now I am in the air, flying. Once again, I become clearly conscious of the fact that my body is asleep and I am dreaming (or else actually experiencing these strange things). As I fly, my body floods with sexual passion; I want to have an orgasm. Even though I recall having read that one is supposed to delay sexual orgasm on astral trips, I don't want to delay. "Why *not* let yourself give in fully?" I wonder. Thus debating with myself, I reach a decision to hold off orgasm for a short while; I continue to fly around the large, warehouselike room.

Below me, I see the man who wrote the book I had read earlier in the week—his face and hair are especially clear. I softly touch his cheek. Flying on, I come to a wall covered with graffiti. I place my hands upon the wall and push gently: my hands go directly through it. I can feel the wall's grainy texture. The letters written on it show clearly through my hands as they pass to the other side. My face and body follow my hands until I am completely through the wall.

Once outside, I fly around the building and, by a door, enter the huge room again. Now a man is calling to me from the ground, threatening to lock the door and keep me inside. I am not at all concerned because I know I can get out whenever I wish by passing through a wall. In front of me is a glass window covered by iron grillework. I have an urge to experience what it will feel like to go through glass and iron. Again I place my hands in front of me and push. This time I feel a great resistance. Some substance like taut plastic film presses back against my hands and face. I am having trouble breathing, as though a sheet of light plastic were pressed against my face. It is extremely unpleasant. I push harder. It will not yield. I cannot breathe. I push even harder. Suddenly, I burst through and find myself outside the building again. The man on the ground is still pursuing me as I fly higher into the air. . . .

Frightened by the sense of suffocation, I contain the fear by reminding myself, "All this is from your mind. You don't have to let it happen; think it away." I decide that perhaps I have had enough astral travel and should return to my body. The vibrations have stopped long ago—an ominous sign. But how do I return? There is one infallible way: simply move part of my physical body—wiggle a toe or lift a finger. However, it is only to be used in extreme emergencies because of the shock it causes the system. I had better go back under power of my astral body. All I have to do is think of my room. Merely picture it.

Good God! *I can't remember my room!* All I have to do is visualize it and I will be there. But I can't see it! I can't think of what it looks like. My mind whirls with blending images of former bedrooms—the one I used to sleep in in Philadelphia, the one in London, and others. Now I am really frightened! I am good at visualizing things. Usually I have great spatial perception, always knowing where I am in relation to other things, never waking up confused about my location, as some people do. Yet here I am, spinning in space, and I cannot see my present bedroom where my body lies. The sole fact I can recall is that my body is in a bedroom in San Francisco. At least I know that much. "San Francisco, California!" I cry. If only I can see my bedroom all will be well. I've got to jog my memory. *"San Francisco, California!"* I shriek.

Abruptly, I am in a bedroom. It is not mine, but it is similar to it. On a wall, I see a familiar etching of a small girl; it is rather like a pen-and-ink drawing I did as a child. Sensing that I am starting to wake, I now feel violently ill. Still dreaming, gobs and gobs of vomit come up into my throat. Choking, I spit them out into my hand; I can smell and taste and see the vomit in vivid color. Continually clearing the junk from my throat with a finger makes it possible to breathe and lessens the strangling sensation. I think, "It has been all right until now, but this symbolism (the vomiting) suggests the experience is not good for me." I walk around the familiar-strange apartment a bit and decide it is definitely time to wake up. At the very instant I am about to do so, a woman in the adjoining room calls out to me: "Just look at this bird a minute!"

I turn and see a dining-room table spread with the most incredible shapes—green-and-white porcelain, and many other lovely things. The woman is offering to me, in her outstretched hands, a magnificent piece of ruby-colored crystal. It is translucent and glowing, as though from inside. The shape resembles an abstract bird. I think, "It's true, I'm dreaming. I can see anything I want. I can ask for anything—something creative." I am sorely tempted to remain. But my next thought is the strong suspicion that the dream woman is an evil spirit who is trying to coax me to stay out of my body longer than is good for me. I will not take that risk. "No, I'll wake," I decide, "I *will* wake." Instantly, I find myself awake in my own bed.

("The Ruby Bird," July 21, 1974)

When I finally did wake up from this strange experience, my eyes remained shut. I was puzzled to observe that my visual field, a light gray, had dark markings at the edge in the pattern of veins. (This image turned out to be important.) The precise memory of my bedroom flooded back and I felt oriented once more. With effort, I forced open my eyes to check the time. It was 10:50 A.M. I had been "out" fifty minutes the second time, although it had seemed like an eternity. Tentatively, my body heavy, I sat up. Did I feel sick? I anticipated that I would because of the vomiting imagery I had just had. No. A bit logy from a larger-than-usual breakfast at 8:30 A.M., but otherwise well—physically. The vomiting imagery must have been a symbolic statement, not a literal one. Perhaps my dreaming mind regarded this out-of-the-body experience as "sick" in a psychological sense, or perhaps "too much to swallow" at one time, especially for an early experience. How strange and light my head felt: I did not then know these sensations were to be expected.

And I felt frightened of my dreams for the first time in years. I had been momentarily terrified. It was as though I had actually been "out there" whirling in space and unable to find my way back to my body. Furthermore, I felt as though an evil spirit had literally been luring me to destruction. Shuddering, I got up.

What a weird day it had been altogether. It had been a struggle to stumble out of bed before 6:00 A.M. to dress to drive Zal to the airport—especially after being up late at the theater. However, there was no choice. Zal was compelled to go back East on an emergency mission for one of our children—problems over "children," whatever their age, seem endless. We had been there on a visit the previous week and had only just returned to San Francisco. I was reluctantly staying behind this trip because there was so much housework and writing to catch up with. Besides, I had begun to bleed midcycle again, always a signal that I have been doing too much air travel. Bleary-eyed, we threw on clothes and took luggage out into the gray morning.

The sun rising over the Bay as we drove along the freeway gave me a lift—pink and golden lights glistening on the water. I dropped Zal off at the airport and headed home, plotting all the writing I could get done on this quiet Sunday. At the freeway exit, I decided to stop and visit our elderly Mama. That way, I could join her for breakfast, since I had to eat anyway, and then I could work all day long without interruption.

Visit completed, full of pancakes and syrup, I arrived home a few minutes before 9:00 A.M. By then, I was so groggy that I could not possibly work. I pulled out the phone plugs, determined not to be interrupted, and crawled under the covers to nap. Stuffed with food, extraordinarily weary, and mildly concerned, I drifted into the drowsy state. The thought occurred to me that this was a perfect time—I was totally alone—to try an out-of-the-body experiment. Sleepily, I began to think about vibrations. . . .

Following the "dream," I moved around rather carefully for the remainder of the day. I had a hangover sense of fear with a dash of fascination. This was more than I wanted to deal with—at the moment, anyway. I thought, "My control is too tenuous in this space, whatever and wherever it is. No wonder people advise guides and gurus. It's spooky alone, and with Zal away there's no one to discuss it with without feeling weird."

All day long the whooshing-whirring sensation lingered close to consciousness. I had the impression that if I merely set head to pillow, the sounds would rush back in full force and I would experience another out-of-the-body trip, like it or not. I carefully stayed upright. I would not risk taking a nap, no matter how sleepy I was. I worked. I walked by the Bay. In the late evening, quite tired, I lay down cautiously. I was careful to avoid resting on my back, as I had deliberately done in the morning. Falling gingerly to sleep on my side seemed the safest thing to do. I was not ready for further encounters the same day—or maybe any other.

How had I reached this point where I once again felt overwhelmed by a "dream" experience? *Was it a dream!* On the more clearheaded days to follow, I pondered the strange experience of "The Ruby Bird." Did I really have a "bad" astral trip? Was it astral travel? Or lucid dreaming? It certainly was not ordinary dreaming.

By then, I knew how to deal with ordinary nightmares. For more than two years I had "confronted and conquered" a lot of my old bogeymen. Then, I had learned how to become lucid in my dreams, to "wake up" my sleeping consciousness so that I could participate actively in ongoing dreams. But the lucid dreams had been uniformly positive experiences. Now here I was confronting another unknown, which had a unique quality of its own. I felt thrown into a new level of experiencing, with chasms below and starry worlds above. Gradually, in the days to follow, I set about assembling what I *did* know of the way I had traveled from lucid dreaming to "The Ruby Bird."

For months I had been practicing alerting myself to specific images within my dreams.[2]

I had watched for *frightening images* that could trigger awareness that I was dreaming. Once, as I was walking down a street in a dream, I realized that a car-bug was following me; I became so alarmed that I was frightened into awareness of dreaming.

I had watched for *incongruous images* in my dreams. In "The Great Steering Wheel" dream everything had seemed normal, yet I do not usually feel the sun on my face and wind in my ears when I am inside a car. This incongruity was a clue that I was in the land of magical sun and wind.

I had watched my dreams for *bizarre images.* In "The Bluebird Tree" dream that I had three months later, I overlooked several incongruities: that I was outdoors in bare feet, rare for me; and that I was living in an alley behind an iron gate, an inaccuracy. I did, however, recognize the bluebird tree as radiating the bizarre dreamlike quality I now know well, and was forced to the conclusion that I was dreaming.

Finally, I had watched for *images that provoke analysis.* In one dream, I observed a fairly ordinary dream image of a fat woman, and began speculating with myself, "I wonder why I'm dreaming *that?"* And suddenly I was lucid.

Then I found, to my delight, that some dreams were *starting* lucid. There was no particular image that shifted me from an ordinary dream state to a lucid one. They simply began lucid.

As I practiced the technique of lucid dreaming, it became easier for me to go into that state of mind during sleep. It seemed to me that seeking images to trigger lucid dreaming was a stage of development and eventually the lucid state might become permanent. Maybe after lucidity becomes a habit, dream consciousness comes so easily that people forget the means by which they acquired the habit in the first place. At least that would explain why I could find so little information in the literature on how to become lucid in dreams. The trickiest part seems to be to experience one's *first* lucid dream. After that, lucidity is a skill that one can cultivate. At present, I average about four or five lucid dreams a month. But lucidity still comes and goes in my dream state. Sometimes I have lucid dreams in clusters on one night, or two; other times I go for weeks without even one such dream.

Thus, at the time of "The Ruby Bird" dream/experience, I had been deliberately invoking lucid dreams for months. I knew how I had achieved that skill, even though it was not totally established. Clutching my dream records, I turned to the literature on astral projection, exploring it more fully than ever before, to see what explanation it could offer for the "trip" that had shaken me.

Comparing and contrasting the accounts written in my own hand with classic and contemporary literature, I found some surprising correspondences and differences. For example, my records show that when I wake up from a lucid dream, I am most frequently on my back, next most often on my left side, and least often on my right side. I never sleep on my stomach, finding it impossible to do so.[3] According to the literature on astral projection, back sleeping is a favorable position to produce an altered state of consciousness. Several astral travelers recommend it,[4] while Tibetan yogis who practice "Yoga of the Dream State," in contrast, advise one to "sleep on the right side as a lion doth."[5] I had been on my back throughout "The Ruby Bird" dream/experience.

Although my findings agreed with the literature in reference to the greater probability of astral projection while lying on the back, they disagreed about the importance of the direction one's head is pointing. Most occult and folk traditions insist that the most propitious direction is with the top of the head pointing north, with the next-best position being with the head pointing east; both of these are believed to facilitate the flow of electromagnetic vibrations through the body.[6] My records show that it does not seem to make much difference what direction my head points. The first bedroom I had in San Francisco was arranged so that my head pointed east; in my present bedroom it points north. There is no noticeable difference in the number of lucid dreams or out-of-the-body projections. Awake, I travel (while *in* my body) a great deal and find that these experiences occur in a variety of body orientations.

Another difference I noticed between my "Ruby Bird" experience and astral trips reported by others is the condition of the stomach. The majority of astral travelers recommend an empty stomach, even fasting.[7] A few have devised special diets to facilitate projection.[8] On the occasion of my frightening astral experience, I had been inordinately stuffed with food. Perhaps extremity is the key. Or perhaps being overfull served to make the physical vibrations slower than the "astral" vibrations; this difference is thought to be conducive to astral projection.[9]

As I continued to compare my experiences with those recorded by others, I was startled to uncover a remarkable parallel to an astral traveler of fifty years ago. Oliver Fox (a pseudonym used by a British lawyer named Hugh Callaway) describes a frightening experience of his in his book *Astral Projection.*[10] Even as I had found myself whirling in space unable to return to my body, he had been "locked out" of his body as he dreamt of walking by the sea. Making, as I did, desperate efforts to return, he finally awoke in his room in a cataleptic state. Using supreme effort to move his little finger, he was able to break the trance. Then, in a way similar to my vomiting in my dream, he sprang up from bed and was overwhelmed with nausea. In his case, however, he felt deathly sick in the waking state, then depressed and tired; it was three days before he felt normal again. When the path seems mysterious and perilous, it can be reassuring to know that others have taken it and survived.

Even the sensation of suffocating, as though plastic film were pressing against my face, turned out to be duplicated in other people's accounts.[11] Occultists and Theosophists, in particular, offer explanations for the phenomenon of difficulty in breathing during astral trips; they conceive of the astral body as being enshrouded by a kind of veil or membrane, which may be left behind during projection.[12] This veil, instead of being left behind, may cling to the astral body throughout the trip, or, finally, the veil may cling to the astral body at first, only to be shed later, much as I "burst through" the sense of plastic that choked me. I found that my lucid dreams were full of imagery that could be viewed as a body veil—often curtains with an open weave or made of lace, or else glass, walls, ceilings, and floorboards that I pass through.

According to my notes, the day preceding the night I have a lucid dream is almost invariably one that is crammed full of people and activities. Many days are quiet and peaceful for me, but on the days preceding lucid dreams I am often especially busy. I might also be tired, anxious, exhausted, sick, or feeling fine, but I am usually stimulated with many activities, ideas, and people. Furthermore, I found that when Zal and I sometimes make love in the middle of the night, rather than before going to sleep or in the morning, the afterglow frequently includes a lucid dream when I return to sleep. High-level arousal seems to precipitate lucid dreaming for me.

After observing this effect, I was fascinated to read an autobiographical account by René Descartes of certain dream experiences that had changed his life. When the seventeenth-century French philosopher and mathematician was twenty-three, he had a series of three dreams, the last of which became lucid. Asleep, he experienced a revelation that not only changed his life but influenced the history of science; the rationalist movement began in a lucid dream.[13] Descartes had had this experience during a highly stimulated state of mind, when his "brain had caught fire" with extended travel and exciting ideas. This link of experience across more than three centuries with a gigantic historical figure seemed to me both extraordinary and reassuring.

Another correspondence between my records and those I was delving into was a tiny, amazingly accurate detail. I have mentioned that when I finally awoke from "The Ruby Bird" dream/experience, I noticed that the light gray visual field before my closed eyes had dark markings in the shape of veins. They could be described as resembling jagged streaks of lightning. I happened to know that they were veins because several months previously I had had an eye examination with a special instrument that shines exceedingly strong light into the retina at such an angle that one's veins become visible. I was much surprised to come across a reference in an esoteric book to the same phenomenon.[14] This centuries-old tradition describes how a guru teaches his disciples to send their souls through seven realms outside of earth. According to this tradition, the first sign that the soul has truly been outside of the body and into the astral world is the presence of "flashes of lightning" in the visual field.

Somehow, in some way, the experience with "The Ruby Bird" had made my eye veins—lightning flashes—visible to me again. Astral travel, if that's what it was, had the same physiological effect as extremely strong light directed into the retina. Occultists would say that I had indeed been in my astral body traveling to the source of all light. Whatever the explanation, I saw once more that I had had a human experience, with typical characteristics, that people have been having for centuries. It is almost unexplored territory in "mainstream" psychology. We need to know about it. If it is a psychological effect, we need to know that; if it is astral projection, we had better know that, too. We may be at one of those crucial juncture points of discovery.

Thus, by assembling my own experience with lucid dreaming and comparing it with the recorded experiences of others, I saw that I had been on an inevitable path to out-of-the-body experience. I had trained myself to look for fearful dream images; I sought out incongruous dream images; I alerted myself to the bizarre; I began to analyze the dream during the dream itself; I had tried to bring on lucid dreams by deliberately dreaming of flying, since the one seemed to trigger the other; I had tried to coax lucidity by reminding myself about it while I drifted off to sleep; and I had deliberately slept on my back when I wanted to become lucid. Discovering how to avoid the emotional extremes that shook me awake during lucid dreams and how to avoid the forgetfulness that led back to ordinary dreaming, I studied the symbolism that typically precedes lucid dreams. I watched for chances to turn ordinary dreams into lucid ones, and I succeeded—perhaps too well.

A final definition of the lucid dream state has yet to be established. It has been called "dreaming true";[15] Carlos Castaneda says that Don Juan calls it *"dreaming"*;[16] Oliver Fox calls it a "Dream of Knowledge";[17] Sri Aurobindo, a "dream of experience"[18] (with the implication that it *is* an experience on another plane of existence). I myself like the phrase *conscious dreaming.*

Some writers assert that all lucid dreaming is a journey to the astral plane, while others say it is a self-induced trance state with the imagination producing physiological changes. Still others see it as the reception of divine powers. My scientific training held me skeptical; yet, beyond any doubt, I saw that there is a kind of learning that is not contained in psychology books, a different kind of knowledge. I reached out for the refreshing and joyous feeling lucid dreams gave me.

These lucid dreams were a delight. I used them to fly, to feel passion, to visit places or converse with figures of real or imaginary people. I summoned images of interest to me during lucid dreams— an illustration for a children's book I was working on, an imaginative character for a story, an original design. Sometimes I practiced skills, dealt with anxieties or anger, and tried experiments with ESP. All of this was pleasurable.

So far, astral projection, the logical extension of lucid dreaming, had been terrifying. Then, as I considered all the evidence I had gathered from the literature and my own accounts, I had a kind of revelation: astral projection is simply another level of the unknown. It is only the unknown of the moment.

When people stand at the boundary between what is known and what is unknown, they always feel afraid. The threshold is in sight. To step over the edge is the task of the hero or heroine. If the threshold is crossed, the way ahead is inevitably filled with trials and misadventures. The zone of magnified power is always dangerous. How could I have thought it would be otherwise? But I have learned the lessons of my childhood fairy tales well. If I keep faith in the value of the journey, there will be helpers as well as demons. With guidance I may encounter the great treasure or find it within. I ventured forward, then, to the newest unknown.

Feeling ready to look at "The Ruby Bird" dream/experience

again, I examined the symbolism during the ordinary dream portion, where I "forgot" that I was asleep and dreaming. Translating the picture language of the dream images into words and feelings and substituting my personal associations to the pictures for the action of the dream, some of the meaning became apparent: I waited (at the elevator) to go "up" with two extreme aspects of myself—an infantile self and an elderly, frail self. The older self needed relief (to go to the bathroom), and my current awareness followed. I was concerned about my older self's ability to handle the ups and downs of the route (the ramps). Once I was airborne, my awareness of being in the dreaming state returned. Images of rising—in elevators, on ramps, or when flying—are, as I have repeatedly pointed out, forerunners of dream consciousness.

I came to understand that many aspects of "The Ruby Bird" were typical of lucid dreaming. Even as I had been swept away by the stream of water in the "Paddeus" dream, so I was caught up by a great gust of air in "The Ruby Bird." In these dreams the current of energy took over, and "I" was tossed upon it. The being caught up, the images of rising, the lightheadedness, the vibrations—all of these I had experienced before in lucid dreams. The intense color, too (in this case of the crystal bird), was characteristic; its translucent glow had an unearthly beauty.

There remained, however, several aspects of "The Ruby Bird" that were unique for me: imagery of leaving my body had never before been so intense, nor had the sensation of passing through walls, iron, and glass been that vivid. And I had never before, in all my years of recorded dreaming, experienced choking imagery. I was struck with how it was repeated—first when I passed through the glass and later while vomiting and removing the matter from my throat. Unparalleled, too, was my experience of being "lost" from my physical body. My research into the literature had helped me understand and accept these as occasional, natural repercussions of astral travel. (Much later, as I will show, I would discover other—better—explanations.)

"The Bluebird Tree" dream, in particular, helped assuage my fear of this new unknown. These bird creatures—the one of ruby crystal and the one of blue feathers—were a sharp contrast. The alluring bird of crystallized light was quite different in appearance and feeling from the one of downy feathers who lit up my dreams three months later. The sense of bewitching danger I had felt at beholding the Ruby Bird yielded to enchantment as I stroked its fluffy blue fellow.

What these bird creatures signify to me, I cannot say completely. I am sure that, in part, they represent my own winged soul —the part of myself that can fly upward, that is half hellish danger, half heavenly rapture. No doubt they are the same bird—now rock hard and glittering, bloody red; now soft, warm, and enveloping sky blue. When first appearing as the Ruby Bird, it was near, yet I resisted it, as though offered from evil hands; in its second appearance, as the Bluebird, it came to me and I welcomed it, as bliss personified. This bird-soul image of mine—red or blue—emerges from my depths. Its varied forms are pictures that connect me to my own inner power.

Now, when I feel frightened by the thought of astral projection, I will turn it off as best I can by avoiding back and left-side sleeping and by not thinking about it as I fall asleep. In safe surroundings— with Zal, for whom few things are too adventurous; my happy home in San Francisco; my deep investment in my work—I venture carefully toward this newest unknown. Especially when I have a comforting image like the Bluebird, I will start thinking about projection and orient myself to make it more likely. When lucid dreams are absent for a while I will miss the delicious sense of freedom and pleasure they give me and so I will deliberately court them.

The resulting projection may be magnificent. Once, I found myself flying along the seashore, high above the beach on a moonlit night. The wind blew my hair and billowed my gown. The water sparkled and the moonlight shone on the wet sand as the waves rolled back. I was enraptured. I knew that I was dreaming (or actually projected) and kept saying to myself, "It feels so good! Oh, it's been so long! So long since I've been out and free. So long!" On another recent night, in the midst of an ordinary dream, I sensed the rising of the magical breeze as I lay on a bed with a lover. I was curled in front of an open window in the light of the full moon as the breeze wafted a sheer curtain. Realizing that I was dreaming, I cried out, "Fly me to the moon!" Up and up I lifted, transported. . . .

Here in space, again and again, as I did in this dream, I find myself encountering a new image: a guide—a friend who glows from an internal light—who teaches me something of the way to move in the astonishing space of my nightly explorations. Most particularly, I have discovered that it is not at all necessary to delay sexual gratification (as I did in "The Ruby Bird"). I can burst into ecstatic orgasm and continue to dream and learn. In fact, my experiences have revealed to me that *yielding* to the power that flows in conscious dreams is but a step to a higher exaltation. The lure is still there, the path is still dangerous, but the glory, ah, the glory. . . .

13 THE WESTERN QUARTER OF THE DREAM MANDALA
Chief Deity: The Strawberry Lady

When I cried out, "Fly me to the moon!" in a lucid dream, I put my arms forward and sailed out of the bedroom window into the night sky. I stretched higher and higher. Rising rapidly upward, I reached toward the moon as though to touch it; I had never flown so high before. As I approached, the gleaming white globe grew reddish in color. My body, already whirring with the sense of flying, now pulsated with sexual passion—as usual in lucid dreams—and suddenly I seemed to be once more in a bedroom. Before me stood two people, one a woman who was discussing the trip to the moon. She wore a most unusual dress: it was the color of a ripe strawberry, with its skirt actually shaped and marked like a strawberry. The same rich red material decorated several articles in the room. In particular, I noticed a lampshade also in the shape of a lush strawberry. The light emitted through its translucent cloth glowed deep scarlet, imparting the red tone to the entire room. I was transfixed by the scene and awoke, my body throbbing with passion and my mind drenched with strawberry red.

The color red has played an important role in my dreams throughout their recorded history of the past twenty-nine years. Although brilliant colors of every hue make frequent appearances in my dreams, lucid or not, red has occurred again and again.

Pondering the meaning of red usually leads me to associations to a redheaded girl in my grade school and, later, junior- and senior-high-school classes. I did not like her very much, although she was a neighbor and I often played with her. The relationship was competitive, and when we squabbled in games, one of us would take her dolls and go home. I remember once trying to slap her and she me in a fury over some childish issue. On another occasion, when a parent was driving several children home from Bible school, she was hesitant to get out of the car. When she was finally persuaded to move, we saw that she had been sitting upon, in order to hide them, the box of gold stars that had been missing from class that day.

Later, in high school, this redhead attempted to solve our universal problem—how to be more popular—by enthusiastically endorsing whatever opinion was being voiced at the moment. Regardless of how much she was forced to contradict herself, she would wholeheartedly agree with whatever was being said; one never knew what she herself believed.

Thus, my associations to that particular redhead were negative and full of anger. Although I last saw her some twenty-five years ago, she still figures as a minor character in my dreams now and then—evidently she must be an important symbol to me. I think perhaps she represents to me an unattractive approach to life, the portion of myself that might be tempted not to be totally honest, the angry part that is also overly eager to be liked and therefore not genuinely open.

The next redhead to figure in my life fared no better. When I was fifteen going on sixteen and working for the summer as a waitress in Atlantic City, New Jersey, "Red" was the short-order cook.

A charming, jovial fellow, he romanced me through the summer evenings, often taking me out when the soda glasses were clean and the grill shut down. I felt flattered to be pursued by this popular young man; and despite rumors eventually relayed to me by friends that he was married and a father, I accepted his denials, wanting very much to believe him, and we continued to date. When I returned to the Philadelphia area for school in the fall, however—as happens with so many summer attachments—we saw little more of one another. He wrote sweet notes; he telephoned; he even visited on occasion (after several broken promises). But I finally decided that our relationship caused me more pain and tears than pleasure. I broke it off completely. Later I found out that he was, indeed, married.

Meanwhile, although our caresses had never advanced beyond mild petting, he had aroused another type of passion in my fifteen-sixteen-year-old body. Once I dreamt that a tick with red curly hair like his was crawling across the blanket of my bed and I awoke in terror. No analyst was needed to interpret the fear and ambivalence his tentative sexual advances had evoked. Another time, when the relationship was waning, I dreamt that a movie marquee displayed an advertisement for a movie entitled *Always Waiting*, a situation I found myself in frequently with him. Later, as I began dating a boy whose family name was Green, I dreamt of looking out my living-room window and being surprised to notice that the leaves on the tree in our yard were turning from red to green—the opposite of what one would expect—an incongruous image that nowadays might trigger awareness that I am dreaming. I recognized it then as a picture of my shifting affection. This "Red," too, had filled me with passion—sexual passion rather than anger—and, like my schoolgirl friend, he had been less than honest.

Despite these experiences with redheads, I have always admired red hair, particularly a deep shade of auburn. When it is natural, I like its unusual hue and how it seem alive with dancing lights. As a child, my own hair had traces of this shade—though hardly discernible now as the silver spreads. In my dreams, I often notice this color of hair—once, a whole dynasty of redheaded people—or other tints of red on objects. I have even had chances to explore the meaning of red to me during some lucid dreams.

For instance, I once found myself in a lucid dream in a bedroom with two women. As one of them had red hair, I immediately seized the lucid opportunity to inquire, "What's the significance of red hair in my dreams?" She replied rather saucily, "It depends. It's not always the same. You don't control all the dream, you know." Soon I was in a car with Zal and some other men, lapping some luscious honey, oblivious to any dream symbolism, and floating away on ripples of rapture. . . .

On another lucid dream occasion, I was sailing up high into the sky when I felt myself starting to wake. I remembered that it is possible to prolong the lucid dream state by focusing on some small detail of the scene before it completely fades.[1] I quickly selected a minute design in red that I could see on the pavement far below me. Holding the visual pattern in focus, I threw myself toward it. As I hurtled downward through the air, I shattered into orgasm. When I had this dream of "The Red Design," and also when I had the dream of "The Ruby Bird," I was experiencing midcycle bleeding.

Studies of the dreams of women during menses[2] often report an increase in the color red throughout the period of menstruation. This incidence of red is reported to be greater than in dreams of the same women when they are not menstrual and greater than in dreams of other women who are not menstrual. These researchers see the frequency of red in dreams of menstruating women as an incorporation of the daytime experience of seeing blood into their nighttime dream content. Occultists, speaking from a different point of view, insist that at the stage of astral consciousness a red tone saturates the atmosphere. Recently, researchers have reported that red-saturated imagery tends to appear at a certain depth of altered consciousness; red imagery follows an earlier stage of blue tones.[3]

Whatever the explanation may be, red permeates my dreams from time to time, and it has a precise symbolic meaning that I came to understand in a particular lucid dream. There, already conscious that I was dreaming, I was making love with Zal. We had somehow arranged our bodies so that he was lower than I and I could look into a mirror while he caressed me. Watching my image as I felt the passion flow, I could see my face change. I was surprised to see how reddish-auburn my hair was. In a flash I realized that all the redheaded people in my dreams are myself! "Red is my natural color!" I exclaimed in a burst of insight. As the fire mounted in my body, and I grew slightly dizzy, even my cheeks took on a rosy flush. Red, I understood, is my sexual color; it is the red of passion, the redness of my thoughts extending to the tip of each hair. I melted down to where Zal was. . . .

In this dream, I myself had become the Strawberry Lady. Cheeks rosy, hair red, I personified my sexual passion as the Strawberry Lady had done in an earlier dream. I chose her, therefore, to be my dream deity of the Western Quarter. As with my other dream deities, I sketched her form and thought about her meaning. Her sexual symbolism was obvious to me, but I find her discernible in many identities: sometimes her energy takes on human shape, as she did when I flew to the moon; or she may metamorphose into an animal or a bird—I tend to think that it was she in the guise of the Ruby Bird. Now I will notice her presence in red garments, then in fruits or objects, now in abstract designs, then in pure primary hue. When her power appears in the color of hair, I see that my own thoughts or mental set have become aroused, "red" with passionate anger, or, more often, red with sexual passion. For I have found that feelings of passion inevitably arise at a certain stage of lucid dreaming.

I saw more and more clearly the pattern in my increasingly frequent lucid dreams. The settings, the characters, the objects, the lovers changed, but the sequence of sensation was constant. At some point in the lucid dream I will find myself feeling as though in a trance (the Mirror Gazer) and possibly lightheaded (the Lightheaded Dancer)—all the initial changes that I have described in the Eastern Quarter. I will very often become airborne (the High Flyer), and, if

The Strawberry Lady—*chief deity of the Western Quarter of my Dream Mandala.*

the lucid dream lasts long enough, it will surely culminate in an orgasmic outburst (the Strawberry Lady). I must emphasize that this series of events was not suggested in the literature that I examined. To the contrary, most people who have described their experiences in lucid dreaming, although they often report flying imagery, state emphatically that intense emotion or even a mild physical touch terminated the dream state.[4] I believe, however, that these people had not developed the lucid dream state until it was habitual. With practice, it is possible to experience strong emotion, even orgasm, and continue to dream. When lucid dreams endure beyond a certain point, at least for me, orgasm is almost inevitable.

I have examined my records on lucid dreams carefully. I counted the number of times I have experienced orgasm, the number of times I was sexually aroused without climaxing in orgasm, and the number of times my lucid dreams contained no sexual imagery at all. The facts are clear: *in fully two-thirds of my lucid dreams, I feel the flow of sexual energy; this arousal culminates in an orgasmic burst on about half of these occasions.*[5] In the remaining one-third of my lucid dreams, I am occupied with activities other than the specifically sexual. For example, in one lucid dream of the nonsexual type, I floated happily on my back in the air as I composed and recited a poem in French, to the effect that, in the world of dreams, I am forever young, forever beautiful; I am alive, and all is real.

In the sexual type of lucid dream, by far the more common for me, the source of stimulation and the partners vary, but the energy flow is constant.[6] The instruments upon which my body flows in these lucid dreams are many. Most often, Zal is my lover. But he is not always so—images of other men, imaginary or real, appear. Once, I confess, it was my father, although I had to tell myself repeatedly that his image was a part of myself that I had to integrate—the father part—to make intercourse possible. Other dream lovers have included a kind of male angelic creature, a rare woman, or half man–half woman, and myself. Animals, plants, and objects all become more sexualized in my lucid dreams. A pink rosebud, a sparkling fountain, a pipe with its bowl warm from being smoked, and many other such things have served as sexual implements in lucid dreams.

I have been made love to by some strange beasts in these dreams. The ultimate of the animal-intercourse series was a strange sort of horse-goat who made love to me from behind. It might have been frightening, but I was amused to see, by peeping over my shoulder, that the tip of his gray beard was like Zal's and the edge of the Ben Franklin–style spectacles he wore were like those Zal wears.

Sometimes I am my own lover in lucid dreams. Once, like a hermaphrodite, I found I possessed a penis myself and by bending into a circle could take the silky organ into my own mouth to climax. More often, I am airborne while the waves of sexual energy rise higher, and at some ultimate moment the tension is broken by a body movement. I will be climbing upward or hovering in the air, and suddenly arch backwards into orgasm. Or I lie upon my stomach as I float and merely lift my legs up behind me as I burst. During these ecstatic episodes, I often gaze upon beautiful sights. Once, for example, I watched a golden yellow egg that hung in the air near me: it was etched with a castle scene, an intricate, tiny world. Or I roll over and over, spinning in space. Once, as I lay on my back in the air, I circled round and round clockwise. At the instant of orgasm, I opened and shut my fingers rapidly as my body shattered. Often I will bring on the orgasm by ascending to great heights and then, turning, plummet back to earth or ocean. On impact with land or water, I explode into orgasm.

Even if I am deliberately bringing on orgasm by one of these movements, I often select Zal's image to trigger the final electric release. Wafting about in the currents of air, I wonder what to do for orgasm, and he will appear and call to me from the ground; I rapidly descend to merge with him. In one special recent lucid dream, Zal and I were leaving a party:

Outside, the night looks so pretty that I say to him, "I want to fly!" He seems reluctant, so I take his hand, pull him up onto my back, tuck him in securely, and take off into the night sky. As though I am a living carpet, we fly from place to place while I point out the wondrous sights. "Oh, it's so lovely—the colors, the wind, the whirring, the flying . . . and the dreaming!" I exclaim as I realize my condition. The white night lights are so strong that I have to squint my eyes to protect them. At last the lightning and thunder of our bodies begin and we spin together into pieces.

Having brought such delight to my waking love life, Zal is often the image of choice in my nightly ecstasies.

The pleasure that shudders through my body is not limited to the genital area. Like a pebble dropped into a pool, the ripples start from that spot and spread outward in great waves of bliss. During

Amitabha—*chief deity of the Western Quarter of Tibetan Buddhist mandalas.*

the most intense of these nocturnal orgasms, even my vision is involved. Whatever scene is before my sleeping eyes, its color and pattern will break into parts, flash, and spin. This kind of "visual orgasm" is indicative of the totality of the response.

It was because the energy of the Western Quarter reaches such an orgasmic peak that I chose the Strawberry Lady to represent this stage in my Dream Mandala. With her rich red color, with her strawberry gown, bathed in red light, she embodies my sexual passion.

For the Tibetan Buddhist, *the ruler of the Western Quarter is the conqueror of passion, Amitabha.* * He often appears as a monk. Like my Strawberry Lady, he, too, is red. His element is fire, and he is as brilliant as the setting sun; he is called the Buddha of Infinite Light.

Amitabha is said to come from the Western Paradise, the realm

* pronounced Ah·mē·*tah*·bă

The Western Quarter of my Dream Mandala—*the Strawberry, Symbol of the Strawberry Lady.*

The Ruby Bird—*dream bird of the Western Quarter of my Dream Mandala.*

of happiness, where he is supreme lord. His throne is borne by peacocks. Both of his hands rest palm upward in his lap in the posture of meditation, and he carries a lotus, his symbol. The lotus stands for compassion, the purified form of passion.

Like the other deities, Amitabha is sometimes robed as a king,[7] or as a monk, or he may appear in *yab-yum* union with his consort, She in White Raiment; or in horrific form.

I placed into the Western Quarter of my Dream Mandala the strawberry, symbol of the Strawberry Lady, who is chief deity. In place of a peacock, I substituted my Ruby Bird; instead of a lotus, I set my pink rosebud. She of Fiery Passion has attendants who are represented in the final version by colored dots.

The energy of the Western Quarter is associated with the heat of passion. This passion, like the other hindrances to enlightenment, can be transmuted into a wisdom.

Tibetan Buddhists believe that passion can become compassion, that one can learn a *discriminating wisdom,* to see with warmth and clarity, to respect differences in and the uniqueness of each person and each situation.

My own view is somewhat different. The Strawberry Lady symbolizes for me the height of sexual passion; she is a contrast to Amitabha, who symbolizes for Tibetan Buddhists the *conqueror* of passion. However, I see these figures as comparable. For it is *by means of* my passion that I am able to go beyond passion. I am no celibate cut off from intercourse by rules and oaths. Joyful in my relationship with my husband, I find I can "conquer" passion with passion. Like followers of some of the Tantric and Taoist cults, I can use the very sexual energy within my body to obtain a higher kind of ecstasy. Sexual energy, I find, is intimately connected to spiritual energy.

It is no accident that many of our dreams are filled with sexual imagery, symbolic or explicit. Freud had observed this fact in 1900, long before modern researchers in dream laboratories verified that penile erections accompanied the dream state.[8] Sexual arousal is now known to be a natural part of dreaming. An erect penis and a moistened vagina are partners of our dreams. Every night, several times each night, we experience a cycle of sexual stimulation. The only exception is dream content that is so anxiety-producing that sexual arousal is impossible. Normally, our bodies are in a state of sexual readiness throughout the duration of each dream. I believe that this may be our bodies' way of making energy available for higher purposes. The nightly waxing of our sexual powers may be a natural evolutionary process that leads us to mystic experience.

Whereas sexual energy is merely stirred during ordinary dreaming, it becomes highly active in lucid dreaming. My experience with intense sexuality in lucid dreams is a result, it seems to me, of consciousness during dreaming. Not only am I aware that my body is asleep and dreaming, but I am also aware that my body is sexually aroused. Even as I know I dream, so I sense the fire of passion. Waves of erotic feeling wash over me until I am overwhelmed with orgasm that can truly be described as ecstatic. The blissful aftermath expands in beauty and brilliant light. My body and mind reverberate with swirls of energy. The activated sexual energy has flowed upward and transformed into mystic experience.

The Pink Rosebud—*dream flower of the Western Quarter of my Dream Mandala.*

Thus we have a range within the dream state. At one end there is ordinary dreaming and unaware sexual arousal; in the middle we have lucid dreaming and aware sexual arousal; at the other end we have lucid dreaming and aware sexual arousal that is transformed into a mystic state.

This use of sexual energy for mystic experience is, of course, what the yogis have claimed to be doing for centuries. They speak of "awakening" the sleeping serpent power that they call *kundalini* from its coiled position at the base of the spine. Rising through the spine, the "serpent power" activates the psychic centers, beginning with the sexual center and ending at the crown of the head. Followers of Tantric yoga attempt to arouse this same power by use of sexual partners rather than by isolated meditation.[9] The Chinese Taoists "circulate the inner light" in an analogous manner;[10] some cults prefer celibate meditation and others advocate exchange with partners. Even Western magicians and psychics report increased sexuality as an early sign of their development.[11] Sexuality is the initial stirring of psychic energy.

I believe that *this process of energy circulation occurs naturally during dreaming.* The more we become aware of the process, the more freely the energy can circulate. Sexuality is inseparable from the life force. Over the years, I have learned to ride my own waves of sexual energy. When, in dreams, the inner ocean rolls, I mount the wave to mystic bliss.

At the conclusion of a recent dream that had become lucid, I was hovering in the air above a bed in which Zal lay sleeping on my left (as he actually was):

My hands rest lightly on a sort of trapeze bar, suspended without any visible support. Using the bar as a pivot, I swing and flip and twirl. The entire background is saturated in a deep, rich garnet. As I perform acrobatics, I think about all the things I am enjoying doing in life; I plan other things; I feel full of life and exquisitely happy. Announcing, "I've got some books to write and speeches to give! And I'm well, very, very well," I release the bar and dive through the air. Body buzzing, I plunge downward head-first toward the bed where Zal sleeps, and burst into orgasm. Before my eyes flashes a pattern—like a honeycomb of hexagrams with red and blue markings inside. Enraptured and peaceful, I awake.

So, more and more often, I move the current of life throughout my whole self. I have become the Strawberry Lady; I have reached out to accept the Ruby Bird. And I am beginning to find that these ecstasies are not confined to dreams.

14 THROUGH THE SCREENED PORCH TO THE INNER CIRCLE OF THE DREAM MANDALA

... I seem to be in a house that resembles the one that we now live in, although not exactly like it. I am standing at the foot of a staircase, talking with someone, when I have the peculiar sensation that someone else is behind me. Bending backward (rather than turning around), I see that it is our Chinese housekeeper, Hsiu-Ming. Leaning forward again, I continue to talk, yet feel uneasy at the presence listening behind me. I lean backward again (the doubleness) and stare at Hsiu-Ming intently. As I do so, I realize that she is a dream figure! Now her outline grows crisper and her form brightens in color.

I have an overwhelming desire to go outside. Hsiu-Ming and I move toward a screened-in porch. She says to me, "We're older," meaning that it is later in time, the future. "Po-trero Hill. Po-trero Hill," she adds (referring to an area where there have been recent murders). Outside the screened porch I can see that it is night and dark. I want very much to get out but there seems to be no door.

Pointing, I indicate a likely spot for a door. Hsiu-Ming, in her resourceful and helpful manner, cuts an opening in the screen with one of her fingernails. Wondering whether I should have had the passageway made more to the front than to the side, I squeeze my body through the space in the mesh.

A blast of cool night air strikes me (the coolness). Bending my knees, I push off from the ground and into the air, still fully aware that I am dreaming. At first I have trouble rising—it has been a long time since I have flown—but soon I have my balance, and I project high above the house and the trees (the High Flyer). I rise higher yet, feeling the air rush by my face. A fast-moving beat throbs in the background; I hear the whoosh of wind, and hear, more than feel, the vibrations.

Far above the house and the trees and the tiny figures watching me, I turn in the air and look back to earth. Now I have an overwhelming wish to plunge toward it. Knowing that I am dreaming and that it is perfectly safe to do so, I gather my energy and hurl myself straight downward. As I plummet, with the wind whizzing by me and the surroundings blurring, I see that Hsiu-Ming and some other person have become alarmed, concerned for my safety. I rein in, and, pausing in midair, I do a tiny jig, as though to reassure them, "Don't worry, it's a dream. I won't be hurt."

Then I continue my fall, down, down, faster and faster, until I land with a soft plunk in a man's office. My body is pulsating from the flight and I feel the flow of passion (the Strawberry Lady). I allow the man to touch my body lightly. He says kindly, "You're a little tired. Lie down." Still aware that I dream, I know that now I will have a "change of consciousness," and possibly of dream scene. My tired feeling is probably from being lucid so long. I determine to try to hold on to consciousness through this next shift. Shall I have an orgasm? Shall I "go to sleep" and continue to dream? Shall I wake up?

Head spinning (the lightheadedness), I recline on a couch to rest and suddenly I am awake in my bed, body aglow, feeling happy and good.
("Through the Screened Porch," January 21, 1976)

Squeezing through a narrow space, such as I did in the slit cut into the screened porch, is an important image in lucid dreams. It seems to suggest a movement from one state of being to another. Occultists would say that it represents the separation of the astral body from the physical body. Whatever the explanation may be, the fact is that many of my lucid dreams involve such imagery.

The sensation of falling asleep that I have in the ending scene is typical, too. Falling asleep in a dream is an overture (and sometimes also a finale) to "falling awake" in a dream.

The ultimate trigger of lucidity in this dream was the slight sense of anxiety I felt with the presence behind me, followed by examination of the figure provoking it. There was no need to "confront and conquer" when I realized that Hsiu-Ming was a dream image, for she immediately became supportive, as she is in waking life. Here, she provides the opening through which I squeeze and then launch into flight.

The image of myself slipping through the hole in the screen is similar to that of passing through walls, as I did in "The Ruby Bird" and many other later dreams, but going through the screen had an additional sensation of *passage.* I stood eager and trembling to be "out," to fly, and, when the opening in the screen was made, I went through it with relief. Like a child being pushed out of the birth canal, I had a feeling of *emerging*—and joy.

In fact, I find that some of my lucid dreams are preceded by ordinary dreams with explicit imagery of being pregnant or giving birth. In one:

✳️ I am a pregnant mother in a hospital, about to deliver. I begin to feel strange and tell the nurse. She puts both hands on my stomach. I can feel a body emerging from my own body. The nurse calls out, "Doctor, we've got a fill!" I lie back down on a cart and am wheeled to the delivery room. The sensations are so intense that I realize I am dreaming. I remember that I've thought about having another baby and now here I am experiencing it in a dream. As I enter the delivery room, I can feel myself beginning to wake, and although I try to focus on a small detail of the scene, I am unable to hold it and I awake.

In another such dream that became lucid, the dream continued after "childbirth":

✳️ I am pregnant and at a dentist's office, about to be given an anesthetic for some dental work. Both Zal and the dentist are concerned that the anesthetic might bring on labor. I am only one day from delivery and I *know* that I will give birth right then. As I drift under the anesthetic (the Lightheaded Dancer), the scene shifts to a cool park where, lucid, I make love with the beast with beard and eyeglasses like Zal's. . . .

Emerging from a hole, then, whether it is the birth canal of a woman, or a space cut into a screen, seems to be part of my personal imagery for "birthing" a lucid dream. If the occultists are right, I am also giving birth to my astral body.

Sometimes the hole through which I pass in these dreams is "mother" earth:

✳️ I am on a ship in a dream with Zal. After many complicated adventures, we are going through crowded passageways of the ship and get separated. I go outside, yet somehow I am underground and see a staircase. Ascending it, I exit through a hole in the earth. There, people across the water on a dock point to falling

snow (the coolness). As I walk around the surface, in the
light snow, I know I will have difficulty getting back to the ship.
I had better return. Will I be able to reopen the hole in the
earth? It has somehow closed over after I came through. For a
second I feel afraid, then decide that if I was fated to be able to
open the hole, I will. Feeling the edges of it with my fingertips,
I push. A kind of trapdoor swings open and I go through it, down
the steps and back to the ship. . . .

More often, my movement in these dreams has been *upward*—
through a hole in the roof, or forward and up, as through the screen.
Sometimes, as in the dream of the trapdoor on the ship, the movement is upward and later downward. In the birth-giving dreams, the
movement is *downward* through the hole. Once it was dramatically
so:

Near the end of an ordinary dream, Zal and I are together in a
garden, traveling down a zigzag path. The pretty green grasslike
plantings on either side of the path all look alike, until, at a certain spot, they appear wavy.

This is a clue to the presence of a special opening. I want to
mark the place more clearly, so I have a plant removed. Zal
thinks it should be replaced. "But there must be some way to
recognize it!" I say to him.

This special spot where the wavy green grass covers a hole in
the earth is where it is possible to go through to the "other
side." Zal and I kneel and scoop the earth away with our hands.

Nearby stand several people watching us. One is a man
named Captain Marvel and another is a reddish giant (the redness). The people plan to test the giant's strength by putting
him through the hole (I spell the word *hole* as *whole* in my original dream notes).

When we have uncovered the opening, Zal and I each squeeze
through this hole in the earth. Hovering in the air on the other

side, we seal the hole from underneath with our hands. On this side, all is white and snowy (the coolness). We scoop handfuls of snow and push it into place. As we work, we back up, away from the hole.

I think how the reddish giant must be less afraid to come through the hole in the earth with people that he knows—us—waiting for him on the other side. Back and back Zal and I move, now falling. More and more rapidly we go.

The white, sunny color in front of me begins to spin and break up into small patterns (the visual "orgasm"). I sense the cold on my face and on the edge of my hands; it is the air rushing by me as I fall backward. Realizing that I am dreaming, I become excited and start to wake. Now I can see a little light through my lids and it interferes with a total carried-away feeling. But the light and patterns continue to whirl. I wake up as warmth returns to my hands and face. I feel aglow.
("Through the Hole in the Earth," May 5, 1976)

The sense of emerging through a hole, of giving birth or being born, is a vivid symbolic prelude to what happens on "the other side." The movement of my dream body upward or downward proves to be important. When I am not waked by the almost inevitable orgasm, when I can hold tight by focusing on a detail of the dream scene, when I can continue to dream and not forget that I am dreaming—when all this can be done, I enter the other side, wander there, and learn. The "hole in the earth" leads to another world. Passing "through the screen" marks the transition.

In the Dream Mandala, we have traversed three rings: the circle of flames that became, for me, the great steering wheel that drives me to an altered state of consciousness; the girdle of diamond scepters that became the ring of raindrops in my mandala, representing the coolness I feel as I pass into this state; and, finally, the innermost circle.

For this inner circle of my Dream Mandala, I chose the hole in the screened porch. It symbolizes for me the sense that I have of emerging into another world as I become lucid. The entire range of images of giving birth, of being born, and of squeezing through a hole in the earth are represented by the slit in the screen.

For the Tibetan Buddhist, this innermost circle is a garland of lotus petals. The lotus (*padma* in Sanskrit) is a symbol rich with meaning. Born from the mud, this flower reaches above it to unfold in pure, white splendor. It represents a harmonious unfolding of spiritual vision. It is also a symbol of creation; in its center, its corolla, the "other plane" is revealed.

The lotus is the prototype of all mandalas; all centralized systems of spiritual universes can be depicted in lotus form. The Tibetan deities, because they are at their journeys' ends, having reached enlightenment, are seated upon "lotus thrones" with *closed* petals. For us, *open* petals of the garland of lotus leaves invite us through the entranceway, welcoming us to the spiritual world.

Here, within the garland of lotus petals, and inside the palace

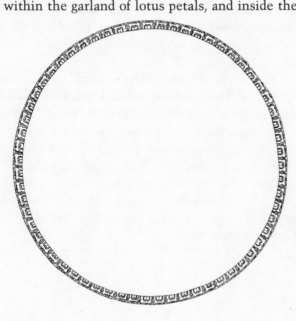

The Innermost Circle of a Tibetan Buddhist Mandala—*the Garland of Lotus Petals.*

walls, seated upon their lotus thrones, the deities are arrayed on individual open lotus leaves. The center of a Tibetan mandala is a stylized lotus in bloom. Originating from the holiest deity at the Sacred Center, the other deities emanate, on their lotus petals, from the central image. The core of a mandala may display only four petals disposed around the corolla. Our sample mandala, however, contains eight lotus petals in its central section; more elaborate versions of mandalas sometimes contain eight hundred petals with numerous gods and goddesses seated upon each one.

The lotus is not only the prototype of all mandalas, it is also the prototype of the psychic centers. For Tibetan Buddhists, as well as for Hindus, each psychic center, called a *chakra* (Sanskrit for "wheel" or "disc"), is often referred to as a lotus. Invariably, the psychic centers are represented as having a certain number of lotus petals. For example, the crown *chakra* is said, by some authorities, to have a thousand petals (others say thirty-two); the forehead *chakra*, two lotus petals; and so on.[1]

Thus, for the Tibetan Buddhist, the lotus is multidimensional in meaning and application: it appears as the symbol of psychic centers to be opened; it is the personal symbol of Amitabha and his "family"; it is the innermost protective circle of mandalas, the garland of lotus leaves; and from it, unfolding in the center of a mandala, are born the divine figures.

For me, the hole in the screen serves a similar purpose. I drew, then, into the inner ring of my personal Dream Mandala, the cross-hatched mesh of the screen. Within its opening, the hole thus created, lie the stone walls of the house on Willow Grove Avenue. Inside these temple walls of mine—the area of magnified power—unfold the deities of my dreams. These are the figures that vibrate with life and magic for me. Since I am not even sure what a lotus looks like, I have seated these dream deities of mine upon rose petals. Rose petals have more meaning for me, associated in my mind with love and beauty.

New spiritual states are born from some mysterious space in the

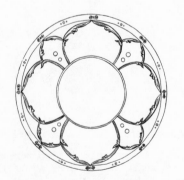

The Central Section of a Tibetan Buddhist Mandala.

The Psychic Centers of the
Human Body—*from Rajasthan,
eighteenth century.*

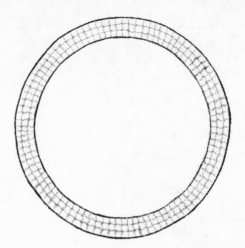

The Hole in the Screen—*the innermost circle of my Dream Mandala.*

depths of each person's heart. So, also, are born the figures of enlightenment in visible form—the deities—from the center of the lotus or rose. The entrance to a new beginning, a rebirth, is through these open petals. They open toward us to embrace us. Even as I step through the hole in the screen and feel "born," the Tibetan Buddhist moves in his or her imagination in meditation, and physically in initiations, into the center of the opened flower. Here is the birthplace of the gods.

15 THE LAND OF BREEZE AND LIGHT

I hold a cat in a blanket on my lap, in the midst of a long ordinary dream. The blanket is wrapped around the cat's body as though it were a tiny baby, with only a portion of the face peeping out. I wonder whether there is space enough for it to breathe well. Undoing the blanket, I am distressed to discover that the cat's skin is covered with small bumps, as of a skin disease. I see that the top of the cat's scalp is loose and I push it back into place.

Later in this complex story, I am wandering around a huge space, rather like a warehouse. There are many extraordinarily beautiful things for sale: handsome furniture, an organ with keys constructed from mother-of-pearl, and other intriguing pieces that I examine. . . .

Suddenly I have a strange feeling that something is happening in the next room. With a sense of urgency, I hurry around a corner. I can see light emerging from the room and think perhaps I will find its source. Reaching the doorway I see that the room is a spacious one with windows on all sides that stand open; bright sunlight streams in. Long sheer curtains billow up in the breeze that enters the open windows. A wave of delight washes over me as I recognize that I am dreaming. "The magical land of breeze and light!" I exclaim happily.

Standing in the center of that airy, light space, I see a woman wearing a red gown (the redness). The breeze blows against my body and face (coolness). I begin to feel slightly dizzy (the light-headedness) and I rise up into the air. Now my body is a-tremble with a "sound-feel." It is a tactile-noise, or an audible-touch —both at once. A whirring-tingling rumbles in my every cell.

This sound-feel is a familiar sensation to me, often accompanying conscious dreaming. Yet now, hovering in the air in this lucid dream, I notice that the center of the vibration is more intense in an area that is lower than usual; it is stronger in my legs than in my head. With a flash of insight, I realize that my legs are still "buzzing" from the acupuncture treatment I had had that day. And suddenly I understand! With a sense of revelation, I exclaim, "The 'buzz' from acupuncture and the vibration of my lucid dreams are the same! I only hear it and feel it in my ears when it reaches that high. It's the same feeling!!"

In rapture over my dream discovery, I translate the intellectual excitement into physical terms. With a spasm of pleasure I wheel over backward in space and shatter into a powerful orgasm (the Strawberry Woman). When I am "conscious" again, I have landed in the same setting. Still aware of my dreaming state, my revelation, and all that has happened, I watch with interest as a tour group goes by. Deciding I had better record all of these interesting events, I grope in my purse for a pen. Immediately I awaken, feeling wondrously well. My legs are buzzing in full force.

("The Land of Breeze and Light," November 2, 1976)

The discovery that I made in this dream excited me. At the time it occurred I had been having full-length lucid dreams for several years. I had grown accustomed to the delightful sensation that often vibrated my body during these lucid dreams. The "point of buzzing light" that traveled around my buttocks in "The Bluebird Tree" dream was one version of this whir-tingle that always seems to leave me feeling refreshed and glowing after I experience it. When the vibration disappeared in "The Ruby Bird," I became frightened; its absence alarmed me. I always seem to feel good, safe, and pleasurably aroused when the vibration is present in my body in my dreams. Later, when I underwent some acupuncture treatments for a minor problem, I began to perceive a similar sensation in the waking world. It was my dreaming mind that connected the two—the vibration in my lucid dreams and my physiological response to acupuncture were identical. This discovery, until then unnoticed, I believe to have significant implications for an understanding of the nature and origin of dreams. But before elaborating on its possible value, let me describe more fully the vibration sensation as it occurs in conscious dreaming.

For a long time, I had noticed that lucid dreams were different from ordinary dreaming not only in the intensity of sensations and colors but also in the areas of touch and sound. It is not simply that tactile and auditory sensations in conscious dreams are more beautiful—silk feels even more lustrous, musical tones are even more exquisite—but, in addition, the sounds and feelings take on specific shapes.

For instance, the sound of wind rushing by my face is a typical lucid-dream experience. I can *feel* as well as hear the wind. At first, I did not pause to consider the peculiarity of such imagery. In "The Great Steering Wheel" dream, when I felt the wind and the sun in my face, it seemed perfectly natural. What could be more reasonable than the sound of wind as one flies through the air? And when in dreams I plummet toward the earth from a height and feel the wind streaking by my face, as in "Through the Screened Porch," the sound and the feel of wind are only appropriate. I did not question hearing the rush of water passing my ears as I dived deep into a pool of water in a dream to pick up a special pebble from the bottom. And when I flew in dreams along a seashore and heard the roar of the ocean, it, too, seemed to make sense.

Yet, bit by bit, dream after dream, I came to the realization that *the sounds and sensations of wind and water in my dreams are pictures of the sound-feeling that comes from within myself.* It was not the wind or the water that produced the sound-feeling, nor was it a memory image of wind and water. It was, quite literally, myself. I was *producing* a shimmery sound-feeling that my dreaming mind formed into pictures of wind and water! I explained the sound and feeling experienced in conscious dreams by creating pictorial reasons for its presence. The object that I saw and heard in my dream was a symbolic explanation for what my body was literally feeling and hearing—*itself.*

Gradually, I found that other dream pictures were related to the sound-feel. The roar of a passing train in a dream, the powerful purr of a bus-train that approached, the buzz of a swarm of bees, the rumble of voices in a crowd, a burst of clapping hands—all these I came to recognize as variations of the sound-feel of my lucid dreams. I began noticing fast-moving beats in the background of lucid dreams. I heard pulsations or drumbeats. Sometimes there were far-off sounds of music, as though a radio were playing in the distance. In other lucid dreams, the music was nearby and I swirled in the air upon swells of rhythm.

Sometimes the pulsation shapes itself into rhythmic verse as well as music. In one such dream:

I am sailing in the air to a heavy musical beat. Matching the tune, I begin to sing:

> *I want to know*
> *Why I can fly*

I want to know
Why God can't die.
Oh, tempt me not
With interior blinds. . . .

At this very second, I realize that I am dreaming. I understand with certainty that the words mean that I should not block off portions of myself, the "blinds," but that I should open them to admit light. Overwhelmed by my emotional response to this insight, I cannot grasp the final line. The dream ends with me hanging in midair, hearing the pulsation, and uttering, in time to the beat, great sighs of pleasure and astonishment.

Like almost all lucid dreams, this one left me feeling superb.

Whatever form the sound-feel takes in my dreams—wind, water, musical throbs—it is unified. Rarely will the whirring be audible to my ears without the vibration's being present in my body. However, one or the other aspect—whirring or tingling—may be emphasized in the dream imagery. When the tingling *feeling* is emphasized over the whirring *sound*, my dream mind creates different pictures. For example, in one nonlucid dream when I was being kissed on every portion of my body at once, the all-over tingling sensation it produced led me to the awareness that I was dreaming. In another dream instance, I was hopping down a street when I saw a group of people who wanted to stop me. I rose into the air a few feet to avoid them. The whole crowd reached up and began petting my body, every portion at once, as they chanted "two thousand and one" in a buzzing sort of hum. Here, it was the sensation of being petted everywhere simultaneously that led me to realize that I was dreaming, and I flew away to further adventures. This was a more pleasant picture of the tingle than an earlier dream occasion in which I found myself being overrun by a horde of mice as I lay resting. The tickle of hundreds of tiny feet on my bare skin explained the prickly sensation I was experiencing.

In another dream, it was I myself who was the animal who was tickled:

> I am standing on one side of a room when I decide to cross it, go out a door, and look in the yard for the Bluebird Tree. (This is a type of thinking I call "dream-composing"; without being fully lucid, I design the dream action to follow.) As I begin to cross the room, I catch a glimpse of myself reflected in a glass door (the Mirror Gazer). Instantly I know I am dreaming. Then I realize that I am no longer myself—I am an earthworm crawling across a thick deep-blue carpet. I feel the plumpness of my earthworm hips as I sashay side to side across the plush carpet. Looking out through earthworm eyes, I feel the fuzzy pile of the carpet tickle my body. . . .

The pictures, such as the earthworm one, that my lucid dreams offer as explanations for the sound-feeling that my body is experiencing are endless. I justify the *sound* I hear myself making by images of wind, water, motors, insects, animals, and people that buzz, purr, roar, hum, chant, and whir. I justify the *vibration* that I feel myself making by objects, animals, and people that pet, kiss, and tickle me. Physiological changes are occurring on and within my skin and ears—my whole body—during lucid dreams, and I transform these sensations into pictures. *My dream images are pictures of the sound-feel I am experiencing.*

All this I came to understand in my conscious dreams. What I had not yet realized, before the dream "The Land of Breeze and Light," was that these same sensations, the identical physiological changes, might be an integral part of a much larger process—the mystical process. I did not comprehend that the mystical process may be under way in lucid dreams. I was about to discover that conscious dreaming can be a preparation, a practice ground, for waking mystical experience.

I never expected to encounter the otherworldly shimmery

sound-feel of my conscious dreams in waking life. It occurred sometimes in the drowsy half-world of almost-asleep, it is true, but I did
not anticipate that the whirring-vibration of my dream travels was
accessible to daily life. To my utter astonishment, then, I met it recently, full face, full force, and wide awake—and another piece of
the giant life mandala fell into place.

It was with some reluctance that I climbed onto the acupuncture
table in the first place. My oversensitivity to pain would have kept
me far away had not my aversion to a suggested minor gynecological operation been stronger. Anxiously, I watched our friend
from Hong Kong, a physician as well as acupuncturist, prepare the
first two needles and plunge them into my shins. A sharp discomfort
occurred on insertion, but thereafter it was not painful. A "zzzz"
shot down my left shin to the ankle. Immediately after the needle
insertion, I felt a strange tingle in a spot above my upper lip. It came
and went throughout the half hour while the needles remained in
place. My acupuncturist suggested concentrating my thoughts on
my pelvic area, as though healing energy were flowing through the
needles and up to the pelvis. He left me alone while I meditated
thus for the next thirty minutes. Gradually the buzzing line worked
down my left leg and into my toes and crept up as far as my knees.
I felt it on the right leg, too, but much less. Eventually it worked
upward to my hands, bringing a warm glow with it. Very relaxing.

    Treatment finished, I was absolutely exhausted. I went home to
bed, slept for three hours, and had to be waked to go out to dinner. I
felt dazed—as though I had had a number of glasses of white wine—
giddy but euphoric. There was still some tingling buzz going on in
my left foot. A mellow, floaty evening followed. That night I dreamt
I was going down a very steep ski slope. In the dream, I told myself I
hadn't realized how exciting skiing could be. (Again the wind and
the sense of flight.)

    Next day was a normal, rather hectic one. And that night, normal dreams—no perceptible difference. The following day I went for the second treatment. (My acupuncturist believes that the treatment is cumulative and therefore is more effective when massed at the beginning, so I was to come every other day.) The second treatment had much the same effect, although the leg points used were different and the hands were added, giving me an achy, heavy feel. I was very tired again, though not quite so much so—a response that many people have at first, my acupuncturist assured me. He examined my tongue carefully. It has always been coated with a thick white fur, as long as I can remember. The next day I felt in quite good spirits, despite some annoying circumstances, and that night I had a long, vivid lucid dream, the first in several days:

At the end, I am flying in the air, finding a wonderful book, having an orgasm, and turning into a huge godlike person bending over a ledge. I see a crib covered with a white veil that faces a mirror. I know that "I" am asleep in that crib. I snatch off the veil and find another one beneath it. Layer after layer I remove until finally I can see me, as a baby, sound asleep, both directly and in the mirror. I lean over very close and gently kiss the baby-me on the cheek. The scene shifts and I am working on a textbook, wondering where to record this dream. I decide I'd better wake up and actually write it, so I do.

This dream left me with a lovely afterfeel of uncovering some new aspect of myself.

The third acupuncture treatment, on the following day, was similar in feel and results. The needles in the hands made me achy and tired. The needles in the original points in the shins felt rather pleasant with the "zzzz" coursing through them. I was physically exhausted once more and returned home to sleep for several hours. Waking, I was still so enervated, I was almost nonfunctional. The weekend days and nights were quite normal. Off and on, I felt an occasional "zzzz" in my legs. It puzzled me because I hadn't expected to feel any such sensation except during the time that the needles were in position.

The fourth treatment marked the beginning of a revelation. I had gone into the office feeling pressured and irritable with Zal over some household friction. My acupuncturist switched tactics. He inserted needles in the ear. Now *that* is painful! The first few times that six needles went into my left ear and two into my right, I literally screamed. Nothing could be worth that kind of agony! Instantly my head was flooded with sensations of spreading warmth and tingling. It moved outward from the ears toward the back of my scalp and down into my jaw and neck. Simultaneously, my legs began buzzing again. It was quite an effect. There I sat like a porcupine, eyes closed and meditating on my pelvis, with head tingling and legs zinging. The thing that stunned me most, however, was the way I felt when I left the office. Gone was the mood of irritation. After half an hour of needles in the ear, I felt marvelously calm. Yet energetic. The result was such as I imagined it would be if an amphetamine and a tranquilizer worked at the same time. Peaceful but zingy. Literally. My entire body was still tingling. Off I went to get my pap test taken: the results were to determine whether or not I must have the gynecological operation immediately. All that day, I felt energetic and magnanimous. And the next day, I felt exceptionally well. My body buzzed continuously.

That night I had yet another lucid dream. My lucid-dream rate usually runs about four, at the most five, a month. To have two lucid dreams within less than a week was unusual. It was here that I dreamt of the Land of Breeze and Light. When I awoke, I immediately recognized the bumps on the cat as a reference to the tingling all over the surface of my skin. The cat's loose scalp had to represent the peculiar zinging that worked its way under my own scalp. *These dream images were all pictures of the physical sensations I was experiencing!*

The dream discovery that I made during "The Land of Breeze and Light" dream fascinated me: the vibration of lucidity feels the same as the buzzing of acupuncture. If acupuncture, as it is believed, is a stimulation to the central nervous system, then there must be a stimulation of the central nervous system during lucid dreams. The feeling that acupuncture creates in me is identical to the feeling I get as a natural part of lucid dreams: a sensation of vibrant aliveness throughout my body.

I returned for my fifth treatment the following day in a state of anticipation. Maybe the pain of ear insertion was worth it after all. Again the pain, although less this time, followed by the spreading tingling and warmth. Again a marvelous mood and energy all day long. Again, at night, another lucid dream! In this case, in the course of a long ordinary dream:

I am seated in a wheelchair at first; then I fly up into the dark-ish sky. Down I come, and skim parallel to the sidewalk, a few feet above it, looking carefully to see what I can see, knowing full well I am dreaming. The color of the sidewalk is gray with a rough texture. I notice that I can see better with my left eye, that it is more open than the other eye. Suddenly I hear what I take to be a flutter of wings above and behind me. I not only hear it but also feel it, like a muscle flurry in the back of my head in the occipital region, more to the left side, either on the scalp or under the skull, I can't be sure which. As I feel-hear this flutter, I see something like dark cloud shadows on the pavement at the same instant. This is followed by the sensation of lifting, heels upward, from the flat stomach-flying position, and by a strong orgasm that wakes me.

Here, the superior sight with the left eye in the dream was probably a function of the fact that the buzzing sensation from acupuncture was stronger on my left side.

As I lay awake in the middle of the night after "The Flutter of Wings" dream, with Zal snuggled to my side, I could still feel the whir-tingle intensely. At first I thought it was a remnant feeling from the dream. Then I realized it was the acupuncture buzzing. There could be no doubt. My previous dream discovery was true: the feeling *was* the same. And it was *inducing* lucid dreams!

There was a pattern to the buzzing now. I lay there quietly listening to my body, trying to discern its rhythm. When I held my consciousness in my head, I could feel the buzzing on my face and scalp, extending forward and backward from my ears like long fingers, and surrounding my head. When I shifted consciousness to my legs, I could feel a current simultaneously running through both legs in a complex pattern of about eight seconds on, one second off, then two or three seconds on again, one second off, and the whole cycle repeated. After several minutes of this, Zal shifted in bed, I roused more, and the feeling vanished. As soon as I relaxed and felt myself back into my head once more, the buzzing returned full force. I finally ceased listening to it and drifted to sleep.

The next morning I examined my tongue, as had become my habit. Almost totally bright pink! The fur was disappearing from the tip backward. All day long my energy and mood continued good despite some friction with Zal over the difficult household situation we were coping with—the presence of a frail Mama, whose rapidly progressing senility was a great problem. Rhythmic dances filled my dreams that night.

The sixth treatment led to a climax. I had been feeling in a marvelous state throughout the entire week, despite the difficult circumstances with Mama. Mood already good, energy high, I found that the sixth treatment enhanced the effect. Until now the center of the buzzing sensation had been in my calves. A kind of whorl of activity, a generator, spread a line of zinging downward into my foot and upward to my hips. It felt rather like a Fourth-of-July sparkler looks. Then a new whorl had appeared in the pelvic area, and simultaneously a smaller whorl in the middle of the foot. On both sides of my body these three centers seemed to be spinning and generating

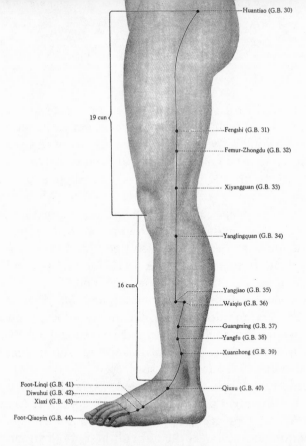

The Gall-Bladder Meridian—*from a modern Chinese acupuncture book.*

energy with a single line connecting them. I drew a picture of it to show to my acupuncturist. "Oh, yes," he said, matter-of-factly, "that's the gall-bladder meridian."

Since I had not read in the literature about acupuncture, I had no idea what a gall-bladder meridian was, let alone where it was. The only preconception I had had about it was that I would probably feel something while the needles were in place. I had no thought that I would be living with a continuous response. Later, I would be intrigued to discover a number of both modern and ancient confirmations of my experience.

My reaction to every acupuncture treatment seemed to culminate on the day *after*, rather than on the day of, the treatment. My sixth session had been on a Friday: again I danced in the dreams of that night. On Saturday, I continued to feel energetic. That night I

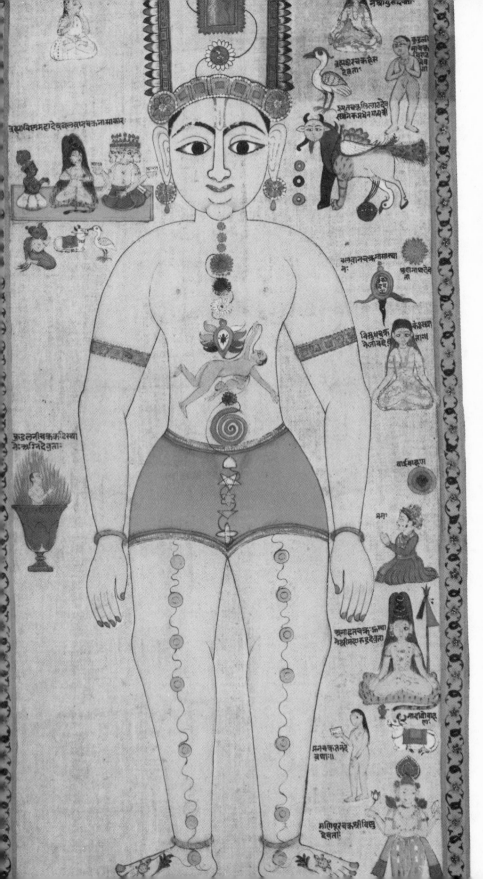

Psychic Energy System—*from Nepal, seventeenth century.*

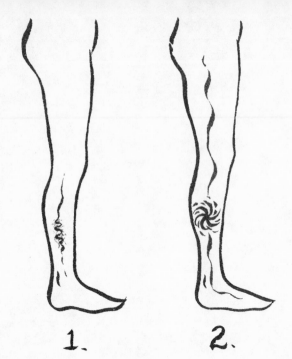

Development of My Vibration Response—*as I experienced it over a two-week period.*

1. 2.

had another powerful lucid dream—the fourth in the same week! All day Sunday the buzzing continued. By evening it was zinging up both sides, still heavier on the left, and more concentrated in the whorls at the pelvic area than in the calves. Now I felt a new whorl on each side under the ribs. In my dream that night I had taken a train in the wrong direction. When I got off I was in the wrong place, a dangerous area. I felt trapped. I took a great chance and hopped on a train that was about to pull out. I was amazed and delighted to find that it was going exactly where I wanted to go. I had taken a chance and made a perfect move. Besides the symbolism of making the right move in the current treatment, the sounds and rumble of the train were pictures explaining the zinging sound-feel that penetrated my entire body.

That night I lay awake again listening to the sounds and feeling the vibration of my body. I was literally tingling from the soles of my feet to the tip of my scalp, from the interior of the marrow within my thighs, calves, and groin outward to the surface of the skin in a rhythmical, pulsating pattern. The three whorl centers and

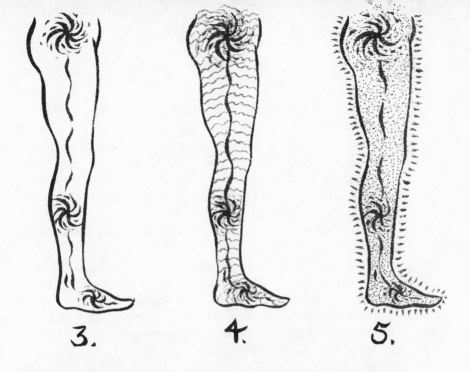

3. 4. 5.

the new fourth center connected by a buzzy line seemed to be generating branches outward. After a pause, my whole right leg, the entire meridian, quivered and trembled. From this central tremor there was a spreading outward of the zinging sensation to the entire surface of the skin. At first it spread in lines, like the branches of a fishbone from a central column. Then it became like thousands of sparks originating as a "zzzz" that felt almost audible, and spreading to the entire surface, particularly concentrated around the buttocks and the genital area. It spread upward on my sides to the face, focused above the ear, and spread backward like fingers to the scalp and forward to greater and greater extensions, taking in the area around the eye and spreading from the cheeks to my lips. The most active center now seemed to be in the head. It was akin to sensations of an emotional shiver on the surface, except that it originated from deep inside the tissue. It produced a kind of creepy crawly feeling of the scalp and a tingling of the face as though I were blushing —very like a strong lucid dream.

Now the rhythmic pattern went like this: the entire right-hand side vibrated for two seconds, then the left-hand side would join it. Both sides vibrated together for another two seconds. Then usually, but not always, the right side would stop. The left side continued to vibrate alone for two seconds and then all was quiescent for two more seconds. With a loud "zzzz" the cycle would recommence.[1] The whir that began inside me spread outward to the surface so that I felt as though there were a million points all over my skin buzzing simultaneously. I felt as though I were glowing—radiating. It was incredible.

Then, as I lay in bed listening to the pulse of my body, the vibration pattern extended into a kind of mini-mystical experience. At a point when the entire body was tingling, the thousands of spots on my skin dancing at once, it turned into a wave. I could feel my heart at the center beating, and with each heartthrob a wave, a current of this sound-feel, rippled outward into a great circle. I no longer felt myself to be a body. A little spot of consciousness, from my closed eyes upward, existed, but the rest was pulsing ripple, a heartbeat that sent waves of energy into the atmosphere, and I was not I, but a throbbing circle of life. . . .

I existed in that space for a long time before I finally fell asleep once more. In the morning Zal and I had to make a trip to Los Angeles. He was consulting during the day, and we planned to spend the evening with a friend. My acupuncture response was still in full force. "You think I'm just sitting here beside you in the car," I told Zal on the way to the airport, "but I'm whirring away inside and tingling all over outside." I described the wondrous feeling. He said with some concern, "Maybe you've had enough acupuncture for a while. But you sure are glowing!" He was not the only one to remark on it that day. The sensation of radiation from every pore of my body must have been perceptible, for two male colleagues we encountered told Zal how beatiful I was. Believe me, that is not an everyday occurrence!

The same night, Monday, I had yet another lucid dream: this time I was flying very high in the air over an expanse of ocean with sunlight sparkling on the water and beautiful whitecapped waves. I listened for the sound and, sure enough, it was there, this time like the roar of the ocean, and my legs were zinging. . . .

Since we were out of town Monday I had to skip my treatment (now into its third week). Without it, the otherworldly response that had invaded my waking state began to calm down. By Tuesday evening I had begun to feel a little shaky, like an addict without a shot. My normal feeling of mild tiredness returned. My tongue began to put on its white coat again. When the next acupuncture session came on Wednesday, and I felt the surge of whirring-vibration return, I welcomed it back like a long-lost friend.

The treatment has continued for over a year, at much more widely spaced intervals, and I've never again had such an intense response to it. But there is a lovely, steady low-level whirring; my mood and energy remain much improved, as well as my health in general. The lucid dreams have returned to their normal rate as I adapt to the steady waking whir-tingle. There are ebbs and flows in this higher plateau. Other people have experienced acupuncture without the extraordinary response that I had. I think that my extreme reaction was due to my body's having experienced the sensation previously in lucid dreams. My general health improved dramatically; the pap test I had taken after starting acupuncture treatment had come out, incredibly, totally clear. The greatest benefit, however, has been the discovery that the marvelous glow of lucid dreams that refreshes and relaxes me and makes me joyful is obtainable in the waking state.

The conscious dreamer, floating in the air (or out of the body), swirling in mind, flooded with passion, flowing with sound and vibration and light, hearing music and poetry, and experiencing a mini-ecstasy of understanding his or her place in the dream state, may be on a lower rung of the ladder of full-fledged mystical exaltation. Surely there is a parallel with the mystic's visions, his sense of levitation, feeling waves of connectedness and oneness with the world, hearing celestial sounds, feeling vibrations, seeing white light, "receiving" divine music and poetry, and experiencing an ecstasy of revelation over his or her place in the entire scheme of the cosmos. Our dreams may be one path to reach that state of altered consciousness that mystics call ecstasy.

I have discovered that I can shimmer while awake as well as in a dream state. Like a giant purring cat, my entire body flows with happy energy, and it is hard to believe that I was ever without it—a purring cat with a pink tongue. The zing of my dream space now exists in my waking space. The next step in this process is even more astounding. Sometimes I feel as though I can step "through the screened porch" at will. Like an experienced world traveler, I cross the border of sleep and carry a treasure from the sea of dreams to the waking shore.

16 THE NORTHERN QUARTER OF THE DREAM MANDALA
Chief Deity: She of the Bell Tones

I am seated Japanese-style on a round black cushion on the gold carpet in my dressing room. To my right, the window is covered with a lace curtain that filters the late-afternoon sunlight and billows up with a fresh breeze. The room feels light and airy. Behind me are built-in storage drawers and cabinets; before me is one of the wooden closet doors, its grain rising upward like flames. To my left, the dressing-room door is slightly ajar, the doors to my bedroom are shut, and the telephone plug is pulled out. I am alone in my private world of meditation.

Having felt extraordinarily well throughout a busy day, I looked forward to this moment—secluded and tranquil at last. The special meditation that I have been practicing has proved so effective that for the past two weeks I have been setting aside two hours each day for it. Of course, I have meditated before, off and on, for years, but usually that was meditation of the familiar twenty-minute variety; I had felt no significant difference then, except for a mild relaxation. But this new practice was different, in technique and in results. The very first time that I rolled my eyes in the prescribed pattern and inhaled while tracing an imaginary route within my body, I felt a surging reaction within my brain. This was no ordinary meditation. The aftereffects of practice left me exceedingly energetic and joyful.

Now, on my cushion—my *zafu*—with my eyes closed, I turn my attention to the area below my navel. Ripples of vibration are moving back and forth across my pelvic region. Tightening and lifting my anus, I inhale and draw the vibration in my pelvis downward to the perineum, into my tailbone, and—in my imagination—raise it up along the length of my spine to the top of my head, pausing at the crown briefly. Then I "lead" the vibration downward through my forehead along the ridge of my nose to meet my uplifted tongue at the palate, and descend, by way of my throat, the imaginary line to my pubic bone, finally turning upward again into the central pelvic cavity. All the while I am synchronizing my eye movements with the directed breath and attention along the imaginary pathway. The vibration is literally present in my pelvis; its movement is imaginary.

Again and again, I rotate my eyes, my breath, and my visualization in this circular route around the body. Always waiting until the pelvic vibration is strong, I mount its highest wave, ride upward with it to a peak, pause, and swoop down to join the source once more. Like a splash on diving into water, the buzzing current wells up with a roar as I, in imagination, reach its pelvic home.

Between the rounds, I contemplate the aftereffects—a sensation as though waves are splashing from side to side in my brain; now a hot vibrant feeling shudders along the entire right side; then an intense spot of heat appears in my left knee. I watch a small purplish orb of irregular outline before my inner eye. It sometimes has a brighter spot within it. Against a grayish-yellow-green background, the entire light seems rhythmically to shrink and expand. Whenever the light is present, the vibration in my pelvis is especially prominent.

How extraordinary! Now the spot of light is growing smaller and smaller as I feel something like a wave move from the back of my brain toward the front. The darkish light, larger, then shrinking in size, seems to come in pulsations from the back of my head forward. Pop! Pop! Pop!—a very soft noise. What's that peculiar sound? I become aware that I have been hearing small popping sounds off and on for the last few minutes. It almost seems as though the noises were coming from inside me. No, it can't be; it must be some of the usual creaks in this old house— some of the wood in the drawers behind me must be cracking. It doesn't sound like an ordinary creak, however, more like a crackle that is separated into pieces. Like something being pulled apart or stretching, it continues—and it is moving!

Good God! It *is* inside of me. It's at the top of my head—before it was behind me. It must have been at the back of my head then. Pop—pop—pop, slowly, inexorably, *something* is moving inside my head!

With the certainty that, whatever it is, it is inside of me, I become excited and not a little frightened. "Relax! Relax!" I tell myself. "Whatever it is, it is happening. You might as well let it take its natural course. Fighting it will only hamper and confuse things. Relax and love God."

Spellbound, I listen to the soft sounds moving forward in a line. Like a spectator at a fantastic event, part of me sits and observes while the rest of me experiences the amazing sensation. Creeping, as though a seam were carefully being pulled apart stitch by stitch, the line moves forward until it reaches the edge of my hairline.

Now the crackling line moves downward onto my bare skin. Like the tiny feet of an ant crawling in a direct path, the sensation goes inching forward and down the surface of my brow. I could swear it is an ant, but I know there is no point opening my eyes to check, for each step of the ant's "foot" is accompanied by a soft pop. Slowly descending, the crackling line reaches the area called, in ancient writings, the "third eye." A further soft pop and suddenly my whole nasal passage and sinus cavities snap clear. All is quiet. I sit still.

Then, bit by bit, a kind of discharge of single "bubbles" wells up from the back of my head and follows the same pathway. Up, up, and over my head to my crown, and forward, forward, the bubbles move in a silent drift to stop their track at the "third eye" where the popping had stopped. Then all is normal once more. I pull myself out of the meditative state a little, open my eyes, and marvel. My whole body is singing with vibration, especially strong in the pelvis, and I feel wonderfully well.

After waiting several minutes, and with no sign of discomfort, I decide it is safe to proceed to the fourth set of breathing rounds. Once again, I gather the pelvic vibrations and lead them upward with my breath and eyes around the mental roadway in my body. When I finish the set, I quietly contemplate the aftermath: now a *flood* of bubbles rushes along the same route. As though following a trail in the snow that had been broken through by a sledder who went before, the bubbles flow. No longer crawling like an ant, or like single bubbles, they *gush* in a fast-moving stream, again and again. A fountain of bubbles issues repeatedly from the back of my head, up and over the crest, to course down my forehead. Rivulets of bubbles pour out and splash down to my third eye.

Entranced for several minutes watching this internal spectacle, I finally become aware that I must have been meditating for a long while. I have to check the time. Gradually, I summon my attention to turn outward, open my eyes, and focus on my wristwatch: 6:20 P.M.! I have to leave the house in ten minutes! This meditative state has gone on for over one and a half hours, without a single thought of the time. I pull myself together, get up,

dress, and dash out to drive to my appointment. As I go, drop-
lets of water bubbles run down my forehead. I do not "wake up"
—for this is no dream!
(Notebook, June 2, 1977)

During the busy evening that ensued, I temporarily set this
inner adventure aside. Only an occasional trickle of bubbles reminded
me of its presence in my system. Home late, to sleep, to dream, I
might have thought by the following morning that I had dreamt the
whole thing. But when I opened my eyes early the next day, like a
cinder thrown from a fire, the energy sprang up to the top of my
head, sputtered, and then, waterlike, cascaded down my brow. It has
never gone away.

This experience of "opening" my "channel" followed closely on
the heels of several months of acupuncture treatment. The acupuncture sessions had made such a vast improvement in my sense of
overall well-being—a physical vibrancy and an emotional and mental lightheartedness—that I was reluctant ever to do without those
sensations again. I had never before realized how good I *could* feel.
Never suspecting that my body was not functioning optimally, I had
gone along content to just not be sick. Asthma was ended; acne had
cleared; minor viruses came and went. I ate much more healthfully
than as a youth, I exercised far more often with the dancing, and I
grew stronger. Yet there was always a mild weariness, quick to set
in—a late-afternoon droop that required napping—and I simply assumed that the constitution I was born with I was fated to, and
adapted myself to it.

After experiencing the vibrant aliveness resulting from acupuncture, I grew discontented. That was how I would like to have felt all
the time! Continued acupuncture had raised my level of well-being
yet did not return it to that earlier sensational height. I did not
want, either, to be addicted to *needing* the treatments. Traveling frequently as I do, I wanted a "portable booster" available to me. It occurred to me that it might be possible to meditate on the acupunc-

ture points, now that I had learned where they were and what they feel like when activated, and thus, perhaps, to stimulate them mentally.

When I confided this idea to my acupuncturist, he said, "Oh, yes, there is a system for that; it's called *Ch'i Kung*" (literally, working the *ch'i*, the life energy force). He explained how a practitioner with proper training could learn to circulate the energy flow along certain channels, and produce effects similar to those of acupuncture. The process, however, took several months, was difficult, and could be extremely dangerous. He knew of no books in English on the subject. Naturally, I couldn't wait to try it.

I am, I admit, voracious for experience—a bit of a pig about it. Anything I like—a delicious dinner with wine, making love, pretty clothes, intriguing books, recording dreams, interesting lectures, theater—I go into wholeheartedly. If something is good, more is better—until I get a stomachache. And the stomachache, in its infinite variety, is inevitable. A gourmet birthday dinner at a splendid restaurant with my favorite dishes and wines will make me merry all evening; and afterward I will be up half the night with cramps and diarrhea. Too much lovemaking can leave me sore. After a buying spree my clothes are jammed so tightly into the closet, I can't find what I want and everything gets wrinkled. My books and volumes of dreams still pile up in the study and bedroom so high it's hard to know how to store them. Activities proliferate until there is hardly room to think. I cannot seem to tell when enough is just right and more is too much.

With this attitude, I plunged into the meditation project. Delving into old and occult bookstores, asking "way-out" people, questioning scholars, poring over translations from the Chinese, I unearthed at last the books that told how.[1] Ignoring the wise warnings that the method must be supervised, I began practicing the esoteric aspect of *Ch'i Kung*, called *nei tan*, the "inner alchemy" of Taoist meditation.

It was—and is—an exciting project. Like an explorer preparing

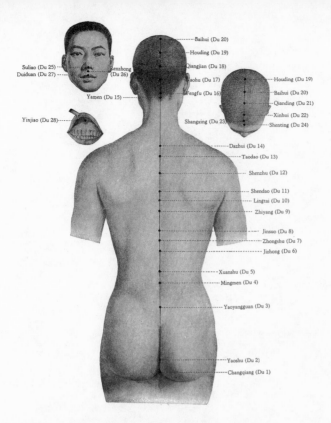

The Back Midline Channel, Tu Mo—*from a modern Chinese acupuncture book.*

for a journey to a treacherous unknown land, I spread out the "maps" and examined what had been recorded of this territory.[2] Ancient diagrams of the "inner circulation," schemata of the steps of "inner alchemy," and their modern descendants—charts of the acupuncture meridians—were posted on my bedroom doors. I studied them intently; I memorized the landmarks, I learned the names of the hills and valleys. Then I turned from the maps to examine the lay of the land, to study the terrain of my own bodily processes.

Here, hypersensitivity served me well. Each little tingle, each crinkle of pain became a focus. I located it; I identified it; I related it to the whole system. Being familiar with the vibration-whir that has stirred within me in waking hours ever since I began acupuncture, and before that in lucid dreams, I found it easy to discern, whenever it spread, the route by which it traveled to another area. Having good spatial perception and visual imagination, I could translate the

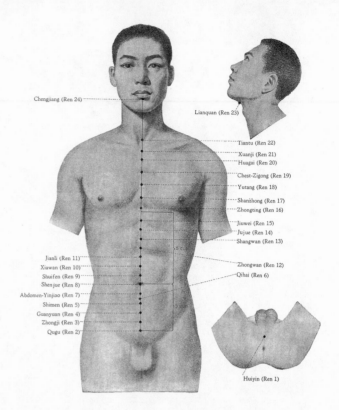

The Front Midline Channel, Jen Mo—*from a modern Chinese acupuncture book.*

verbal descriptions and two-dimensional diagrams into the organs and spaces of my own body.

My body became my teacher. As the meditation process evolved, as imagination gave way to experience, as *picturing* a current moving along a pathway yielded to *feeling* a current running a course, there were many surprises. I had always thought that the term "energy flow" was a metaphor, that it meant a general life force, without a specific referent. The Chinese named it *ch'i;* the Hindus called it *prana;* the Greeks termed it *pneuma;* the Latins, *spiritus.* Perhaps, I thought, one would sense a warmth or a diffuse "aliveness" as one focused on an area, but nothing more specific than that.

With the channel-opening described above, I was astonished to discover that "energy flow" is literal. It is specific. It is as clearly different as a lamp's being turned on is different from its remaining off. When I place my tongue in the proper position to meditate, it is like putting a plug into a socket. A connection is made and the power *literally* moves around my body. It is tangible; it is audible; it seems almost visible.

I was surprised, too, to find that the movement was, at first, slower than I had imagined it to be. When the current became reality within my body, it *crept,* in comparison to the pace I had pictured for it. As I began to "orbit" the energy, I would count from one to six as I moved in my mind's eye from my tailbone up the spine to my crown. After the current actually moved within me, I perceived that it lagged behind my mental counting. So, I slowed the count to suit the fact, and was able to match my imagery to what was happening within.

I was learning from myself. The current relentlessly pushes its way into new nooks and crannies; it has a "mind" of its own. Once I set it upon the main backline and front-midline channels, as though on an interstate highway, it shows me where the branching routes are, the state roads and the country lanes.

Every day, every meditation period brought a new discovery, a new insight. Each night, each dream period brought a clearer symbolism of the powerful changes I had unleashed within myself. So many puzzling things began to make sense to me. A delicious adventure, I gobbled it up—and got another stomachache, and eye ache, and neck ache, and headache.

I overdid the meditation. Greedy for even more of the exhilarating sensation it induced, I meditated two and three hours a day for more than a month. I became so full of energy that I gave up naps. Then I grew so energetic I could barely sleep; I began to feel shaky. My system became so overheated that my tongue turned bright yellow. The sensations of creeping and dribbling intruded so much that it was hard to ignore them and work. My eyes ached and fuzzed; I felt strange dull pains; I began to feel quite anxious. Even as it is hard for me to tell when I am overeating because everything tastes so good at that moment, I had difficulty recognizing that I was meditating too long and too strenuously because it felt so good while I was engaging in it. Taoists would say that I was overcirculating the energy faster than my body could absorb it. Reluctant to relinquish the positive results, yet fearful of the discomforts and mindful of the dangers, I knew that I needed help.

I sharply cut back on the time I spent in meditation and inquired ceaselessly for specialists in Taoist meditation. In the mysterious way that these things happen—Jung would call it synchronistic—a master of Taoism appeared.

Master K—— had come from mainland China to live in California. Thoroughly versed in the technique of Taoist meditation, generous and gentle, he reviewed my practice and corrected my errors. He prescribed special exercises he believed would strengthen my body to sustain the power that had become so strong it seemed to batter my insides; he taught me self-massage to lower the pressures after I had inflamed them by meditation. With the wisdom based on centuries of knowledge, he demonstrated the practice over and over, so that I could see directly how and where and why to circulate the energy. I learn continuously from him. The aches subsided and the vibrancy remained.

I have "overeaten" a time or two since, but I have learned to recognize the symptoms sooner. I respect the power of the inner current enough to treat it well, to ration its roaming, and to exercise it gently. And the process of meditation proceeds well, unfolding in my waking body everything I had dreamt of and had not known was possible.

I saw at last that the lucid dreams of my past few years were forerunners of the current that now flows through my waking body. No wonder I felt refreshed after conscious dreaming—the current of energy was circulating itself during lucid dreams. Today, awake, I can activate the same current and, to some extent, direct its rejuvenating power. No wonder that I felt tingling and heard buzzing in those lucid dreams. The current tingles and buzzes as it moves from place to place within my system—now in my genitals stirring passion, now in my legs making me feel airborne, now in my cheeks creating whirlpools and breezes, now in my brain stirring eddies of lightheaded ecstasy, now on the surface of my skin like a drizzle of rain, tingling alive in every pore, now plunging down my front to make me feel, in my dreams, as though I am plummeting to earth. I believe that the same current that I now feel in meditation moves naturally, unimpeded, in our ordinary nightly dreams. In our conscious dreams, we are able to hear and feel its activity. And, if we are lucky, we can coax it to the light of day.

Wide awake, I experience sensations that I had first perceived in my lucid dreams. For instance, when the current is very strong and its peak passes down my throat, riveting the tip of my tongue to the palate as though connected by a poker, shaking and vibrating all the way down to its root, a mass of energy sometimes "sticks" in the depression at the base of the throat (where the Hindus and Buddhists both locate the throat *chakra*). Like a great, whirling lump, the mass of energy wedges there, unable to break through, giving me a sensation of difficulty in breathing or a sense of some matter caught in my throat, exactly as I experienced in "The Ruby Bird." The pressure builds until, at last, the current plows through into the chest.

Wide awake, I have felt the point of buzzing light that I first perceived in "The Bluebird Tree" dream. It climbs my calves, creeps through my thighs, crawls across my groin; it wends its way up my arms; it trickles like ringlets down my neck. Like a burning fuse at the end of a wire, the buzzing light moves within me daily.

Most often now the current originates from the soles of my feet, welling up from the area that the Chinese appropriately call the "bubbling springs." Or it commences from the left great toe. Rumbling out, hot and bubbly, it starts its upward journey. It is like my dreams of dancing on hot mud, of walking on pulsating sands, of twirling on my toes; it is like all my dreams of dancing.

Once, during meditation, when the current broke into rivulets running down the sides of my head and neck, working its way into

She of the Bell Tones—*chief deity of the Northern Quarter of my Dream Mandala.*

sideburnlike hairlines in front of my ears, I began to feel whorls of energy emanating from my cheeks exactly as I had had in "The Woman of Fixedness" dream.

During another meditation period, when I felt the current rippling out from the crown of my head, in the spot that the Chinese call the "hundred crossroads," it broke into tributaries, finer and finer, until, a wispy line, it curled in front of my ears, across my cheek, to the corner of my lips. Into my head flashed the image of a dream woman of years ago. She was one of the figures that impressed me considerably at the time, and, as is my practice, I had sketched her. She was a primitive woman who encountered a slave tribe who were "keepers of the snakes." In this complex dream:

The main job of the tribespeople is to guard the safety of the snakes. The snakes, wearing harnesses and leashes, go out walking and swimming, followed by their slave protectors. One woman, who is beautiful and intelligent, wears a deep-blue scarf wrapped around her head. She speaks not in words, but in musical tones, exquisite, bell-like sounds. Filled with awe, I watch her through a screened door where she stands opposite me. From the corners of her lips, near her nose, issue fine golden spikes, like pussycat whiskers. She opens the door. . . . ("She of the Bell Tones," July 1, 1975)

Now it was I, body radiant, who felt fine golden whiskers brushing my own cheeks. My dreams had pictured the physical sensations that were now emanating from my body. The current had been flourishing then, in those dreams of long ago.

As I feel the current more and more in the waking world, my dream language keeps pace. I dream that I am dancing, twirling, leaping, ballerina-style, and awake to find that the "bubbling springs" in the soles of my feet are whirling wildly. I dream that I discover a threadlike golden hair growing from the tip of my spine and awake to feel my tailbone tingling. A dream of a cigarette burning at both ends preceded my awakening to find that the current was alternating between my head and pelvis in a steady rhythm. My dream language becomes clearer with every dream. I see that the "meaning" of my dreams, their symbolic content, is lying over a base of physical sensation. *My dreams are multilevel—and their foundation is the movement of the current.* My dreams speak now in a more transparent language and I understand much of it.

Of course, it works the other way as well: my meditation experiences are reflected in my dreams, even as my dreams predict the meditation experiences. Shortly before the pathway through my crown opened, I dreamt of a stream of water dripping on the top of my head; *after* the pathway opened, and the whole area was sore for days, my dream characters were hit on the head with rocks and hammers, leaving them as sore as I felt. The night *before* I had the opening in the solar-plexus area during meditation, I had dreamt of having difficulty driving my car through some locked gates, but finally I managed to do so, and pulled into a seemingly impossible parking place. I awoke with a sharp, squiggly pain through my solar plexus, replacing the former dull ache. The night of the day *after* my front midline channel opened and the energy squeezed through my solar plexus and crept beyond my navel during meditation, I dreamt that I put on a leotard that had a front panel set into it made of beautiful pale-blue open lace. A few nights later, I dreamt that I wore a transparent blouse that revealed my breasts—the "openness" of my front. My dreams are forecasting the process of meditation; my dreams are reflecting the process of meditation.

As I circulated the energy upward and downward during the day, I dreamt at night of roller coasters, escalators, steep hills, ski slopes, deep-grooved tracks, sharp curves on roadways, flights of stairways up and down—all telling of the ascending and descending of the inner current during my ordinary dreams; as I grew accustomed to its presence, the slopes of my dreams became gentler. In my conscious dreams, the pattern of flying upward followed by plummeting back to earth took on new meaning as the current flew up my spine and plunged to its home deep within my pelvis. This new language that I am translating from my dreams requires a book of its own to set forth; it is to be shared another time.

Within myself, I "turn the great steering wheel" and circulate my energy. Awake and conscious, I meditate and move to the other space that used to exist for me only when I was asleep, in my conscious dreams. The circular route of energy within my body becomes a living mandala; the shell of skin becomes the temple walls within which the personified powers breathe and perform.

The greed of overdoing, of wanting more of every good thing until I almost burst because I am too full, is well suited to the energy of the Northern Quarter. For in Tibetan Buddhist mandalas, the ruler of the Northern Quarter, *Amogha-Siddhi,* * *is the conqueror of greed.*

* pronounced Ah·*mōg*·ă·si·dē

Amogha-Siddhi—*chief deity of the Northern Quarter of Tibetan Buddhist mandalas.*

(*Siddhi* is a Sanskrit word meaning magical spiritual power.)

Amogha-Siddhi is seated in the meditation posture with his left hand in his lap holding his symbol, a cross formed from two *vajra*s.[3] He holds his right hand aloft, palm toward the viewer, in a gesture that signifies, "Fear not!" He is of the cold, stormy quality of the North.

Dark green is his color, like the "sun at midnight." The serene mystic green of his body, and the green light that emanates from his heart, are meant to represent a combination of the deep blue of the night sky with the yellow light of an inner sun.[4] Amogha-Siddhi's element is the wind, moving air. Seated upon his lotus throne supported by *garuda*s, the mythological birdmen, he represents the sum of all previous actions, our *karma.*

When the energy that Amogha-Siddhi symbolizes is expressed neurotically, it appears as greed, envy, and jealousy. The person manifesting this energy neurotically needs to keep up with everything, eager not to be left out. This same energy, transmuted, becomes a wisdom that accomplishes all works. Having attained the All-Accomplishing Wisdom, we no longer act out of self-interest, to gain profit, or with desire for results. We act for the benefit of all, doing what needs doing and destroying all obstacles.

Thus, Amogha-Siddhi in his cool color, with his gesture of fearlessness, in his serenity of action, is the conqueror of greed, envy, and jealousy. He leads to the Successful Performance of Best Actions. He, too, appears in myriad forms, as a monk, as a king, in *yab-yum* union with his consort, or in wrathful aspect, alone or united, haloed in flames instead of radiant light.

The Northern Quarter of my Dream Mandala—*the Bell, Symbol of She of the Bell Tones.*

For my personal Dream Mandala, I chose, as chief deity of the Northern Quarter, my primitive tribal woman, She of the Bell Tones. Although she is not green, her deep-blue headdress, like the night sky, and her golden whiskers combine to produce that shade. I hope that she will remind me of my tendency to overdo, to gobble greedily, to want and act too much for myself. Perhaps she will help lead me to the wisdom that acts instead for the well-being of all; the wisdom that, fearless, is a giving rather than merely a grasping; that is balanced, active, and serene. I placed her symbol, the bell, into the Northern Quarter of my personal Dream Mandala. Her various related dream images, attendants and their consorts, are symbolized by colored dots.

She of the Bell Tones is a numinous figure for me. Her musical voice sings to me of the vibration current. I recognize that there are several possible explanations for what I have experienced during meditation: a hypnotic effect produced by intense concentration while relaxed, pure suggestion, spiritual influence, etc. I find myself particularly receptive to the Taoists' view because of the profundity of my body's response when I followed their ancient precepts. She of the Bell Tones represents for me the power—whatever the explanation for it may be—that stirs within me now. Like the element of wind that can blow everywhere, the current can move and transform. And its beauty is at times almost indescribable:

I am in my bedroom—exactly as it actually is—getting dressed early on a Sunday morning, when I hear church bells begin to chime. Their tone is exquisite. They vibrate and resonate like Tibetan gongs, on and on and on, rippling the air around me. I marvel at the extraordinary sound and wonder where it originates because I have never heard such melodious ringing before.

I decide, "It must be Chinese church bells from a nearby church." The ringing is so lovely that I throw the windows open wide to be able to hear it better. Again and again and again, the chiming reverberates through my whole being.
("Chinese Church Bells," August 11, 1977)

This dream fragment was so realistic that, when I first recalled it in the morning, I thought it was the memory of a waking event. Gradually it dawned on me that I had never heard a tone so beautiful during my waking state, and, inasmuch as there are no Chinese churches with bell towers in the neighborhood, I was forced to recognize that I had dreamt the incident.

If the exquisite Chinese church bells of my dream follow the pattern of my meditation development, I may yet hear such music in meditative states. Even as much of my meditation experience has been forecast in conscious dreams, so the ethereal notes may resound once more. Surely they resonate in my dreams—"She of the Bell Tones" and the realistic "Chinese Church Bells." They echo the magical power of the current of life.

17 THE BRANCHING WOMAN

Toward the end of a complex ordinary dream that includes scenes of my mother becoming dizzy (the lightheadedness in a dream character other than myself, an earlier step than feeling lightheaded myself) and rain (the coolness), the scene shifts:

I am climbing up a beautiful hill on a clear, sunny, breezy day. Ruminating as I go on the novel *Jane Eyre,* which I had read a few months previously, I think of how Jane's dream was crucial to the resolution of her story. Colorful flowers surround my path, and, as I pass by, I reach out and grasp some of the lovely blooms. A few of them crumple as I pick them, and I caution myself—dream-composing—"I don't need to let that happen. I can pluck them more carefully." Although it is difficult to do in the dream and I occasionally crush a flower despite my care, I manage to gather an armful of exquisite, unblemished blossoms.

Reaching the top of the hill, I survey a majestic scene. As my gaze lowers, I see that, down in front of me, there is a long stone wall, and, through a rather large hole in the stones, beyond the wall, lies what I know to be a royal river. I watch with fascination as small boats filled with dark-skinned people slip past the opening in the wall. I somehow am certain that these people are members and relatives of the royal family.

As they float by, some of the people in the boats glance up and, noticing me, smile warmly. I can sense that I wear something special on my head—perhaps a kind of hat of flowers. Seeing outward through my own eyes, I do not know what my headdress looks like, but I can feel its weight and sense a shape as I move my head.

Suddenly, a child in one of the boats points to my headpiece and shouts in quaint, childish style, "Xerxes give it to her!" The people begin to murmur in tones of awe, "Xerxes, Xerxes," as they in turn pass by the hole in the wall and regard me. I have a strange feeling—I feel as though I am some sort of goddess or good spirit. Then a very beautiful dark-skinned girl standing in one of the boats smiles radiantly at me and entreats, "Stay, Xerxes!" With a wave of intense pleasure, I awaken.
("Xerxes and the Royal River," October 5, 1972)

This dream of Xerxes is one of those that left me with a baffling afterglow. Although it has been five years since I dreamt it, the incredible sense of being someone important whom even I did not fully comprehend still clings to my recollection of this dream. As though I had *experienced* being a goddess or good spirit, the image of myself wearing some mysterious thing upon my head that proclaimed my position bewitched me. I felt myself having been—for a dream moment—a mythical being.

My only conscious association to Xerxes as a historical figure was that he had been a king of Persia—itself a secret, intriguing realm to me. Looking up *Xerxes* in the dictionary I read that he had ruled Persia from 486 to 465 B.C. and that he was known as Xerxes the Great.

At the time I dreamt "Xerxes and the Royal River," Zal and I were in Papeete, Tahiti, having completed our world tour and taking a rest before proceeding back to the States.

There in Papeete, midst the profusion of tropical blooms that probably stimulated those that grew on my dream hill, I was unwinding at last, feeling relaxed and tranquil. Sunbathing, swimming, working on my dream record, making love—as we had in the early morning just prior to the dream—I took the dream of Xerxes, at the time, to reflect my state of loving peacefulness. I saw myself gathering beautiful things, climbing high, seeing beyond obstacles to fantastic vistas, and feeling appreciated.

So concluding, although the experience of *being* the mysterious creature intrigued me, I set the dream aside and thought no further about it. Several years had to pass before I recognized in the "Xerxes" dream a crucial element in an emerging pattern of self-discovery. And then another few years went by before I understood that these dream pictures of headpieces were portrayals of the movement of the current through my own head.

I had overlooked many pivotal pieces to the puzzle during my years of dreaming. The image that finally jarred me into awareness was a highly idiosyncratic one: the head of a woman from which grew branches, almost like antlers, each dividing and subdividing into a thick full growth. I call her the Branching Woman.

Since I have quoted the dream of the Branching Woman in detail elsewhere,[1] I will simply mention that I found myself in a dream at a professional conference standing to announce that, "I would like to discuss the concept *branching*. I have had several dreams in which there was a growth. There was a woman's head. . . ." and I proceeded to elaborate. Nobody in the dream paid much attention except Zal, who kissed me on the cheek and told me how well I had done.

The Branching Woman—*chief
deity of the Sacred Center of my
Dream Mandala.*

At the time of "The Branching Woman" dream I was actively
formulating my ideas about dreaming. In the waking world as well,
no one but Zal seemed to be listening and appreciative. The image
of the Branching Woman, as those mysterious glimpses of our inner
selves can do, mesmerized me. Had I dreamt of her before? I had no
memory of having done so. Leafing through my journals and note-
books, I discovered that, sure enough, time after time in the past
years, I had dreamt of analogous images and sketched them into the
margins of my dream records: one was a picture of myself with my
hair standing straight up by internal willpower; another was of a
redheaded girl, an insignificant character in the background, who
wore a cap with leafy branches issuing from it that swished as her
head turned; yet another was of myself as a secretary with two

curled horns atop my head; the "Xerxes" dream seemed to be part of this head-growth pattern; there were numerous others.

I traced the Branching Woman's family tree. I saw that there had been a long-emerging aspect of myself, whose evolution was delineated in my dream record, that I had passed by blindly. Pondering the meaning of growth from the head, I finally realized that it was my own creative thinking that was growing, dividing, and subdividing, stretching rich and full, reaching outward. The tender, growing tip of antler-branches was the growing edge of myself.

Comprehending that both hair and antler-branches are kinds of growth, I came to understand for the first time many specifics in my dreams. I saw that, for me, in my intimate dream language, a *set* of hair was a *set* of my mind. I noticed how often in an ordinary dream, immediately before it became lucid, I or another dream character was having her hair set in an unusual style. Then I would find myself conscious—that is, in an unusual *set* in the dream state.

If hair set was equivalent to mental set, then headpieces, head growths, and hairstyles were equivalent to my mental contents, my thoughts. It is as though *whatever I or another dream character wears or grows or arranges upon the head is an outer expression of my inner condition.*

It seems so obvious now, I wonder how I could have missed it for so long. As a teenager, I recorded numerous dreams of women who wore heart-shaped hats, clusters of hearts, or one large heart, crownlike upon the head. In retrospect, it is easy to see that these were shorthand visual expressions of my own head filled with thoughts of romance, and my wish for a valentine of my own. The Branching Woman spoke of my conceptual occupation with creative growth, reaching out in every direction with exciting discoveries. Headpieces of all sorts in my dreams referred to the contents of my mind. *An inner quality of thought is expressed by an outer form of the dream image.*

The condition of hair itself, I came to understand, was an extension of my inner condition. Thick and glossy hair that reflected back from my dream mirrors said something about my state of mind different from what limp and straggly strands did. Rich brown, deep auburn, silver, or golden hair—each had its shade of meaning. Cutting hair could be positive or negative, depending on the outcome—whether the new style was becoming, too cropped, or uneven. Hair and headpieces are observable outer extensions of inner mental states in my dreams.

By generalization from this discovery, I noticed that head growths on animals and vegetables, as well, were significant. In one dream, I saw a vegetable that was shaped rather like a carrot but white instead of orange and with long tendrils issuing from its crown. The vegetable seemed like a living being and danced about the table, unwilling to be cut up for food. I sketched this dancing vegetable and, as I did so, became aware of how intrigued I was with elaborating upon the tendrils that grew from its top. Suddenly I understood that the tendrils, too, were a head growth. I realized that they represented the tender quality of my then-vegetarian daughter. At the time I had "The Dancing Vegetable" dream I had been peeved with her and, not realizing how "tender" she was, was startled to see how violently she reacted to the situation. I have already mentioned that when I drew the Polka Dot Horse I found myself concentrating on his mane and associating to his rhythmic sexual flow. Thus, I saw that head growths from animals and vegetables were also outer expressions of inner qualities, just as head growths from humans were.

As my Taoist meditation progressed, I discovered that there was an additional level of meaning to hairstyles and headpieces in my dreams. The rivulets of energy that spilled over my brow and trickled down my neck, first in waking meditation and then during most of my waking hours, translated into ringlets and unusual arrangements of hair in my dream characters. In one such dream I admired the lustrous silver tresses of a woman who had her hair arranged into an elaborate and unusual style—it was shaped like wings near her face and fell in ripples of long silver waves down her neck. The shining silver of her curling hair portrayed well the silvery feeling as the current wends its way into finer and finer channels.

The dream of the woman with wavy silver hair turned almost immediately into a powerful and satisfying lucid dream, the one in which I twirled upon a trapeze bar suspended above my bed. Earlier the same night I had had a peculiar dream segment:

I have broken a tooth and hurry to the ladies' room to examine the damage. Looking into the mirror, first at my teeth, I am startled to realize that the top of my head is missing. Without eyes, I can see that the bottom of my hair is rolled into curlers, the old-fashioned kind of metal curlers used for permanents, while the entire top of my skull is gone and inside my head is a mass of glutinous tissue. Instead of finding this disturbing, I am intrigued.

I touch one of the curlers on the right side and it produces a buzzy, electrical feeling. With pleasure, I exclaim, "This is the perfect opportunity to examine the inside of my brain!" Careful not to touch the curlers, as it might set the electrical current going so strong I could not concentrate, I peer into my open skull. I can see the tip of my brain pulsating.
("Visible Brain," August 8, 1977)

When I awoke, I was not surprised to feel the current in my head.

Dreams such as these helped me to realize at last that the extensions from the heads of my dream women, including myself—their hair, or curlers, or hats, or crowns, or antler-branches—were based upon physiological sensations as well as expressions of inner qualities. The symbolic significance of the mental growth of ideas, or passionate thoughts, or peering inside my head, or whatever was being pictured at the moment of the particular dream, was still accurate. *There was meaning to the individual dream picture, but all along, underneath the symbolism, runs my current.* The energy of life moves forcefully in my dreams. Circulating through my scalp, stirring my brain, it shapes now a Lightheaded Dancer, then a Branching Woman, or a mythological creature with mysterious bonnet. *Dream symbolism is superimposed upon the movement of the current.*

This realization that dream pictures were related to the movement of the current fit perfectly with another fact—a change—that I had been observing in my dreams for the past few years: the women in my dreams were shifting. I had not only sketched the Branching Woman, I had sculpted her of clay as well. It had seemed important to shape her head growth in three dimensions, to literally reach out in all directions. I set the finished statue upon my bookcase—a spot of honor and import. She helped call my attention to the fact that the female figures in my dreams were taking on a different form.

Two years after I had shaped the Branching Woman in waking life, I was astonished when a colleague at a program where we were fellow speakers chanced to say, "Oh, I loved the photograph of your statue of the Branching Woman that appeared in the *San Francisco Chronicle.* I cut it out of the paper and made a slide of it to use in my art lectures. She's a perfect example of the Horned Goddess."

Although I had never heard of horned goddesses, I was, of course, familiar with Jung's concept that modern people have "archetypal" images in their dreams. Even as we bear in the womb, briefly, the tail of our ancestors, so we are said to carry in our minds the remnant memories of our ancestors' experiences. These primary memories are believed to emerge in dreams and myths. Turning to the literature that Jungians have collected from various cultures on the archetype called the "Great Mother," I saw how goddesses often wear upon their heads "ideograms" that express the quality that the goddess represents. The Egyptian goddess Isis, for example, wears as part of her crown the horns of Hathor—the goddess of love to whom the cow is sacred; Hathor is often represented with a cow's head. On Isis, Hathor's horns are meant to express the quality of nurturance within Isis. Every culture has evolved an image of this sort: primitive cave people drew shamans with antler

Isis—*the Egyptian goddess who wears a crown consisting of the horns of Hathor, the cow-headed goddess, embracing a sun disc.*

headpieces; American Indians sculpted similar forms; ancient Hawaiians depicted Pele, the volcano-fire goddess, with tresses flaming upward. I saw that my Branching Woman could well be related to the Great Mother in her good aspect, as goddess of birth and fertility for all growing things—plants and animals and humans.

In recent years, I had been noticing that the women in my dreams differed in quality from the women of my earlier dreams. My dream population was changing. The cast of characters in my dream world when I was fourteen had been mostly ordinary folk.[2] Unusual characters were rare. When I was forty-one, the dreams that I had analyzed carefully still contained the people I related to most often in waking life.[3] However, many unusual characters were also present. Highly idiosyncratic figures who were powerful creatures appeared; most of these were women.

A typical example of one of these females appeared in an ordinary dream in which I had gone to a television studio to be interviewed:

I am having difficulty locating the appropriate room. A show with tribal people begins, so I watch it. Among the participants is an exceptionally beautiful black woman who wears a headdress made of rosy pink silk, trimmed with crystal beads that glint in the studio lights. Next to her sits an older tribal woman, perhaps the young woman's grandmother; she admonishes a grown son.

This older woman wears a white shirt dress unbuttoned down the front, revealing her ripe, shapely breasts. She states, "They do not call me Ivory-Bosom for nothing." The many people of the tribe and in the studio murmur admiringly, "Look at those breasts!" Indeed, despite her age, the older woman's breasts are firm, erect, and perfectly sculpted. Somehow she has been denying them to her grown son.

The younger woman speaks to the older woman, urging her to

consider the needs of the whole tribe. In response, the older woman's breasts, as we watch, begin to churn and fill. I can see it happening underneath her skin. I realize that this woman alone must be nourishing the entire tribe from her breasts. As they swell to abundance, the breasts overflow with streams of milk. Then, no longer shut out by walls, the skies around us fill with a milklike rain that falls upon and nourishes all. ("Ivory-Bosom," June 21, 1975)

Students of mythology will recognize the archetypal imagery reflected in this dream of a nourishing earth-mother figure, yet I, myself, had no familiarity with such images when I dreamt of Ivory-Bosom. Then, at the time, I could respond to the sense of being cared for, because this dream came to me during a stressful period. (It was a few days after we had moved from our flat to a house, and there were the usual complications and exhaustion of re-establishing households; I was just beginning to recover.)

Looking back, it is easy to see that the young woman in the rosy pink headdress was an ancestor of the Lightheaded Dancer. Her glistening, light-catching crystal beads spoke of the light that circulated in my own scalp, although I did not hear it at the time. Her darkness told of my deeper self; her rosiness, of my passion.

The plenteous milk-rain that fell from the skies as Ivory-Bosom's breasts filled is another version of the ring of raindrops that, drizzling or drenching my skin, describes the vibration that sets my whole body atingle and heralds the commencement of conscious dreaming or awakens me with a feeling of rejuvenation.[4]

The figures of goddesses and strong women who appear in my dreams are very giving. In another such instance, after having fallen asleep exhausted:

I feel myself dancing in a hallway. I know that I am being guided by a woman, although I cannot see her. The sensation is strange, as though I am in a kind of trance. I experience the dream more from inside myself than from outside; I *feel* it more than see it.

Sensing the presence of the guide, I dance down the hallway. I am periodically aware of the fact that I dream—consciousness ebbs and flows. When my awareness is present, I throw myself down upon things in the hall, knowing that I cannot injure myself. I can feel something odd inside my mouth, as though my front teeth are false, and set upon a plate backed with wax. I will have to be careful or there is a danger the plate will come loose, I think.

Then the guide says to me, "Now you can let something come up." She encourages me, prompting, "Good! Good!" From deep inside some part of my mouth, I can feel a kind of pus-filled ball working its way out. At last it emerges and I spit it out into my hand to examine it. I can see a clear close-up view of the ball now, but still not the entire scene. Spellbound, I watch as the ball unfolds into a kind of metal bell. And then it seems as though the bell itself were spreading open to form a flower.

The guide, sounding rather like one of my dance teachers, says, referring to the pusball—bell-flower, "That's been inside you since way back—oh, at least since the time when you had acne." I understand that it is a great accomplishment to have managed to exude this pustule. I have removed a source of infection from within me that had been deeply buried for a long time.

I feel marvelous and want to repeat the experience. "But I'd miss not seeing," I tell the unseen guide. "Well, then," she replies, "if you want to see, you can require it and you'll have it." The scene shifts to a house on a hill where we are to catch some transportation. I awake, finding myself pressing hard with my lower teeth against my front teeth.
("Pusball—Bell-Flower," May 3, 1975)

The Bell-Flower—*dream flower of the Sacred Center of my Dream Mandala.*

The Pale White Child—*dream deity of the Sacred Center of my Dream Mandala.*

Needless to say, this dream renewed me, too. Awake, I felt as though I had completed, with the help of the female guide, some crucial life's work.

Male figures are still important in many of my dreams. Their number and power have remained constant; several are good and guiding figures. (One gray-haired gentleman with glasses, for instance, taught me in a dream various ways to project out of my physical body.) The men remain staunch dream characters; it is the females who have shifted dramatically.

Instead of the hurt, suffering little girls who populated my past dreams, the women have gained a strength of their own. At times, I *observe* the fantastic creatures, as I saw the Branching Woman and Ivory-Bosom. I once descended in a dream, clinging to damp stone walls, to an underground grotto. There, in a tiled chamber, across a clear pool where marvelous statues glittered submerged under the water, I watched a beautiful woman with fresh flowers in her long dark hair—garbed like a priestess or goddess—talk to a boy. Another time, I saw a sick, dying queen, hidden by a long dark cloak and a hood, flee on horseback with her newborn baby to a place where he could be spirited away to safety. I have observed women and men with miraculous children: one, for instance, was a pale white child whose lower body was like a fish and whose upper torso was that of a boy; on his head grew hundreds of tiny Buddha-heads. I have watched fertility rites in scenes of splendor.

I saw another remarkable woman in the course of a long dream:

After having saved a man from drowning, I am at a political rally when, suddenly, a princess appears. She is most unusual: her head and naked upper torso are that of a shapely woman; her lower body is that of a delicate fawn. All of her—skin, fur, and long, flowing hair—is snow white. Across the white fur-skin at the base of her throat is a circlet formed of drops of scarlet. Upon her head grows a crownlike arrangement of small rounded horns (marking her as a descendant of the Branching Woman).

Beside her, huddled alongside her flank, are four small children that she embraces with an outstretched arm (no doubt a reflection of our four "children"). A voice speaks:

Does the love of the want fall short?

Does the love of the strife fail strength?

Determined to capture this scene, I rouse myself to awaken and write it.

("The Fawn Princess," August 10, 1974)

Sometimes, as in the dream of the guide and the pusball—bell-flower, instead of merely observing the unusual woman, I am the recipient of much kindness. Strong women, some six feet tall, comfort and rest me in my dreams. One pillowed my weary head upon her thick gray hair. Another, a physician, showed me a way to rub my body to heal myself.

At other times, the source of mystery and strength and wisdom seems to emanate from within myself, as with "Xerxes" and other similar dreams that came later. In one of these I spoke eloquently to great crowds; in another my own eyes seemed to be a source of light that directed illumination whenever I looked. I have, in dreams, participated in mysterious rituals and initiation rites, with other women, that imparted power.

I believe that this change in the quality of dream character is a direct reflection of my shift in self-concept. As my ability to cope with the problems of my life increased, the strength of my dream women grew. Dreaming of more capable women, I felt and acted even more capably while awake.

Thus, I have evolved a series of strong dream women, many of them goddesses. A kind of liberation of my dream world has occurred. No longer am I identified with the suffering child in a male-dominated dream society; I identify with the strength of the women in my dreams, and, at times, as in the "Xerxes" dream and later ones, the source of strength emanates directly from within myself.

These changes in my dreams parallel the changes in my waking world. Once, the stage curtains of my father's marionette theater hid me from view and all I had to do was repeat the lines correctly and pull the strings properly. Now I stand alone, center stage, and am unafraid. As a child, I operated the control sticks that made the puppets dance; then I learned how to dance myself—in life and in sex. Now my very cells seem to dance as the current continues to vibrate through them.

I find myself, aged forty-three, midstream of life, evolving inwardly and outwardly. I have discovered that I can relax the rigid control I found essential in adolescence to contain the raging forces within. I free my body to the rhythms of the dance of life; I free my mind to rely upon my own experience. I permit myself to ponder notions that my scientific training held in disrepute and to step into a land where there are few maps—the realms of lucid dreaming, astral travel, and deep meditation—wherever and whatever these states of mind are. I write with freer mind and draw with freer hand. Stories and sketches leap easily from dream to pen. I let my thoughts wander on a looser rein, even as I let the current roam.

A recent dream expresses well this sense of growing freedom:

At the end of a long ordinary dream, I am flying in the air high above cities, fully conscious that I dream. Below me, I see scenes from my life, as though I am reviewing my life's events from this perspective. One scene is of a boy and a girl kissing in the center of a large tree. I can make out an exceptionally clear scene of a city by some water, a lake or a river. Carefully noting the details so that I can later determine whether it is an actual location in the waking world, I stretch out full-length and fly over the water. The light is shining brilliantly on the water, stronger on the right-hand side, I notice. After a long flight, I hurtle myself downward and splash into the water, as my body floods with sexual pulsations.

Feeling pleased with myself that I should understand, I think, "I'm going into the water now because I hear a noise." There is a sound, crackling and sizzling like fire, on the top of my head. My face is awhir with strong vibrations. Then, in a rush, I feel a stream of energy exiting from the sizzling spot on the top of my head. All is quiet. Through the lapping of the blue water I see the reflection of a lovely flower shape. I awaken, feeling superb.

("Stream of Energy," April 14, 1977)

The image of myself and the stream of energy is related to the Branching Woman and all her relatives. The lovely flower shape, seen through the blue water, seems to be a version of the earlier pusball-bell that transformed into a flower. The opening within my-self continues.

In deep slumber, then, the current races through my relaxed body, taking first this form, then that form, in my dreaming mind. In my conscious dreams, I literally feel, hear, and see its movement. In deep meditation, the current rumbles through my relaxed body, bringing its refreshing bliss. Awake or asleep, when my body is re-laxed and yet the current is aroused, flowing freely and vigorously, I am renewed. Asleep, I am conscious of dreaming; awake, I let my-

The Woman with the Stream of
Energy—*dream deity of the Sacred
Center of my Dream Mandala.*

self fantasize more freely. Day and night are blending and both are beautiful.

As the current moves more and more easily through the centers of my body, I find that archetypal images emerge ever more often. The archetypes of my dreams are many, yet they are, I believe, all derived from a single source: the moving current. I think that the varied shapes of our dreams tell us of the location and the blockage or movement of the basic life energy dwelling and circulating within us; the picture in our dreams speak of the physiological changes in our sleeping selves.

In fact, I believe that *the reason archetypes exist at all is that the physiological basis of the images—be they dream pictures or mythological creatures—is identical: their forms depict the movement of the current.*

Individual symbolism varies. I dream of a Branching Woman or a Fawn Princess who has personal significance to me. An ancient Egyptian may have dreamt of Isis with her Hathor-horned crown that had personal significance to that dreamer. But both of us see an image with a headpiece because at that moment the current is circulating in our own heads, creating the image that fits our framework. Essentially, the process of the movement of the current in the head is the same.

Archetypes are similar in varied cultures because the human experience—the movement of the current—is identical. All persons, ancient and modern, experience in dreams the circulation of the current. If we are lucky, we lead the current to our waking world.

Branching Woman and her sisters, strong, good, wise, and beautiful, speak of a strength that has crystallized within me. I have absorbed some of their power in dreams and brought it to daily life. Still sensing that I am on the verge of the greatest gamble of all, I now feel safe. I have passed a barrier. I am unafraid because I have been there before in my dreams. . . .

18 THE SACRED CENTER OF THE DREAM MANDALA
Chief Deity: The Branching Woman

We have arrived at the Sacred Center, the birthplace of all images. Here dwells the most precious figure. From it, every other figure emerges, shines, and then melts back into the central figure once more. Having crossed the three protective circles, entered the temple walls by the eastern gate, and traversed the four quarters around the Dream Mandala, we meet, at last, in the center, the mother of all dream figures.

Even as the limbs of a great tree encompass its life history, so do the figures of our dreams depict our inner evolution. Sometimes, when I walk down the cool, damp pathways of Muir Woods, beneath the cathedral-like arches of the giant redwoods, I fall under a spell cast by the quiet, the plash of water over rocks, and the call of birds. In the hush of dappled sunlight, I gaze at a particular tree and observe, eternally captured—at least for so long as that tree exists— the pattern of its life. See, here's an old wound. Look there, where its thick bark was charred by the fire of 1908. See how it grew around this obstacle, spreading its life force to incorporate it, and going forward. Always and ever, its branches reach toward the small shafts of sunlight that pierce the dense overhead growth of the taller trees. Stretching and stretching, sending forth new shoots, it tries in yet another direction to reach its own spot of golden light.

Our psychic growth, like the branches of the tree, is recorded for all our time in the pattern of past dreams. We can trace it well, observe old wounds, follow the circuitous routes of passage we have taken until now. We, too, reach toward sunlight to nourish our growth. If our world is too crowded, if the dark is too solid, we end up stunted and shriveled. We, too, must have light to survive. Only, for us, the life-giving light is internal as well as external.

I have watched with wonder this inner light emerging through the twisting evolution of my own dreams. Delving back into the volumes of my records over the past twenty-nine years, I am amazed and fascinated to see the unfolding patterns of symbols, to trace their meandering routes that, at the time of their dreaming, were blocked to my vision. Now, as though able to see from an aerial view, when before I was earthbound, the life pattern is clearly visible. I feel as though I begin to truly understand.

I have already spoken of the movement in my dream life from characters who were passive and negative to those who were more often active and positive. I have described dreams of fear yielding to dreams of anger, giving way, in turn, to dreams of wonder. The cast who played dream roles when I was fourteen have shifted from ordinary folk of my immediate environment to include characters of archetypal depth and richness. The women in particular became goddesslike figures of supreme inner strength, reflecting, and in part producing, the shift in my own self-concept. The deities of my Dream Mandala are *goddesses*, not gods, suggesting a psychological identity fulfilled.[1] The sophisticated, complex symbols of today have all had their own antecedents—a primitive ancestor, so to speak, a cave-person relative. Simple and crude, even savage, these figures have been forerunners of their mature descendants.

The same evolutionary pattern is, I believe, unrolling in my dream images of light. For some three years I had noticed that my lucid dreams would often contain imagery of light. Now, this is not simply the general change in quality—the brightening of images or the translucency of colors—but also there is a specific *source of* light. For instance, in the "The Bluebird Tree," dream, the colors were brilliant; in addition I *felt* a point of buzzing light that traced a pattern around my buttocks while I *watched* a crack of light in the sky. The light often takes the form of a line or a crack, such as illumination gleaming from underneath a closed door or shining through a space like a window. In "Paddeus and the Jungle Fighter," the light came from beyond a moving window, and in "The Land of Breeze and Light," it streamed in through open windows on all sides of the room. When I go in dreams through "the hole in the earth" I always move *toward* the light on the other side. Often the light I notice in lucid dreams seems to reflect from the sparkles of moonlight or sunlight upon the waves of ocean or river, or from the moon itself. In a most unusual dream, on a dark night, I stood on the top of a high tower and watched troops attacking people below. I alone could see because light emanated from inside my own eyes; I swooped down to rescue the victims.

Since I have been practicing Taoist meditation, I often select in dreams, whether they are lucid or not, the pathway or staircase (representing the channel along which the current moves) that leads upward toward an intense light. Once, in a dark dream, a great light flashed on and off, illuminating a whole countryside. In another, I saw a strange globelike apparatus in the sky that sparkled and glowed, fascinating me.

Parallel with the growing awareness of the important role that light takes in my dreams, there was an understanding of the symbolic function of images of eyes. In my personal dream language, I have determined that dream pictures of "eyes" reflect the condition of my "I"—that is, my self-concept. This "eye/I," my self-concept, has shifted over the last twenty-nine years, evolving, even as the images of women have evolved, and the change is traceable through the shapes that eyes have taken in my dreams.[2]

As with the figures of women, my early images of eyes, and my responses to them, were commonplace. I would notice the color of a dream figure's eyes; some were pretty, some repulsive and ugly, others intriguing. As I matured, the images of eyes took on more and more unusual forms. Once, when I was thirty-five, in a dream I cared for the injured eye of a half-drowned butterfly. By then, I knew my symbolic dream language well enough to recognize the injured creature as myself, and was relieved that my dream treatment proved effective.

Unusual eye images increased. When I was thirty-seven, for instance, I dreamt:

> A girl friend and I are catapulted from a swing at its forward arc. We zoom into the air and are then caught up and blown along by a great gust of wind. As I hurtle through the air, I can see below me, pedaling hard on bicycles trying to keep up with us, two girl friends from junior high school.
>
> The wind is blowing swift and cold (the coolness). At first it carries us back in the direction from which we came; then it shifts again and we are going in the right direction, sailing above snowy fields. Below us, I can see great flocks of pure white peacocks, all of them running across the snow. I notice that one of them, especially pretty, is apart from the crowd, with spots of blood at its mouth. Two other peacocks, taller than the rest, are running face to face. Suddenly, the wind dips us down and I am carried very close to them.
>
> The heads of the peacocks are beautiful—snowy white with sprays of feathers forming crowns. One in particular is extraordinary. I see him in profile with a single golden eye ringed with white feathers. The eye is glorious, glowing. I give an exclamation of delight as I glide down through the air toward the mov-

The Peacock with the Golden Eye—*dream bird of the Sacred Center of my Dream Mandala.*

ing figure. Just as I am about to land beside him, I awake. ("Peacock with the Golden Eye," November 9, 1972)

The image of the Peacock with the Golden Eye stayed with me hauntingly, yet I did not then connect it with the evolution of my own "eye," my self-concept.

Only after months of dreams of one-eyed people, and sometimes three-eyed people, did I connect the "eyes" ("I"'s) to myself, as in a dream when I was thirty-eight:

I am dressed to go out, wearing a fur coat, and checking my appearance in the mirror before leaving. As I do so, I notice, just below my hairline, almost hidden by the hair, a third eye. I wonder what it is for. Testing its vision, I decide it is not too good for seeing. My ordinary eyes look a bit puffy, as though I have been crying. I conclude that perhaps this is the eye of enlightenment, and think I will show it to Zal, but decide to wait until later. . . .
("The Third Eye," December 2, 1973)

Then, like music rising to a crescendo, images of single or triple eyes accelerated, in dream after dream. Once, for example, dreaming about goddesses, I saw a woman who was being taught to be a guru. She had one large green eye in the center of her forehead; my own hazel-green eyes could finally see the connection to myself. Finally, in an ordinary dream, I saw a woman with one large, round, globe-like eye stippled with a pattern of red; she was making an announcement. I was struck by her single eye; as I wondered about it, the dream became lucid, and, in a rush of insight, I comprehended that one eye symbolizes, for me, one "I," a unity, a whole person. The Peacock with the Golden Eye had offered the same message.

It was then I understood that in my dreams an eye is my I; eye = I. I am the awful I from which I shrink in terror; I am the half-drowned I that needs care; I am the red, the green, the yellow, the golden I. I am the one of three I's, the one of the global I.

By now, I have grown accustomed to seeing a third eye gaze back at me from my dream mirrors. A typical example of the form eyes currently take is a recent lucid dream:

> I am on the edge of a roof, looking into a mirror. At first I cannot see any reflection; startled, I say, "That means I'm dead." Then, smiling to myself, I correct the conclusion, "No, that means I'm dreaming." Now the image begins to take shape in the mirror as I watch, and I examine it carefully. The skin seems to be coming in rumply, oldish, scarredlike. I say to myself, "Oh, don't do that," and it clears as I look. The color of my ordinary eyes is, I observe, this time a deep blue. On my forehead, between my brows, is a mark that I know is a kind of rudimentary third eye. . . .
> (Opening scene, "Japanese Tea Garden," April 26, 1977)

I cannot resist quoting a portion of one more recent lucid dream with third-eye imagery:

At the end of an ordinary dream, I am in a bedroom looking into a mirror in the early morning. I am surprised to observe how large and dark the pupil on my left looks. As I examine it closely, I realize with a start that I have three eyes. They are straight across, with the third one directly between the others. I laugh softly to see this, realizing it means that I am dreaming.

I look into the mirror again and the reflection shows a man, with two eyes, a broad face, and curly hair. I say to myself with amusement, "And now I'm a man!" Then the image shifts once more to myself with the three eyes; I continue to examine them, the left with its larger pupil. Again the image shifts, and now, instead of a middle eye, in its place between my brows is a round spot. At first uncolored, the dot grows white and begins to pulsate. At that, my whole body starts to throb. I feel the familiar surge of passion, and, hurrying downstairs, search for Zal. . . .

("The White Dot—Third Eye on the Woman-Man," August 28, 1977)

This dream contains several images connected with the movement of the current: the larger left pupil suggests the greater intensity of the current on my left side; the curly hair of the man who is also myself speaks of the current in my own head; the third eye—white dot that pulsates is the strong pulsation that occurs at the root of my nose as the current passes. I felt it first in meditation and now periodically during my waking hours. Some dream theorists would see the image of myself—a man as an inner unification of male and female aspects, the merging of opposites within me. The stairs that I raced down as the passion built in my body suggest to me the current as it descends into my pelvis.

Thus I came to realize that no matter what dream symbol I selected to trace—eyes, light, a Branching Woman, headpieces, red hair, dancers—each one led, eventually, to the movement of the current within me. It was as if I had begun at the source of the Penob-scot River, and then started over again at the Hudson River, and then commenced once more from the corner creek and followed the route to the Schuylkill, to the Delaware River, and then, continuing to its mouth, made the astonishing discovery that each separate stream led at last to the same Atlantic Ocean.

Twisting, turning, merging, each one expressing its own nature, but blending with the larger body of which it was a part, these dream images alone—isolated in a single dream—had limited sym-bolic meaning. Seen from above, as part of a total system, their rela-tionship stood out; they led to the same conclusion: *each dream image was a momentary expression, at a certain spot in my own body, of the vast flow of life energy.*

For most people, as it was for me for most of my life, this con-nection of single dream images to the current of life is obscured. I believe that the tensions of our lives, the rigidities of our bodies and spirits, prevent us from experiencing all but a trickle of the dynamic power latent within. During dreams, when our bodies are relaxed and our minds release their grip, the inner energy stirs, but its movement may be chaotic and its pathways clogged, its centers tan-gled and silent.

I did not realize it at the time, but I was systematically unrav-eling the knots in my own psychic channels.[3] One by one, I was working upward through my body, loosening and expanding each psychic center.

The dancing that had always given me pleasure through my first marriage had surely kept active the "bubbling springs" on the soles of my feet. The dramatic change, however, began with loving Zal. When my body finally became sexually responsive with him, I grew to know sensuous flow and orgasmic ecstasy. My lower centers be-came fully awakened.

When I began belly dancing, not only was I continuing to stir pelvic energies, I also puffed my diaphragm, stretched my stomach in and out, and rolled it up and down—slowly, inexorably raising my awareness to the navel and solar-plexus centers.

If it had not been for my dream life, my awareness might have become permanently blocked at this level. But, in my dreams, I glimpsed something beyond the joy of sexuality and the delight of dancing: I *flew*; I fell into spells; I saw and experienced extraordinary sights; I knew that I dreamt even as I dreamt. As I struggled to encounter that world of brilliant color and mighty power more often, I succeeded in re-evoking the special state of mind. I heard whirring sounds; I felt buzzing vibrations; I flew upward and swooped downward; I exploded into light; I seemed to move in and out of my body.

As these marvels unfurled in my dream state, I gradually became aware that I was, now and then while awake, experiencing uncanny insights. I sensed in these intuitions—trivial on the whole, yet impressive to me—a kind of "gathering" of strength.

These psychic experiences made me willing to consider styles of thinking that my training as a psychologist had ignored. I read more widely, searching for something that was congruent with my experience that could help me to understand it. I played with ideas as I had with my dolls and later with my marionettes; I invented stories once more; I let fantasy back into my waking life. This, too, was a growing flexibility.

When I experienced acupuncture, I discovered that the tremendous energy within myself need not be confined to dreams. I had turned to acupuncture in a time of stress, and found more than a treatment; I found a revitalization. My energies were released from their local homes, dispersed, and surged around the universe of my body. Never before having realized that I could feel so vibrant, except in a lucid dream, I sought a way to cling to the sense of well-being and uncovered Taoist meditation.

Then, as I practiced Taoist meditation, I circulated the energy that released a torrent. No longer confined to a magnificent orgasm or a sprightly dance, the current soars through my body in waking time as well as dreamtime. My body tingles in every crevice, rumbles up my legs and across my pelvis; liquid fire laps up my spine to sparkle from my crown, and, glowing golden as the current passes my eyes, it cascades downward, refreshing me. My whole body purrs, alive and aglow. The point of buzzing light from "The Bluebird Tree" dream is a waking reality; I feel its movement every day. It is the current that my dreams foretold.

If I had not gone back in my dreams to the house on Willow Grove Avenue, I would never have truly discovered myself. As though stumbling upon a trunk in that dim and dusty attic, opening it, and finding that it is laden with jewels that fill my world with light, I found the key to understanding myself in those dreams. Had I not re-entered the cold stone walls of that house in dreams, I would not have rediscovered my heritage: a rich fantasy life. Fantasy, in a healthy form, helped me learn how to steer myself, first in dreams and then in waking meditation, through the ring of raindrops, through the hole in the screened porch, where all things seem possible.

The cold stone walls of the house on Willow Grove Avenue became the temple walls demarcating my space of personal power. Perhaps I had needed the suffering that my sensitive skin brought me as an adolescent to attune me to subtler vibrations. Only later did I realize that the skin boundary of my own body was also, in a sense, temple walls. Within them, I traversed the quarters and encountered my dream deities.

If, then, I had not written this book to arrange the images of my dreams, I would never have explored their patterns so carefully and seen, eventually, the *grand* pattern. I looked to my dreams and I discovered myself.

Now, in the waking state, I am at a new beginning of experiences that previously I had only seen snatches of in lucid dreams. Almost every single experience I have had in Taoist meditation has been experienced beforehand in a lucid dream. Every bodily sensation I have felt first in a lucid dream I subsequently had in meditation. I dream of dancing on hot, bubbling mud; I meditate and the current rumbles out of the soles of my feet with an identical sensation. I dream of dancing on my toes, ballerina-style; I awake and my toes are tingling with the current; I meditate and the current springs up and rushes to my great toes with the same sensation. I dream of a Lightheaded Dancer or a Mirror Gazer and grow dizzy; I meditate and grow lightheaded. I dream that I lift aloft and fly; I meditate and feel the bright, burning tip of the current fly up my spine.[4] I dream that I wear twinkling golden nail polish on each fingernail; awake, I meditate and my fingertips tingle with radiance. I dream of being petted all over my body simultaneously; I meditate and feel a sort of shiver run across my skin and raise my hairs with a sensation of being lightly petted.

I understand! I understand at last! My lucid dreams have the same content as my meditation periods because both are part of the mystic process: *lucid dreams are microcosms of the mystic experience.*

The current is set in circulation in dreams and in meditation (presumably in other ways, as well), and, with its flow, the current brings the same physiological experiences. These bodily changes, brought about by the moving current, solidify into momentary dream images; the same current may create visions in meditation. Each dream image or vision has personal symbolic meaning (and learning to read that meaning has been a joy), but each picture also arises out of the flow of the current. Every dream image is an expression of the movement of the current captured, like "freezing" a motion picture of a sporting event into a still portrait.[5] What we call archetypes are manifestations, made by other people in other cultures and other times, condensed and solidified from *their* current moving in them in identical ways to the way it moves in me. *The movement of the current congeals into a dream form, a single manifestation of infinite possible forms.*

Furthermore, I saw that in working my way around the mandala, I was doing more than arranging dream images based upon an ancient schema. I was *literally* working my way around my body. I had been blind to the most obvious fact, until I had almost finished writing this book: *the movement around the mandala is identical to the movement of the current around my body.*

Beginning at the Eastern Quarter, the dancing figures of my dreams—the Temple Dancer, the Dancing Cat, the Lightheaded Dancer—all spoke of the current as it rumbled in my own feet. All my dreams of dancing over the years were probably minor stirrings of the force that gushes from my bubbling springs now. The dancing that produces dizziness, the dizziness of the trancelike state of the Mirror Gazer, was the first step of my lucid dreams, crystallized into the Eastern Quarter.

Moving to the Southern Quarter, to my High Flyer in all her variations, animal as well as human—the Polka Dot Horse, the Butterfly, the Bluebird—I was recording the second phase of lucid dreaming: the sense of flight. I did not then think how the current was rising in my own legs as I dreamt.

Reaching the third phase of my lucid dreams, in the Western Quarter I placed my Strawberry Lady and my images of love and passion. The luscious fruits and flowers of love were placed here without realizing that by then the mounting current had reached my pelvis and, swirling through my genitals as it does with every dreamer, brought me to beautiful orgasm.

Into the Northern Quarter I went, setting my dream images of sound and tactile sensations, personified in the image of She of the Bell Tones. The exquisite notes I heard, the rush of air and water, the throb of poetry, the pulse of dance music—all fit here. So, too, went the feel of wind and wave, kissing lips, petting hands, the feathery strokes of my lucid dreams. Even yet, I did not recognize that my current, reaching so high in my sleeping body, was rushing by my inner ears and tracing fine tremors over the whole surface of my skin. Dreaming, my mind transformed the pulsing, quivering current into pictures that resonated and tingled.

Only now, deep into the meditation that began long after I started to write this book, can I see. Now, as I turn to write of the Sacred Center, I understand. Now, as I consider the Branching Woman in her numerous forms—her headpieces and hairstyles, animal manes, and vegetable topknots—I finally comprehend.

In a revelation, I recognize that in reaching the Sacred Center, the current of energy that circulates in my dreams has ascended from the soles of my feet, through my psychic centers, and reached my own head. There it radiates, shaping a dream figure with a headpiece, before it plunges into its downward path. Awake, meditating, I feel the same current streaming, *branching*, like the Branching Woman, only downward, to every side of my skull, down my neck, down my cheeks, down my forehead and nose, where the tributaries merge at my tongue and descend.

With my newly opened eyes, I see that my Branching Woman is my version of an ancient archetype, not merely of the Horned Goddess, but on an even grander scale; she is the psychic center of the head, my own thousand-petaled lotus, flowering, blooming, open to every direction.

The same current must have been flowing through the skull of some ancient Hindu when he depicted the psychic center of the head as a thousand-petaled lotus, unfolding, hanging downward, pouring radiant light into the meditator; some Tibetan Buddhist, too, drew the head center as a lotus, this time with thirty-two petals emanating rainbow light; a Chinese acupuncturist of long ago probably felt the same current when he named the topmost point *pei hui,* the "hundred crossroads";[6] the Taoist sage who first drew the head of an enlightened one with an "upper cauldron" inside it, merging the lights of the sun and the moon, must have felt that current, too. For me, the antler-branches of Branching Woman were an early dream version of this same theme. The image that emotionally touches each dreamer is the one that is *inborn,* of our own sensations, our personal version of the current as it illuminates.

The Branching Woman, then, is the chief deity of the Sacred

Center of my Dream Mandala. From her, flanked by her attendants and consorts, emanate my other dream deities. She, in her rightful place, marks the center of my growth—the insight I had as I reached the middle of the mandala. Her image guided me to self-discovery. She is an appropriate representative of the ruler of the Sacred Center, who is the conqueror of ignorance.

In Tibetan Buddhism, this conqueror is named Vairocana,* the "Brilliant One." Pure white, he is seated upon a lotus throne borne by a lion. The flowing mane of the lion seems most apt in view of my own dream images of flowing manes and hair. In Vairocana's hands on his lap he holds the Wheel of the Law, symbol of the teachings of Buddha. At times, Vairocana depicts this symbol by holding his two hands in a circular form meant to indicate that he is turning the Wheel of the Law; that is, spreading the teachings. Branching Woman holds my version of the Wheel of the Law—the small hypnotic wheel.

White is Vairocana's "color," like a crystal from which the other colors emerge as in a rainbow. His whiteness resembles his element: ether, matter, space. *Vairocana conquers the evil of ignorance and delusion* by the wisdom of the Absolute Truth, the All-Embracing Wisdom.[7]

Vairocana, like the other deities, appears in numerous forms, peaceful and wrathful, as a king or as a monk, with or without his consort, Vajra-dhatvisvari. His attendants, including He Who Bears the Wheel of the Law, and their consorts often appear in the Sacred Center depicted in mandalas in the form of colored dots. In similar manner, Branching Woman, as my chief deity, could be flanked by her attendants, appropriately in white color and headdress: the Fawn Princess, the Pale White Child, the many hatted and bonneted women of

* pronounced Vī·rō·*chah*·nă

Vairocana—*chief deity of the Sacred Center of Tibetan Buddhist mandalas.*

my dreams, myself as Xerxes, and with the stream of energy. They all belong to the Sacred Center of my Dream Mandala.

Having dispelled my own ignorance with the image of Branching Woman, I see dream figures as part of a unified whole. And, as after a revelation, these days I perceive everything differently. Recently, I came across a photograph of a tribal shaman with circular designs painted on his cheeks, and I recognized at once, "Oh, yes, that's where the whirlpools were in my cheeks in the dream of Fixedness." A friend recently gave Zal and me a mask carved in New Guinea, and at first glance I saw the dotted lines drawn in the paint across the cheeks and knew it was no simple primitive pattern: it is exactly the path the current takes in slow, bright dots as it crosses my own cheeks. Each primitive drawing, each mystic art form has new meaning for me now because it has parallels grounded in my own experience.

My understanding spreads wider and wider. I notice how some methods of hypnotic induction induce eye movement, such as focusing on a bright, swinging object, in order to bring about a trance state. When dreamers have rapid eye movements automatically, as a normal part of the dream state, they are possibly stirring the current just as I do deliberately in meditation. The optic nerves are closely connected with the brain and its state. The eye movements of hypnosis, Taoist meditation, and ordinary dreaming are surely related to the special state of mind that accompanies them.

More and more pieces fall into place from this new viewpoint. I have a friend, a frequent lucid dreamer, who constructs drums. Whenever he has a wound from working with tools and he becomes lucid in a dream, he visualizes his wound as healed during the dream. Awake, he claims that after "healing" himself in a lucid dream, his wound is always much more improved than it would have been without the dream.

Acceleration of healing could be expected if the current were directed to a particular spot. A hypnotist has reported a case of warts dropping off his entranced subject's hands when told to imagine that heat was traveling to the warts and burning them off.[8] Yogis have claimed for centuries to be able to send their *prana* to any place in their bodies and produce changes in temperature, create and remove bumps, etc. Taoist meditators assert they can send their *ch'i* out and effect similar changes. I have observed a Taoist master produce within seconds, on request, spots of scarlet on his palms and then remove them; and I have felt with my own hand intense heat issue from his neck and crown when he indicated to me that the *ch'i* had reached these areas. All these mysterious events are explicable by the movement of the current in a directed fashion.

Recently, Russian scientists have reported being able to predict forthcoming physical disease with great accuracy based upon the dreams of their patients.[9] Perhaps they are pinpointing areas of congestion of the current that leads to disease. Perhaps when a dreamer does not have figures analogous to my dream deities of the four quarters and Sacred Center in his or her dreams, we can infer that the current of energy is blocked in the area of the body these figures represent: the feet (dancing deities); the legs (flying deities); the genitals (passionate deities); the sensory organs (deities of sound and touch); the head (deities with headpieces and hairstyles). It is an exciting potential for lucid dreamers and meditators to explore!

Not only do my eyes see anew, and embrace new possibilities, but also my body *feels* anew. With my psychic centers open, at least partially, every experience has a first-time quality to me. Like a finely calibrated measuring device, my body reacts to each sensation. Every musical tone, every fragrance, every taste of food is responded to by the current within. This food dampens its force, so I avoid it; that food magnifies it, so I eat more. This fragrance sends it wildly racing; that one leaves it unmoved. A certain tone makes my solar plexus ache; another starts the flow coursing down my head into my cheeks. Gounod's *Faust*, for example, leaves the current placidly wandering; Wagner's *Das Rheingold* whips it to a whirlwind, perhaps because it is more akin to its own thunderous nature. Tibetan gongs, *Shiatsu* massage, exerting pressure on the centers send the current scurrying madly about my insides. Its presence comforts me; when I feel it purring within, shifting now here, now there, I feel good. When, rarely, it deserts me, my energy ebbs in the deadly quiet. Each waking hour I learn more of the current's moods and how to increase its heat and light.

In constructing my Dream Mandala, then, I have made a pictorial map of the psychic energy that moves inside me day and night. My Dream Mandala is a picture of wholeness. I recognize at last that all of my dream figures, in their endless variations, are momentary crystallizations of the movement of the current. It is my hypothesis that in lucid dreams the current is, as it is during meditation, circulating correctly in my psychic channels. When I fly upward in a dream, the current is then, at that moment, ascending the back midline channel in my spine; when I hurtle downward in a dream, the current is then descending my front midline channel. When I burst into orgasmic ecstasy in a dream, the current rumbles in my genitals; when patterns of light spin before my eyes in a dream, the current is whirling in my head. They are all truly one; all dream images are born of the moving current.

These precious images of dreams are like snapshots taken of a

growing child; they catch and hold a fleeting moment. By placing them into the mandala in their proper order, as though arranging photographs of the ripening child into an album, I have traced the pathway of the current these images represent. Yet I need not cling to them greedily, for they are of one source, the source of life. It moves within me ceaselessly, dissolving one image, ever-creating a new image. Eventually, perhaps, I will see beyond all the images to the source itself. If so, it will be because these precious dream deities of mine have lit the inner path.

The burst of ecstasy in swirling light is one aspect of lucid dreaming that has not yet been duplicated in waking meditation. As my experience in meditation grows, as I sense the shifts within my body and I feel the stage of liquid fire begin, I suspect that the great ecstasy is a culminating part of the ongoing process. My dreams suggest its approaching force, as recently when:

Facing page:
My Personal Dream Mandala—completed. The dots represent attendants and minor deities.

I am in a house on a hill with family and friends discussing air crashes that have been taking place. All the shades in the living room, narrow white ones, have been lowered. I raise them, letting in the sunlight. As we talk, I hear a loud whirring sound. I say, "Now, that sounds like it" (an airplane about to crash).

The noise grows louder and I call everyone to me—Zal, children, friends. We all crouch on the living-room floor, face down in a circle with our heads toward the center and our arms around each other. I peek to see what the tremendous noise is and see, sure enough, it is a huge plane directly approaching the spot in the house where we are huddled. At first I think, or someone else says, "God hates us," to let us all die this way. But I think, "No, just love Him."

The noise reaches a crescendo, the room shakes, and the plane crashes into the house and us. My eyes are closed and I can feel myself being blown apart into atoms. Somehow I know that I will not feel any pain with an impact as strong as this. My body is breaking, I am dissolving into atoms and dispersing through the air, and yet I hold my consciousness. The knowledge that my awareness will endure keeps me serene even as we are being blown apart, and I awake.

("The Airplane Crash," July 10, 1977)

This dream of the airplane crash, for all the apprehension it aroused, left me with an afterglow of calm, a serenity. It seems to represent the next step, and I am ready.

From the Branching Woman at the center emerge, on rose petals, the chief deities of my dreams—the Mirror Gazer, the High Flyer, the Strawberry Lady, and She of the Bell Tones. Their consorts and attendants come forth. They shimmer; they fly; they surge with passion; they whir with rhythm; they are radiant with energy. Shining in splendor, they multiply and shift their luminous forms. They rise, take shape, and live in a dream; then they dissolve back into the formless mass, the mother of all forms. These dream figures are born for a night and they die in the morning.

And yet their spirit lives on in me and in all who dream. These divinities have shown me their power; they have left traces in my body and soul. The current that runs through me speaks their names. It bubbles the hot springs in my feet, making my dream figures dance; it climbs my legs and lifts my dream figures aloft; it whirls across my genitals and leads my dream figures to love; it mounts my spine in a fiery river and sends blissful sparkles from my crown; it cascades waterfall-fashion down my brow; it rivets my tongue; and, wriggling, it works its way back home to my pelvis, where it purrs ceaselessly.

The current revolving within—it is my *living* mandala. I bless its presence. I feel that I have touched the edge of its source.

Whatever shifting shapes may come and go in future dreams, whatever new paths the current takes, I know that these figures of the current born have a common origin, a central source. When the end comes, it will be, I am convinced, not an end, but a transition to a new shape . . . a new beginning . . . a new dream.

APPENDIXES

The Five Basic Tibetan Buddhist Deities*

ASSOCIATIONS	VAIROCANA	AKSOBHYA
Realm ruled over (location in mandala)	Sacred Center	Eastern Quarter
Color of body	White	Blue
Element represented	Ether, space	Water
Season represented	All-Pervasive (presumably)	Winter
Time of day	All time (presumably)	Dawn (sky before sunrise)
Personality "evil" to be conquered	Ignorance	Hatred
Wisdom that can transmute the "evil"	All-Embracing, *Dharmadatu* (absolute truth)	Wisdom of the Mirror (impartial reflection)
Gesture (*mudrā*)	Teaching, turning the Wheel of Law	Earth touching
Symbol	*Dharmachakra,* the Wheel of the Law	*Vajra* (*dorje*), diamond scepter
Family	Buddha	*Vajra*
Mystic consort	*Vajra-dhatvîśvarî,* Mother of the Space of Heaven	*Locanâ*
Animal supporting throne	Lion	Elephant
Associated *chakra*	Head (brow, crown)	Heart
My equivalent deities	Branching Woman	Mirror Gazer

* Called Meditation Buddhas (*Dhyani* Buddhas) by some and Celestial Conquerors (*jina*) by others. This chart is a simplified version, compiled from several sources that do not always agree; the sects differ among themselves, especially in elaboration.

RATNA-SAMBHAVA	AMITABHA	AMOGHA-SIDDHI
Southern Quarter	Western Quarter	Northern Quarter
Yellow	Red	Green
Earth	Fire	Wind, moving air
Autumn	Spring	Summer
Noon	Sunset	Dusk (evening, night)
Pride	Lust	Greed (envy, jealousy)
Wisdom of Equality (recognizing self in others)	Wisdom of Discernment (ability to see differences)	Wisdom of Perfected Action, All-Accomplishing Wisdom
Gift bestowing	Meditation	Fearlessness (blessing)
Ratna, the flaming jewel, wishing gem	*Padma*, the lotus (sometimes, the begging bowl)	*Viśvavajra*, the crossed or double *vajra* (sometimes, the flaming sword)
Ratna	*Padma*	*Karma*
Mâmakî	*Pâṇḍarâ*, She in White Raiment	*Târâ*, Saviouress
Horse	Peacock	Birdman (the *garuda*)
Navel	Throat	Perineum
High Flyer	Strawberry Lady	She of the Bell Tones

Note on Making a Personal Dream Mandala

Making your own personal Dream Mandala can become, as it did for me, an act of self-discovery. People who have collected their dreams often complain that they do not know what to do with them once they have them; their extensive dream records become more overwhelming than enlightening. Yet many of my students, when they have organized their dream images into mandala form—when they construct mandalas of their own—say that they have experienced growth in self-understanding.

If you would like to experiment with making a Dream Mandala of your own, you first need a collection of your dreams. (Suggestions for recalling and recording dreams are given in my *Creative Dreaming* and my Introduction to *Dream Notebook.*) With a record of your dreams in hand, you can proceed as follows:

1. *Search your dream diary for the images that are most powerful for you*—those that fascinate, awe, or inspire. These are the images that can transform.
2. *From verbal descriptions, translate these dream images back into visual form.* This does not mean that you have to be an artist yourself (although it is exciting to attempt to make dream images graphic). Search through magazines, books, etc., until you find reasonable facsimiles—images that stir feelings similar to those you experienced when you first saw your dream image. Use these photographs or drawings, or duplicate them—a color duplicating machine is helpful here—as the figures for your Dream Mandala.

   If you make your own dream figures, concentrate on *expression of feeling* rather than a finished product to be displayed. Dream Mandalas can be totally private meditation devices. The important principle is that the pictures should *emotionally move you* and be linked to images from your dreams; that is, they should be internally derived rather than externally applied.
3. *Contemplate the symbolism of each dream-derived picture.* Think about its various aspects and what it might represent to you. Notice what attracts your attention about it, and your feeling response to it.
4. *Arrange your dream-derived pictures by category.* Observe whether they fall into the categories encompassed by the Tibetan Buddhist mandala as described throughout the body of this book:

Hatred and Anger	Eastern Quarter
(or Fear of these)	
Pride	Southern Quarter
Lust	Western Quarter
Greed, Envy, or Jealousy	Northern Quarter
Ignorance	Sacred Center

Perhaps your dreams contain images that seem to go *beyond* these personality "faults," that represent, for you, a "conquering" of them; use such images if you have them. If, however, these categories seem forced or not right, you can try sorting your dream images by elements—water (for example, dreams of tidal waves), earth, fire, air, or space; Or sort your dream images by color—blue (for example, my "Bluebird Tree" dream), yellow, red, green, and white. Use your internal feelings as a guide. You may want to try one scheme temporarily and later experiment with another, or devise your own. Find an arrangement that makes sense to you, where you are now.

5. *Construct a mandala framework for your dream-derived pictures.* Any material can be used for this purpose. You could, for instance, have the outline in this book enlarged; I had my local duplicating service blow it up to a sixteen-inch diameter for the outermost edge, making it easy to mount on an eighteen-by-twenty-four-inch bulletin board. Some of my students simply traced or sketched a mandala outline on paper; others painted their mandalas in color on poster boards; still others constructed them in three dimensions.

One student built her mandala like a mobile. Revolving from a central branch, it was hung with objects—feathers, beads, stones, etc. —that had personal significance for her from her dreams. Another student made hers by arranging selected tarot cards into a mandala pattern.

Dream Mandalas can be rendered in virtually any medium: they can be woven into rugs; they can be applied to screens and scrolls; they can be built of tiles or mosaics into a table or inlaid floor; they might be worked in needlepoint for pillows or embroidered onto clothes and tablecloths, etc.

6. *Place your dream-derived pictures into the mandala frame.* Tibetan Buddhists depict their mandalas in paint on cloth or fresco. Temporary ones are made of colored sand, piles of rice, or with symbolic gestures of the hands. Some mandalas are even produced in a dance pattern. Others are built of wood or bronze in three dimensions; like

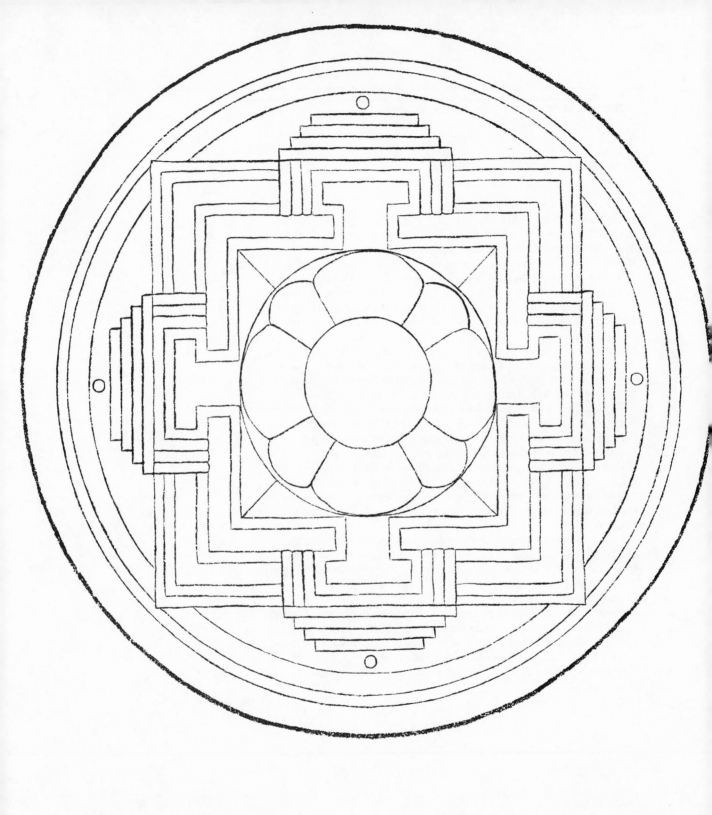

tiny temples, the deities in them look out of windows as though they were inhabitants of dollhouses. The form that *your* mandala takes is limited only by your imagination and the use to which you wish to put your finished product.

For some people, insights come *during* the construction of their mandalas. For others, it is their use *afterward* as a contemplation device that is more meaningful. When used this way, the imagery begins at the center. From a pinpoint, picture the central deity growing; let the other deities expand outward from the central one; when finished contemplating them, let the visualization contract back into the center again and dissolve. Examining our personal dream language and organizing it into the archetypal mandala form can lead to a synthesis; the Way of the Dream Mandala is a way of inner wisdom.

The patterns that are evolving within us—our internal mandalas—are, I believe, able to emerge more easily as we attend to them. By giving our dream images visual form in the waking world, we can appreciate their richness, their symbolism, and their relationship to the whole of ourselves. But we must remember that a completed mandala is only a picture of where we are at a moment of our development. Like a snapshot of ourselves at age six, the picture stays the same; whereas we continue to change and grow. Forming and dissolving anew, we continuously create—and travel around—the ever-changing mandala within ourselves; it is our connection to the great pattern.

Facing page:
Basic Diagram of a Mandala—*to be used for constructing personal Dream Mandalas.*

NOTES

Numbers in italics refer to entries in the Bibliography.

2 THE GREAT STEERING WHEEL

1. Lucid dreaming has recently received greater attention in the literature. For further information, see *14, 26, 28, 37, 75, 77*.

3 THE OUTERMOST RIM OF THE DREAM MANDALA

1. See *Creative Dreaming, 28*.
2. For more information on mandalas in general, see *3*; for Tibetan Buddhist mandalas, see *6, 35, 52, 81, 82*.
3. Carl G. Jung, *47*, p. 250.

4 THE HOUSE ON WILLOW GROVE AVENUE

1. Havelock Ellis, *22*, p. 145, and others have claimed that flying dreams diminish or cease in middle age. This is clearly not accurate for everyone, as my own have returned and increased in number.

5   THE TEMPLE WALLS OF THE DREAM MANDALA

1. This is psychologically equivalent to what Carlos Castaneda says Don Juan calls a "place of personal power."
2. Several sources (for example, *81*, p. 106) claim that initiates literally enter an initiation mandala—which may be drawn as large as eight feet on the ground—during an initiation ceremony. However, Stephan Beyer, an expert on Tibetan Buddhism who has lived in a Tibetan Buddhist monastery, finds this claim inconceivable. He said to me in a personal interview that walking into a mandala would be equivalent to a priest leading a worshiper physically onto an altar; the process is done in imagination, according to him.
3. According to the catalog of Nyingma Institute, Tarthang Tulku Rinpoche is a lama from Tarthang Monastery in eastern Tibet who journeyed in 1959 to Sikkim and then to India to serve as professor of Buddhist philosophy at the Sanskrit University in Benares. He arrived in Berkeley, California, in 1969, where he established the Tibetan-Nyingma Meditation Center and, later, the Nyingma Institute. For further information, write to the institute at 1815 Highland Place, Berkeley, California 94709.
4. According to Buddhist tradition, there are at least three "bodies" in which forms may appear. We are familiar with the physical form. There is also said to be a supernatural, transcending, and radiating form known as *sambhogakāya*. This is the plane of the actualization of visions; they are said to be controlled by the throat *chakra*, whose symbolic color is red—thus the meditation directed at the sunlight through the red curtains. There are believed to be two or three other forms that are of even higher reality than the physical or the visionary; see Lauf, *50*, p. 23.

6   THE TEMPLE DANCER

1. The traditional method of computing the expected date of delivery is to add 274 days—the average length of gestation—to the date of the first day of the last menstrual period. I mistakenly thought the 274 days should be added to the date of *conception*, which I knew, and so believed myself to be going into labor ten days early, when, in fact, I was exactly on schedule.
2. *Always advance toward pleasurable experience in dreams* is one of the Senoi "rules" of dreaming. See *Creative Dreaming, 28.*

7 THE EASTERN QUARTER OF THE DREAM MANDALA

1. Hall and Nordby, *39*, p. 87.
2. The ratios of male to female characters were similar in the two sets of dreams; the absolute numbers of characters were almost identical; the numbers of groups of all males or all females were roughly the same, as were the numbers and kinds of animal figures; my intensity of interaction with a few limited central characters remained stable; and six characters were identical despite the twenty-seven-year span between the two sets of dreams. As to social interaction, the numbers of aggressive interactions were almost the same, passive-negative emotions experienced by characters other than myself remained stable, and my positive emotions in the two sets of dreams were similiar. See "Dream Content —Does It Reflect Change in Self-Concept?" *29*.
3. Changes that I verified between the two sets of dreams separated by twenty-seven years included an increase in the number of mixed groups; a reduction in my role of victim in the dream; a slight increase in friendly interactions; a marked increase in sexual interactions; a decrease in passive-negative emotions expressed by myself; a dramatic increase in active-negative emotions expressed by myself, and also in those experienced by other dream characters; an increase in my experiences of wonder; an increase in the number of unusual dream events; an increase in the number of references to largeness and a decrease in references to smallness; as well as the difference in quality of female character that appeared in later dreams. See "Dream Content," *29*.
4. According to, among others, Anderson and Anderson, *2*, p. 13.
5. All of the paintings that I made for this book were originally sketched in dream records.
6. Aksobhya's color and position vary according to different sects. Some groups depict him as blue; others as white; some place him in the Eastern Quarter; others, less frequently, in the center. I do not think the labels matter, as long as there is a figure to represent his type of energy.

8 THE BIG GAMBLE

1. See "Keeping a Longitudinal Dream Record," *31*.

9 THE SECOND CIRCLE OF THE DREAM MANDALA

1. Robert Crookall, *16*; for example, pp. 54, 104.
2. Giuseppe Tucci, *82*, p. 318.

10 THE BLUEBIRD TREE

1. Reginald L. Hine, *42*, p. 53, says that he has concentrated on a flower of a specific color prior to falling asleep, and, having it by his side while he slept, nearly always had its color or its complementary color incorporated into his dream of that night. Different flowers produced different dreams, which recurred when the same flower was used again. My experience corresponds with his in the sense that the orange-yellow of the trees that impressed me during the day was transformed into the complementary color blue of the bluebird tree that impressed me at night.
2. Described in "Keeping a Longitudinal Dream Record," *31*.
3. Recent reports suggest that Kilton Stewart's account of the dream culture of the Senoi may be exaggerated. See Kilton Stewart, "Dream Theory in Malaya," in Charles Tart (ed.), *Altered States of Consciousness,* New York: Doubleday, 1972 (other references in *Creative Dreaming, 28*). No other sources have documented as extensive a system as Stewart describes. Regardless of the outcome of this inquiry, the Senoi dream "rules" work as principles.
4. Recounted in *Creative Dreaming, 28.*

11 THE SOUTHERN QUARTER OF THE DREAM MANDALA

1. Again, there is some disagreement among the sources. For example, Coxhead and Hiller, *15*, p. 92, claim that the Egyptians believed that the *ba,* represented as a jabiru-bird bearing the face of the deceased, leaves the body during dreams and at death. Muldoon and Carrington, *61*, p. 23, state that the *ka,* the vehicle of the soul in Egyptian tradition, was depicted as a sort of birdlike "double" of the deceased. *Ka* is more commonly cited. The important thing is that a human-headed bird represented the soul. Crookall, *16*, p. 51, says that the Greek symbol for the soul generally bore butterfly wings, while the Burmese symbol for the soul was a butterfly.
2. Robert Crookall, *16*, p. 187.
3. Mircea Eliade, *21*, p. 328.
4. Quoted in Raymond De Becker, *19*, p. 405.
5. Carl G. Jung, *46*, p. 323.
6. Jorge Luis Borges, *7*, p. 45.

12 THE LURE OF THE RUBY BIRD

1. I had recently read Robert Monroe's book, *60*.
2. The types of imagery I describe (which trigger lucid dreams) were suggested by Oliver Fox, *26*, and by C. E. Green, *37*.
3. See Shirley Motter Linde and Louis M. Savary, *55*, p. 171.
4. Recommendations for back sleeping to induce lucid dreams are found in Muldoon and Carrington, *61*, in Monroe, *60*, and in others; even the novelist George Du Maurier, *20*, advises it.
5. See Evans-Wentz, *24*, p. 216.
6. Described in Mariane Kohler and Jean Chapelle, *48*, p. 38, among others.
7. See, for example, the chapter on American Indian dreamers in *Creative Dreaming*, *28*. Also, see Muldoon and Carrington on fasting, *61*, p. 147.
8. Described in Muldoon and Carrington, *61*, p. 146. The original appears in vol. 10, no. 12, of the *Journal of the American Society for Psychical Research*, December 1916, p. 680; after hours of viewing microfilm I discovered that, unfortunately, it adds little.
9. Muldoon and Carrington regard this difference between the rate of astral vibrations and physical vibrations to be the basic rule of astral projection; see *61*, p. 65.
10. Oliver Fox, *26*, p. 37.
11. For example, Case 101 in Crookall, *16*, p. 104, mentions "gasping."
12. Described in Robert Crookall's conclusions in *16*, p. 140.
13. Quoted in full in Raymond De Becker, *19*, pp. 96–100.
14. In Lekh Raj Puri, *54*. Also see Singh Ji, *74*.
15. George Du Maurier, *20*, p. 201.
16. Carlos Castaneda, *10*, p. 118.
17. Oliver Fox, *26*, p. 34.
18. Described in Satprem, *70*, p. 130. We are cautioned here to distinguish "ordinary dreams" from "experiences," which are real events on a particular plane, differing from ordinary dreams by their special intensity.

13 THE WESTERN QUARTER OF THE DREAM MANDALA

1. This is a trick I learned from Hervey de Saint-Denys when I made a translation of his book, *41*. If I focus on some small detail of a fading dream scene, such as a pebble or a leaf, and remain immobile in my

dream body, I experience a slight strain between the eyes. However, this behavior will often also produce a return of color and light to the dream scene and the action will continue, with no discomfort.

2. For example, see Robert L. Van de Castle's article "His, Hers, and the Children's," 83. Van de Castle reported greater frequencies of reds and pinks occurring in women's dreams during the first halves of their cycles—including menses—than in the second halves of their cycles. In an unpublished study of my own, "The Late, Late Technicolor Dream Show," I present findings based on an analysis of color in 130 consecutive dreams of mine. I did *not* find a preponderance of reds and pinks in the first halves of menstrual cycles, but I did observe a greater frequency of warm colors, as a whole, in the first halves of my cycles. The role of color in dreams is still unclear.

3. See Ronald Siegel's article, "Hallucinations," 73. Although Siegel does not directly apply his material to dreams, I believe that the same principles may be operating in all altered states of consciousness; that is, *what we are observing is actually the operation of our own nervous systems under various conditions.* Siegel suggests that his experiments point to an underlying mechanism in the central nervous system that is the source of the universal phenomenon of hallucinations and of the eight colors, eight basic forms, and eight patterns of movement he has abstracted.

4. For example, see Oliver Fox, *26,* p. 44, where he says that "the mere thought of a possible embrace was fatal" when he spoke to women in his lucid dreams or projections. He suggests the motto of looking but not getting too interested, let alone touching, or the experience would end. Others make similar recommendations. My own experience is that this is a stage that passes with adaptation to the lucid dream condition.

5. For instance, in one set of twenty-nine consecutive lucid dreams, in 1976, ten of them involved orgasm, seven had sexual arousal without orgasm, and twelve had neither.

6. I also experience sexual arousal and even occasional orgasm in nonlucid dreams, but the frequency is much less than in lucid ones.

7. There is a cult of Amitabha that is quite widespread. A variant of Amitabha in his kingly form is also called Amitayus; as such, he never appears with a consort.

8. The cyclical appearance of penile erections during sleeping and dreaming was reported by P. Ohlmeyer et al. in 1944; see Ernest Hartmann, *40,* p. 26, for further details.

9. For example, see Philip Rawson, 66, p. 24, where he mentions that the most powerful of these sexual rites requires intercourse with a female partner when she is menstruating and thus her "red" sexual energy is at its peak.
10. For example, see Richard Wilhelm, 86, p. 30.
11. See Colin Wilson, 87, pp. 149–56, for an interesting discussion of the connection between latent psychic powers and sexuality.

14 THROUGH THE SCREENED PORCH TO THE INNER CIRCLE OF THE DREAM MANDALA

1. Sources vary considerably in reference to the location and number of *chakras*, number of petals in each *chakra*, color, etc. A typical listing of some of the associations follows, based mainly on Lama Govinda's *Foundations of Tibetan Mysticism*, 36, p. 144. The details are less important than the concept of focusing imagery in certain areas of the human body.

Chakra Location	Number of Petals	Hindu Name	Area Governed
Root center, base of the spine, in perineum	4	Mūlādhāra Chakra	Outer organs of generation
Abdominal center, about 4 finger-widths below navel	6	Svādhisthāna Chakra	Inner organs of reproduction and secretion (Mūlādhāra and Svādhisthāna are combined in the Tibetan system)
Navel center, at solar plexus	10	Manipūra Chakra	System of nutrition
Heart center	12	Anāhata Chakra	Circulatory system
Throat center	16	Viśuddha Chakra	Respiratory system

Chakra Location	Number of Petals	Hindu Name	Area Governed
Brow center, between eyebrows	2	Ājñā Chakra	Nonvolitional nervous system
Crown center	1,000	Sahasrāra Padma	Volitional nervous system (Ājñā and Sahasrāra are combined in the Tibetan system as one chakra of 32 petals)

15 THE LAND OF BREEZE AND LIGHT

1. Occasionally the right side would vibrate throughout the cycle, but the left side was always stronger when it made its appearance.

16 THE NORTHERN QUARTER OF THE DREAM MANDALA

1. Please note that I do *not* recommend practicing this form of meditation without appropriate supervision. If you wish to read about it, see Philip Rawson and Laszlo Legeza, *67;* John Blofeld, *6;* Chang Chung-yuan, *11;* Wen-shan Huang, *84;* and, most complete, Lu K'uan-Yü, *58.*
2. The two acupuncture-chart references in the Bibliography—the Academy of Traditional Chinese Medicine's book, *1,* and the Chinese Traditional Medical College of Shanghai's *Anatomical Charts, 12*—are particularly good. Many of the paperback books on the subject of acupuncture are inaccurate or illegible. The above-mentioned charts, correlated with modern anatomy and with internal organs, are excellent. See also Serizawa, *72,* and reference *64.*
3. This Buddhist symbol is sometimes called a crossed *vajra,* a double *vajra,* or the *viśvavajra. Dorje* is the Tibetan word for *vajra.*
4. Lama Govinda, *36,* p. 120.

17 THE BRANCHING WOMAN

1. See Introduction to *Dream Notebook, 30,* p. 12, where "The Branching Woman" dream is quoted in full.
2. I, my mother, my father, and my young brother were constantly present.

Assorted schoolmates, friends and enemies, teachers, the principal, movie stars, some unknown characters, and a few animals were also there occasionally. Rarely, a special creature, a beautiful female stranger with long blonde hair—quite unlike my waking self—fairies, and angels with golden hair fluttered into my dreams when I was fourteen.

3. I was still the most frequent character, and, as before, the people I related to most often in waking life were those who most often populated my dreams: Zal, and my two youngest daughters. Other people important in my life, or in my symbol system, were there: my deceased father, my mother-in-law, housekeepers past and present, current friends, two junior-high schoolmates, some political and show-business personalities. In addition, there were among the characters several highly idiosyncratic figures who were powerful creatures, most of whom were women.

4. The milk-rain that falls from the heavens in this dream sounds analogous to the "elixir" that flows from my head (the "heavenly heart") downward in meditation, leaving me similarly rejuvenated. Since the dream occurred long before I began practicing meditation, I suspect that the same process was taking place in the dream state and found its expression in appropriate imagery.

18 THE SACRED CENTER OF THE DREAM MANDALA

1. See M.-L. von Franz's description in her chapter "The Process of Individuation," in Carl G. Jung, 44, p. 196. I had noticed the change in my dream women to strong and unusual figures long before I became aware of the Jungian concept that in a woman's dreams the center of the Self is usually personified as a superior female figure, such as a priestess, sorceress, earth mother, or goddess of nature or love.

2. At first I was unable to see the crucial role that eye images have in my dreams. During my training I was exposed to the psychoanalytic notion that people who report eye images in ambiguous stimuli, such as ink-blots, are expressing paranoid behavior. Thus I did not attend to eye images in my dreams and was missing their symbolic reference to my "I," my self-concept.

3. See Lama Govinda's description, 36, of the Buddha teaching his disciple that the process of liberation consists of "untying the knots" of our psychic centers in the order that they were tied. Thus we cannot concentrate right away on the highest centers; we need to loosen the lower ones first and work our way up.

4. Some time after I had begun practicing Taoist meditation, I came across

Wen-shan Huang's book, *84*, and saw for the first time the direction that one should imagine one is flying upward while inhaling and flying downward while exhaling (p. 67). This is the identical sensation that occurs in dreams when the current is moving.

5. I am indebted to Theodor Schwenk for inspiring this concept. He presents a similar view in reference to the creation of flowing forms in water and air; the application to dreams is mine. See his beautiful book, *71*, p. 122.

6. *Pei hui* is also transliterated as *Paihui,* or *Baihui.*

7. Also called the *Dharmadatu.*

8. William S. Kroger and William D. Fezler, *Hypnosis and Behavior Modification: Imagery Conditioning* (Philadelphia: J. B. Lippincott Company, 1976), p. 345. Kroger and Fezler say that numerous investigators have found that 60 to 70 percent of warts respond to suggestive therapy; several citations are given. In one study (Ullman and Dudek, 1960), eight out of fifteen deeply hypnotized patients had complete remissions of their warts, in contrast with two cures in forty-seven patients who could not be deeply hypnotized.

9. Quoted in Barbara Jeffrey, *43*. According to this report, Dr. Vasily Kasatkin and his team at the Leningrad Neurosurgical Institute have saved many lives by using dreams to diagnose illnesses long before they could be picked up by conventional tests. For example, dreaming of a stomach wound could indicate a liver or kidney complaint before the dreamer is aware of it in waking consciousness. The system is said to be in the process of being perfected.

BIBLIOGRAPHY

The following citations represent selections from the numerous materials I have read on the subject matter of this book. I have not attempted to be comprehensive; these references are those that I personally found to be most interesting or helpful or that are mentioned in the Notes.

1. Academy of Traditional Chinese Medicine. *An Outline of Chinese Acupuncture.* Peking: Foreign Languages Press, 1975; available in the U.S. through China Books & Periodicals of San Francisco.
2. Anderson, Harold H. and Gladys L. *An Introduction to Projective Techniques.* Englewood Cliffs, N.J.: Prentice-Hall, 1951.
3. Argüelles, José and Miriam. *Mandala.* Berkeley: Shambhala, 1972.
4. Beyer, Stephan. *The Cult of Tārā: Magic and Ritual in Tibet.* Berkeley: University of California Press, 1973.
5. Blofeld, John. *The Secret and Sublime: Taoist Mysteries and Magic.* New York: Dutton, 1973.
6. Blofeld, John. *The Tantric Mysticism of Tibet: A Practical Guide.* New York: Dutton, 1970.
7. Borges, Jorge Luis. *Labyrinths: Selected Stories and Other Writings.* New York: New Directions, 1964.

8. Campbell, Joseph. *The Hero with a Thousand Faces.* Bollingen Series, no. 17. Princeton: Princeton University Press, 1968.

9. Campbell, Joseph. *The Mythic Image.* Bollingen Series, no. 100. Princeton: Princeton University Press, 1974.

10. Castaneda, Carlos. *Journey to Ixtlan.* New York: Simon and Schuster, 1972.

11. Chang Chung-yuan. *Creativity and Taoism: A Study of Chinese Philosophy, Art, and Poetry.* New York: Harper & Row, 1963.

12. Chinese Traditional Medical College of Shanghai. *Anatomical Charts of the Acupuncture Points and 14 Meridians.* People's Republic of China: Shanghai People's Publishing House, n.d.

13. Conze, Edward, et al., eds. *Buddhist Texts Through the Ages.* New York: Harper & Row, 1964.

14. Corriere, Richard, and Hart, Joseph. *The Dream Makers: Discovering Your Breakthrough Dreams.* New York: Funk & Wagnalls, 1977.

15. Coxhead, David, and Hiller, Susan. *Dreams: Visions of the Night.* New York: Avon, 1975.

16. Crookall, Robert. *The Study and Practice of Astral Projection.* Secaucus, N.J.: University Books, 1966.

17. David-Neel, Alexandra. *Initiations and Initiates in Tibet.* New York: University Books, 1959.

18. David-Neel, Alexandra. *Magic and Mystery in Tibet.* Baltimore: Penguin Books, 1973.

19. De Becker, Raymond. *The Understanding of Dreams; or, The Machinations of the Night.* London: George, Allen & Unwin, 1968.

20. Du Maurier, George L. *Peter Ibbetson.* New York: Harper & Brothers, 1891.

21. Eliade, Mircea. *Yoga: Immortality and Freedom.* Princeton: Princeton University Press, 1969.

22. Ellis, Havelock. *The World of Dreams.* Boston: Houghton Mifflin, 1911.

23. Evans-Wentz, W. Y., ed. *The Tibetan Book of the Dead.* London: Oxford University Press, 1957.

24. Evans-Wentz, W.Y., ed. *Tibetan Yoga and Secret Doctrines.* London: Oxford University Press, 1967.

25. Evans-Wentz, W. Y., ed. *Tibet's Great Yogi Milarepa: A Biography from the Tibetan.* New York: Oxford University Press, 1976.

26. Fox, Oliver. *Astral Projection: A Record of Out-of-the-Body Experiences.* New York: University Books, 1962.

27. Fremantle, Francesca, and Trungpa, Chögyam. *The Tibetan Book of the*

Dead: The Great Liberation Through Hearing in the Bardo. Berkeley: Shambhala, 1975.

28. Garfield, Patricia L. *Creative Dreaming.* New York: Simon and Schuster, 1974 (hardcover); Ballantine, 1976 (paperback).

29. Garfield, Patricia L. "Dream Content—Does It Reflect Changes in Self-Concept?" In *Sleep Research,* vol. 5. M. H. Chase, M. M. Mitler, and P. L. Walter, eds., p. 136. Los Angeles: Brain Information Service/Brain Research Institute, UCLA, 1976.

30. Garfield, Patricia L. Introduction to *Dream Notebook,* created and designed by Robert Gumpertz. San Francisco: San Francisco Book Co., 1976.

31. Garfield, Patricia L. "Keeping a Longitudinal Dream Record," *Psychotherapy: Theory, Research and Practice,* vol. 10, no. 3 (Fall 1973): 223–28.

32. Garfield, Patricia L. "Psychological Concomitants of the Lucid Dream State." In *Sleep Research,* vol. 4. M. H. Chase, W. C. Stern, and P. L. Walter, eds., p. 183. Los Angeles: Brain Information Service/Brain Research Institute, UCLA, 1975.

33. Garfield, Patricia L. "Self-Conditioning of Dream Content." In *Sleep Research,* vol. 3. M. H. Chase, W. C. Stern, and P. L. Walter, eds., p. 118. Los Angeles: Brain Information Service/Brain Research Institute, UCLA, 1974.

34. Garfield, Patricia L. "Using the Dream State as a Clinical Tool for Assertion Training." In *Sleep Research,* vol. 4. M. H. Chase, W. C. Stern, and P. L. Walter, eds., p. 184. Los Angeles: Brain Information Service/Brain Research Institute, UCLA, 1975.

35. Govinda, Lama Anagarika. *Creative Meditation and Multi-Dimensional Consciousness.* Wheaton, Ill.: Theosophical Publishing House, 1976.

36. Govinda, Lama Anagarika. *Foundations of Tibetan Mysticism.* New York: Samuel Weiser, 1969.

37. Green, C. E. *Lucid Dreams.* London: Hamish Hamilton, 1968.

38. Greenhouse, Herbert B. *The Astral Journey.* New York: Avon, 1976.

39. Hall, Calvin S., and Nordby, Vernon J. *The Individual and His Dreams.* New York: Signet, 1972.

40. Hartmann, Ernest. *The Biology of Dreaming.* Springfield, Ill.: Charles Thomas, 1967.

41. Hervey de Saint-Denys, Jean Marie Léon Lecoq (Baron d'Hervey, Marquis de Saint-Denys). *Les Rêves et les Moyens de les Diriger.* Paris: Tchou, 1964. Originally published in Paris by Amyot in 1867, with author anonymous.

42. Hine, Reginald L. *Dreams and the Way of Dreams.* New York: Dutton, 1913.
43. Jeffrey, Barbara. "Dream Breakthrough." *Woman's Own*, June 1977, pp. 35–37.
44. Jung, Carl G. *Man and His Symbols.* New York: Doubleday, 1964.
45. Jung, Carl G. *Mandala Symbolism.* Princeton: Princeton University Press, 1972.
46. Jung, Carl G. *Memories, Dreams, Reflections.* New York: Vintage, 1963.
47. Jung, Carl G. *Modern Man in Search of a Soul.* New York: Harcourt, Brace [c. 1933].
48. Kohler, Mariane, and Chapelle, Jean. *101 Recipes for Sound Sleep.* New York: Walker, 1965.
49. Krishna, Gopi. *Kundalini: The Evolutionary Energy in Man.* With psychological commentary by James Hillman. Berkeley: Shambhala, 1971.
50. Lauf, Detlef Ingo. *Secret Doctrines of the Tibetan Books of the Dead.* Boulder, Colo.: Shambhala, 1977.
51. Lauf, Detlef Ingo. *Secret Revelation of Tibetan Thangkas.* Freiburg Im Breisgau, Germany: Aurum Verlag, 1976.
52. Lauf, Detlef Ingo. *Tibetan Sacred Art: The Heritage of Tantra.* Berkeley: Shambhala, 1976.
53. Legeza, Laszlo. *Tao Magic: The Chinese Art of the Occult.* New York: Pantheon, 1975.
54. Lekh Raj Puri. *Radha Swami Teachings.* Delhi: National Printing Works, n.d.
55. Linde, Shirley Motter, and Savary, Louis M. *The Sleep Book.* New York: Harper & Row, 1974.
56. Long, Max Freedom. *The Huna Code in Religions.* Santa Monica, Calif.: De Vorss, 1965.
57. Lu Gwei-Djen. "The Inner Elixir (*Nei Tan*): Chinese Physiological Alchemy." In *Changing Perspectives in the History of Science.* M. Teich and R. Young, eds., p. 68. London: Heinemann, 1973.
58. Lu K'uan-Yü. *The Secrets of Chinese Meditation: Self-Cultivation by Mind Control as Taught in the Ch'an, Mahāyāna and Taoist Schools in China.* New York: Samuel Weiser, 1969.
59. Lu K'uan-Yü, trans. *Taoist Yoga: Alchemy and Immortality: A Translation, with Introduction and Notes, of "The Secrets of Cultivating Essential Nature and Eternal Life" (Hsin Ming Fa Chueh Ming Chih) by the Taoist Master Chao Pi-Ch'en, Born 1860.* New York: Samuel Weiser, 1973.

60. Monroe, Robert. *Journeys Out of the Body.* New York: Anchor, 1973.

61. Muldoon, Sylvan, and Carrington, Hereward. *The Projection of the Astral Body.* New York: Samuel Weiser, 1974.

62. Needham, Joseph. *Science and Civilisation in China,* vol. 5, part 2. New York: Cambridge University Press, 1974. Also see vol. 2.

63. Neumann, Erich. *The Great Mother: An Analysis of the Archetype.* Bollingen Series, vol. 47. Princeton: Princeton University Press, 1963.

64. *The Newest Illustrations of Acupuncture Points.* Hong Kong: Medicine & Health Publishing, 1974. Charts and explanatory book.

65. Purce, Jill. *The Mystic Spiral: Journey of the Soul.* New York: Avon, 1974.

66. Rawson, Philip. *Tantra: The Indian Cult of Ecstasy.* New York: Avon, 1973.

67. Rawson, Philip, and Legeza, Laszlo. *Tao: The Chinese Philosophy of Time and Change.* New York: Bounty, 1973.

68. Robinson, Richard H., and Johnson, Willard L. *The Buddhist Religion: A Historical Introduction.* Second edition. Encino, Calif.: Dickenson, 1977.

69. Sannella, Lee. *Kundalini: Psychosis or Transcendence?* San Francisco: H. S. Dakin, 1976.

70. Satprem. *Sri Aurobindo, or the Adventure of Consciousness.* New York: Harper & Row, 1968.

71. Schwenk, Theodor. *Sensitive Chaos: The Creation of Flowing Forms in Water and Air.* New York: Schocken, 1976.

72. Serizawa, Katsusuke. *Tsubo: Vital Points for Oriental Therapy.* Tokyo: Japan Publications, 1976.

73. Siegel, Ronald. "Hallucinations." *Scientific American,* October 1977, pp. 132–38.

74. Singh Ji, Maharaj Sardar Bahadur Jagat. *The Science of the Soul.* Punjab, India: Radha Soami Satsang, Beas, 1972.

75. Sparrow, Gregory Scott. *Lucid Dreaming: Dawning of the Clear Light.* Virginia Beach, Va.: A.R.E. Press, 1976.

76. Tansley, David V. *Subtle Body: Essence and Shadow.* London: Thames and Hudson, 1977.

77. Tart, Charles T. *Altered States of Consciousness.* New York: Anchor, 1972.

78. Thompson, Laurence G. *The Chinese Way in Religion.* Encino, Calif.: Dickenson, 1973.

79. Trungpa, Chögyam. *Cutting Through Spiritual Materialism.* Edited by John Baker. Berkeley: Shambhala, 1973.

80. Trungpa, Chögyam. "The Iconography of Tantric Buddhism," commentary on *Tibetan Thangka Calendar 1977*. San Francisco: Iris Publications, 1976.

81. Tucci, Giuseppe. *The Theory and Practice of the Mandala*. New York: Samuel Weiser, 1973.

82. Tucci, Giuseppe. *Tibetan Painted Scrolls*. 2 vols. and portfolio. Rome: Libreria dello Stato, 1949.

83. Van de Castle, Robert L. "His, Hers, and the Children's." *Psychology Today*, June 1970.

84. Wen-shan Huang. *The Art of Glowing Health*. Hong Kong: South Sky, 1973.

85. White, John, ed. *The Highest State of Consciousness*. New York: Anchor, 1972.

86. Wilhelm, Richard, trans. *The Secret of the Golden Flower: A Chinese Book of Life*. With foreword and commentary by C. G. Jung. New York: Harcourt, Brace & World, 1962.

87. Wilson, Colin. *The Occult*. New York: Vintage, 1973.

INDEX

Images provoking analysis, 120
  see also Symbolism
Imagination, 26–27, 28, 29, 30, 31,
  37
  control of, 42
Incongruous images, 119
Inner circle of dream mandala, 141–
  50
Interpreting your dreams, *see* Ana-
  lyzing your dreams; Symbolism
Isis, 193
Isolation, 24–25
Ivory-Bosom dream, 194–95, 197

Japanese Tea Garden dream, 208
Jung, Carl, 11, 14–15, 17, 193

Karma, 183
Kundalini, 139

Land of Breeze and Light, 151–68,
  205
  the dream, 151–52
Light:
  lucid dreaming and, 83, 179, 205,
    209, 212, 221
  meditation and, 170–71
  out-of-body projections and, 117,
    123
Lightheaded Dancer, 50–51, 54, 59,
  60, 74, 91, 133, 193, 195, 213,
  214
Lightheadedness, 49–51, 54, 55, 60,
  74–75, 99, 101, 186, 213
Lotus, 147–48, 215
Lucid dreaming, 6, 13, 19, 28, 44–45,
  49, 51–52, 54–56, 68, 73–79,
  80–85; 95 and *passim*
  day before, 122–23
  having your first dream, 120

meditation and, 182, 212–13
process of becoming lucid, 72–73,
  76, 99–101, 143
as refreshing, 73–74, 75, 77, 125,
  167
sexuality during, *see* Sexuality
shifting from, to astral-projection,
  120
vibrations of, *see* Current, feeling
  of; Vibration sensation
see also Astral-projection experience

Malaysia, 12, 91
Male figures in dreams, 197, 204
  see also Goddesses and gods;
    names of individual dreams
Mandalas, 33, 214
  explanations of, 2, 14–15
  framework of Tibetan, 2, 54, 59
  as a philosophy, 15
  see also Dream Mandala
Marriage, 41–43, 62–64, 65
Meditation on acupuncture points,
  169–85, 191, 205, 211, 212–13,
  218
Menstruation, 132
Metamorphosis, 109–11, 112, 199
Mexico, 13
Mirror Gazer, 56–60, 101, 110, 133,
  156, 213, 214, 222
Moslems, 14
Mystical experiences, 54, 71, 213

New Delhi, India, 14
Nightmares, 21–22, 34–35, 57–58,
  95, 119
Northern quarter of the dream man-
  dala, 169–85, 214
Notre Dame Cathedral, Paris, 14
Nyingma Institute, Berkeley, 35

ABOUT THE AUTHOR

Patricia Garfield is an author, speaker, and private dream consultant with an exclusive clientele. She received her Ph.D. in clinical psychology from Temple University. Since 1973, she has been a lecturer in psychology at the University of California Extensions at Los Angeles, Berkeley, San Diego, Santa Cruz, and Irvine. She has also served as a dream consultant for the National Geographic Society, the American Broadcasting Corporation, the Canadian Broadcasting Corporation, and Globe Communications.

Her first book for general readers, *Creative Dreaming*, was published in 1974; *Pathway to Ecstasy: The Way of the Dream Mandala*, first appeared in 1979. She and her husband, a psychotherapist, live in San Francisco.